Perspectives on Gender and Work

A volume in
Research in Social Issues in Management
Eden King, Quinetta Roberson, and Mikki Hebl, *Series Editors*

Perspectives on Gender and Work

edited by

Eden King
Rice University

Quinetta Roberson
Michigan State University

Mikki Hebl
Rice University

IAP
INFORMATION AGE PUBLISHING, INC.
Charlotte, NC • www.infoagepub.com

Library of Congress Cataloging-in-Publication Data

A CIP record for this book is available from the Library of Congress
http://www.loc.gov

ISBN: 978-1-64802-244-9 (Paperback)
978-1-64802-245-6 (Hardcover)
978-1-64802-246-3 (E-Book)

Printed and bound by CPI Group (UK) Ltd, Croydon, CR0 4YY

CONTENTS

PREFACE

In thinking about the focus for the second volume of this series, we were struck by the auspiciousness of the year of publication: 2020. As the centennial anniversary of the ratification of the 19th Amendment to the U.S. Constitution, which granted American women the right to vote, we knew that we needed to explore the study of gender at work. History recounts that after almost a century of activism and protest for women's rights, including property ownership, access to jobs, and retention of wages, the right to vote in both national and local elections, or women's suffrage, emerged as the cornerstone issue of the movement. Both women and men joined together to lecture, write, lobby, march, and practice civil disobedience to legislate what many considered to be a revolutionary change to the U.S. legal, economic, and social systems.

Similarly, many scholars have studied, presented, and worked to achieve what many considered to be a radical change in the management and organizational psychology literatures. While much of the early research in these areas used primarily male samples and explored phenomena in workplaces dominated by male employees, some scholars ventured to explore gender in the work as a topic as well as its influence in and on organizations. With the increasing participation of women in the workforce, they identified a limit to the generalizability of our theories and findings, and a need for research that examined what was happening in work organizations. While not considered a mainstream research area, these scholars realized the importance of giving attention to gender at work as an area of study in order

Perspectives on Gender and Work, pages vii–ix

to understand the experiences of women in the workplace and to better inform practice for maximizing egalitarianism and social justice within work organizations. Over time, new generations of scholars have taken on this pursuit and continued gender research to support, empower, and advance women in the workplace.

The year also invokes an optical analogy. Whether referring to the clarity or sharpness of vision (i.e., 20/20 vision) or to reflection on a situation or event to understand what could be done differently (i.e., 20–20 hindsight), it encourages us to consider how we see the world. Accordingly, we wanted to use this opportunity to consider the various ways that scholars have approached the study of gender at work in an effort to identify key learnings from, and gaps in, our current knowledge. We also aspired to look into and across the stories of different scholars who study gender to reveal and share the lessons embedded in their journeys. We thought that by inviting contributions across geographies, disciplines, career stages, and other identities, we could gain diversity of insight into the state of the field of diversity and inclusion, and more specifically, gender at work. Akin to the ongoing struggle for women's rights throughout the world, we saw value in leveraging this unique point in time to take stock of how far we have come, the strides that have been made, and the work that still needed to be done.

And so, for this second volume, we were motivated to feature the personal narratives of recognized scholars in the field who have advanced our understanding of gender at work to appreciate, and gain perspective on, the rewards and challenges of pursuing this area of research as well as directions for future work in this area. To this end, we invited scholars across the globe that we have respected and admired for many years and asked them to contribute in a way that is more personal and reflective than we typically do in scholarly journals, book chapters, and policy reports. Specifically, we asked them to contemplate and discuss their own experiences as a scientist studying gender using the following questions to guide their thinking: (a) "How did you get interested in studying gender at work?"; (b) "What is the study or finding of which you are most proud?"; (c) "What advice would you most want to give to young scholars in the field?"; and (d) "What do you think are the hot topics (related to gender) for the future?" Still, we encouraged our contributors to address these questions in whatever form and format they preferred. We present these personal, thoughtful, and inspiring responses in alphabetical order.

The discussions begin with Derek Avery's reflections on learning about (and eventually studying) injustice as a Black son of a pastor and a clinical psychologist in Louisiana. Next, Yvonne Benschop describes the experience of being a feminist in a business school and the evolution of feminist organizational studies. Mindy Bergman then describes how she has come to understand sexual harassment from both scientific and personal perspectives. Martin Davidson offers the term "second-order bias" to describe his scholarship and experience of biased thoughts and behavior that reinforce inequity in response to supposed remedies for inequity. Nancy DiTimaso's reflections on her most influential work point to the critical role of race in gender inequality. Similarly, Jack Dovidio's understandings of racial intergroup relations more generally informed and guided his interest on gender dynamics. Robin Ely describes a compelling series of "turning points" in her journey as a gender and race scholar. Consideration of the everyday, lived experiences of women across their lives is one of the ways that Alison Gabriel's work has contributed to the field. Peter Glick's story describes the important role that students can play in driving important research questions. Author and co-editor Mikki Hebl reminds us to keep pushing, to keep marching forward. Madeline Heilman's description of "gender-laced memories" reflect a powerful combination of scholarship and history. Sonia Kang's reflections emphasize not only the past, but also the future of research and her own sons' views of gender. The past and future also play important roles in the work and life of Zoe Kinias, whose international journey exemplifies global experiences of gender. Lisa Leslie's contribution compels us to do this work from an objective, rather than an ideological, standpoint. Isabel Metz describes her shift to an academic career; a "pracademic" journey. Gary Powell and Jeff Greenhaus reflect on a long-time partnership that has provided unique insights about the intersection of gender and the work–family interface. Finally, Pam Tolbert's description of her work on gender demography encourages broader consideration of gendered aspects of organizations.

Together, these authors' voices highlight the challenges of studying and living diversity and inclusion. Their guidance for the future underscores the continuing pressures, dilemmas, and significance of this work. We believe the end result is an exciting and meaningful exploration of the study of gender at work that authentically captures the experiences of scholars in the field and inventively pushes our understanding of diversity in organizations.

—**Quinetta Roberson, Eden King,** and **Mikki Hebl**

CHAPTER 1

WHEN DEMOGRAPHICS DISADVANTAGE

Why I do Research on Gender in the Workplace (and Believe You Should Too)

Derek R. Avery
Wake Forest University

You probably do not remember the first time you heard someone say that life isn't fair. Most people whom I know do not (yes, I have asked) and, quite frankly, I don't either. What I do vividly recall is how much this saying proved to be a recurring theme during my upbringing. As a lawyer and pastor, my father could recount literally tons of stories involving someone being treated unjustly. As a clinical psychologist, my mother knew that raising a Black boy in Baton Rouge, Louisiana would require her to instill a degree of psychological hardiness and resilience by making me aware of racial discrimination and its influence (see Wang, Smith, Miller-Cotto, & Huguley, 2019 for a recent review on this process known as racial socialization). Together with my grandparents, they took great pains to ensure that I realized injustice exists and people are often disadvantaged by the demographics

Perspectives on Gender and Work, pages 1–7

with which they are born. Being Black in the southern United States in the 1970s and 1980s, there were constant reminders that my race mattered to other people in a way that wasn't entirely clear to me. These experiences facilitated both my equity sensitivity and an extreme passion for improving the plight of demographic underdogs (i.e., those whose social identity group memberships often placed them at a relative disadvantage to others).

When I began studying diversity-related issues while in graduate school, I was deeply troubled by much of what I read. In short, it is staggering how much (a) attention people pay to and (b) information we infer from social identity group membership, particularly given how little variance these variables tend to explain in outcomes of interest like potential and performance. Though race clearly had been the most salient identity marker in my life to that point, two realizations quickly began to materialize. First, stereotyping, stigmatization, and discrimination extended to a whole host of demographics beyond race. Second, it is impossible to optimize one's impact in advocating for equality if you are not equally offended by *all* forms of inequity. As Dr. Martin Luther King Jr. famously penned in his letter from a Birmingham jail: "Injustice anywhere is a threat to justice everywhere." These realizations led me to begin investigating issues related to other forms of identity with the same fervor I applied to my examinations of those most personally salient to me.

Since that time, I have been amazed both at how much gender bias and discrimination is observed when a person simply pays attention to it and the staggering number of people simply choosing not to recognize it for whatever reason. For example, the United States existed for nearly 150 years before the 19th amendment was passed, thereby *granting* women the right to vote. There have been fewer female senators in this country's entire history than there are male senators today. Only 33 of the Fortune 500 are headed by women though roughly 47% of U.S. workers are female and considerable (and growing) evidence indicates women are at least equally capable of leadership as men on average and often more so (e.g., Hoobler, Masterson, Nkomo, & Mischel, 2018; Post, 2015). Though these statistics reflect my U.S.-centric perspective (as someone who has never lived elsewhere), global data suggest Americans are not alone in moving so slowly toward gender equity. In fact, the United States was recently ranked 53rd out of 153 countries in an equality metric based on economic, educational, political, and health indicators (World Economic Forum, 2020). What's worse, other evidence suggests that 45% of women and 67% of men worldwide believe gender equity (in terms of opportunity to succeed) has been achieved and only a third consider themselves to be a feminist (IPSOS, 2019). This report also indicated that 31% of women and 39% of men recently disagreed with the statement that "women won't achieve equality in [country] unless men take actions to support women's rights too" (IPSOS, 2019), and roughly half the male respondents believed men are being asked to do too much to support gender equality (IPSOS, 2019). I could go on citing additional evidence of gender inequity such as the well-chronicled pay gaps, but you probably get the point. Another unfortunate consequence of our antiquated approach to gender is that I have personally witnessed and heard of more instances than I care to recall where a woman was disadvantaged at work (or pursuing an employment opportunity) for no apparent reason other than her sex and gender. Though I have made it my personal commitment to stand up to any such injustices I witness, it has also become increasingly important to me to make shedding light on such occurrences a focal point of my research.

SOME LESSONS LEARNED

My scholarly work on sex and gender has taught me a good deal. As the chief diversity officer at Facebook recently noted, members of often marginalized groups, such as women, desperately crave validation of their perceptions that things are unequal (Williams, 2017). Accordingly, I have sought to empirically demonstrate the existence of gender bias in organizations, shed light on how it occurs, and identify means by which it might be attenuated. For instance, my colleagues and I have found that women in the United States are 12.5 times as likely as men in general to perceive sex discrimination at work and more than 60 times as likely when fewer same-sex coworkers are present (Avery, McKay, & Wilson, 2008). In response to this type of sex-based mistreatment, our work shows that victims tend to withdraw psychologically by burning out or disengaging, then physically, resulting in behavioral withdrawal such as absenteeism, tardiness, and turnover (Jiang et al., 2015; Volpone & Avery, 2013). Thus, sex-based discrimination is personally harmful to those who experience it and introduces a number of organizational inefficiencies such as selecting/promoting/rewarding less qualified individuals and, ultimately, encouraging the exit of high-potential employees who have perceived discriminatory mistreatment.

Beyond just showing that it occurs (or is perceived to occur) and how individuals respond to it, it is important to understand how sex-based discrimination takes place. One multi-study project, which I collaborated on, indicated that the stereotypes we hold, regarding how women behave, can lead us to discriminate against them (Luksyte, Unsworth, & Avery, 2018). Our first study showed that there are greater expectations for men than for women to be creative. Based on these expectations, we anticipated that evaluators would be more likely to recognize and reward innovation (the implementation of creative ideas) when the innovator was male. Consistent with this premise, evidence from both lab and field settings showed that female innovation has significantly less of an impact than male innovation on performance appraisals. An even more dramatic empirical finding (that, unfortunately, did not survive the peer review process) was that innovation corresponded positively with being targeted by incivility for women but not for men. In sum, whereas men were rewarded consistently for being innovative, women were not. Moreover, colleagues actually may punish their female colleagues for violating the societal expectation that innovation is a male domain.

In looking at ways to diminish discrimination based on sex, I've also learned a few things. First, support from others appears particularly important. Supervisor support, for instance, can help to attenuate commonly reported male–female differences in work stress (Raghuram, Luksyte, Avery, & Macoukji, 2012). Second, all forms of support are not necessarily equivalent. My colleagues and I found that empowerment, which is often advocated as a means of helping to accommodate differences in the workplace, actually tends to be more impactful in elevating individual performance when employees have a greater proportion of same-sex coworkers (Avery, Wang, Volpone, & Zhou, 2013). Third, though my work generally points to sex similarity as a key to employees having more favorable organizational experiences (e.g., Avery et al., 2008; Avery et al., 2013), I've also found that organizational efforts to create an equitable work environment can prove especially helpful in the absence of same-sex colleagues (Rubino et al., 2018). For instance, the justice climate interacted with sex similarity to influence sexual harassment such that harassment was lower when there were more sex-similar peers *or* climates were deemed fairer. Thus, organizational climates are especially important to those underdogs who may not have a critical mass of demographically similar peers.

STILL A LOT TO LEARN

Though I feel my work has helped move the field forward in some small ways, there are constant reminders of how much we have yet to understand the impact of gender in the workplace. I recently had one while taking part in a paper development workshop at a conference. Without getting too specific, the paper applied an intersectionality perspective to explore the novelties of women's experiences as a function of their racial and ethnic backgrounds. The data the authors presented was incredibly eye-opening. Though some scholars have criticized the tendency to study demographics in isolation and how this limits the utility of our theories for explaining experiences, some of the qualitative narratives provided really illuminated this point. My point here is twofold: First, we need more research on sex and gender at work. One tenet of modern sexism is the belief that sex-based discrimination is a thing of the past (Swim, Aikin, Hall, & Hunter, 1995). Evidence suggests this belief is fairly commonplace (IPSOS, 2019) and research needs to continue countering this notion and illustrate how much further we actually have to go to achieve equity. Second, this work needs to recognize that gender does not operate in isolation and that we can only truly understand its nuances if intersectional approaches become more of the norm than the exception to the rule.

Another way I hope the field continues to progress is through the increased involvement of men. I know this statement may elicit disagreement from some feminists and nonfeminists alike given the statistics presented earlier. Nevertheless, there are very few instances (if any) throughout history wherein members of a disadvantaged identity group were able to achieve greater equity without the aid of broad-based coalitions containing members of the advantaged group(s). In recent years, there has been an increase in the calls for greater involvement by men in pushing for gender equality and I greatly agree. There is some very thoughtful scholarship being produced on this topic. For instance, Burke and Major (2015) recently devoted an entire edited volume to comparing and contrasting men's roles as allies and adversaries to gender equity in organizational settings. Part of what this work demonstrates is the complexity associated with attempting to advocate for the advancement of a group to which one does not belong. I know that I have sometimes inadvertently engaged in benevolent sexism in an effort to defend or protect a colleague I perceived as potentially vulnerable. I found Mayer's (2017) discussion of "How Not to Advocate for a Woman at Work" to be a thought-provoking read and have incorporated it in my MBA diversity seminars. It would be great to see more empirical inquiry focusing on identifying the optimal means for men to advocate for greater gender equity.

A final avenue for future research I'd like to see explored is further investigation of the organizational initiatives that can help to level the playing field. For example, it is well chronicled how the introduction of blind auditions greatly increased the representation of women in symphony orchestras (Goldin & Rouse, 2000). By using tools like machine learning, some companies are identifying irrelevant material that exerts the greatest impact of human resource management decision-making and, subsequently, introducing strategies aimed at removing this information from consideration (see Bortz, 2018 for a recent review). It would be great to see organizational scholars take more of a leadership role in this research and seek to extend theory to identify the ways by which our implicit gender biases are manifested in our decisions and behavior.

One of my recent intellectual pursuits has been to try to better understand why people feel the way they do about diversity (e.g., Avery, 2011). I hope that this chapter has helped to provide some insight as to why I feel that studying gender is a highly worthwhile pursuit, what I've learned along the way, and what I hope to learn more about as the literature continues to progress. If you're still reading, you probably agree that this line of inquiry is an important one. Assuming so, I hope you'll consider pursuing this research as well—the field and society need you!

REFERENCES

Avery, D. R. (2011). Support for diversity in organizations: A theoretical exploration of its origins and offshoots. *Organizational Psychology Review, 1*(3), 239–256. https://doi.org/10.1177/2041386611402115

Avery, D. R., McKay, P. F., & Wilson, D. C. (2008). What are the odds? How demographic similarity affects the prevalence of perceived employment discrimination. *Journal of Applied Psychology, 93*(2), 235–249. https://doi.org/10.1037/0021-9010.93.2.235

Avery, D. R., Wang, M., Volpone, S. D., & Zhou, L. (2013). Different strokes for different folks: The impact of sex dissimilarity in the empowerment-performance relationship. *Personnel Psychology, 66*(3), 757–784. https://doi.org/10.1111/peps.12032

Bortz, D. (2018, March 20). Can blind hiring improve workforce diversity? Stripping identifying information from resumes may reduce bias in recruiting—and you don't need expensive software to do it. (A Sharpie works fine.). *Society for Human Resource Management.* Retrieved from https://www.shrm.org/hr-today/news/hr-magazine/0418/pages/can-blind-hiring-improve-workplace-diversity.aspx

Burke, R. J., & Major, D. A. (Eds.). (2014). *Gender in organizations: Are men allies or adversaries to women's career advancement?* Cheltenham, England: Edward Elgar.

Goldin, C., & Rouse, C. (2000). Orchestrating impartiality: The impact of" blind" auditions on female musicians. *American Economic Review, 90*(4), 715–741. https://doi.org/10.1257/aer.90.4.715

Hoobler, J. M., Masterson, C. R., Nkomo, S. M., & Michel, E. J. (2018). The Business case for women leaders: Meta-analysis, research critique, and path forward. *Journal of Management, 44*(6), 2473–2499. https://doi.org/10.1177/0149206316628643

IPSOS. (2019). *International Women's Day: Global attitudes toward gender equality.* Retrieved from https://www.ipsos.com/sites/default/files/ct/news/documents/2019-03/international-womens-day-2019-global-attitudes-towards-gender-equality.pdf

Jiang, K., Hong, Y., McKay, P. F., Avery, D. R., Wilson, D. C., & Volpone, S. D. (2015). Retaining employees through anti-sexual harassment practices: Exploring the mediating role of psychological distress and employee engagement. *Human Resource Management, 54*(1), 1–21. https://doi.org/10.1002/hrm.21585

Luksyte, A., Unsworth, K. L., & Avery, D. R. (2018). Innovative work behavior and sex-based stereotypes: Examining sex differences in perceptions and evaluations of innovative work behavior. *Journal of Organizational Behavior, 39*(3), 292–305. https://doi.org/10.1002/job.2219

Mayer, D. M. (2017, July 26). How not to advocate for a woman at work. *Harvard Business Review Digital Articles.* Retrieved from https://hbr.org/2017/07/how-not-to-advocate-for-a-woman-at-work

Post, C. (2015). When is female leadership an advantage? Coordination requirements, team cohesion, and team interaction norms. *Journal of Organizational Behavior, 36*(8), 1153–1175. https://doi.org/10.1002/job.2031

Raghuram, A., Luksyte, A., Avery, D. R., & Macoukji, F. (2012). Does your supervisor stress you out? How support influences sex differences in stress among immigrants. *Journal of Career Development, 39*(1), 99–117. https://doi.org/10.1177/0894845310377499

Rubino, C., Avery, D. R., McKay, P. F., Moore, B. L., Wilson, D. C., Driel, M. S., . . . McDonald, D. P. (2018). And justice for all: How organizational justice climate deters sexual harassment. *Personnel Psychology, 71*(4), 519–544. https://doi.org/10.1111/peps.12274

Swim, J. K., Aikin, K. J., Hall, W. S., & Hunter, B. A. (1995). Sexism and racism: Old-fashioned and modern prejudices. *Journal of Personality and Social Psychology, 68*(2), 199–214. https://doi.org/10.1037/0022-3514.68.2.199

Volpone, S. D., & Avery, D. R. (2013). It's self defense: How perceived discrimination promotes employee withdrawal. *Journal of Occupational Health Psychology, 18*(4), 430–448. https://doi.org/10.1037/a0034016

Wang, M., Smith, L. V., Miller-Cotto, D. A., & Huguley, J. P. (2019). Parental ethnic-racial socialization and children of color's academic success: A meta-analytic review. *Child Development, 91*(3), 528–544. https://doi.org/10.1111/cdev.13254

Williams, M. (2017). Numbers take us only so far. *Harvard Business Review, 95*(6), 142–148.

World Economic Forum. (2020). *Global gender gap report 2020.* Retrieved from http://www3.weforum.org/docs/WEF_GGGR_2020.pdf

CHAPTER 2

FEMINIST ORGANIZATION STUDIES

A Love Story

Yvonne Benschop
Radboud University, The Netherlands

ENTERING THE FIELD

A hundred years after women won the fight for the right to vote (1919 in the Netherlands), we have come a long way in changing gendered power relations in organizations and society. Yet, contrary to popular, postfeminist beliefs (see below), gender inequality is not a thing from the past and continues to manifest itself in today's organizations in many different ways. The field of gender in organizations, or feminist organization studies, as I like to identify my intellectual and scholarly home, is the place where knowledge is developed about how gender, in intersection with race, class, and other forms of social inequality, shapes and is shaped by organizations and processes of organizing. I draw on feminist organization studies to identify and analyze these inequalities in organizations with their underlying power processes; to articulate the goal for change towards gender equality, diversity, and inclusion; and to design, implement, and evaluate inventions to realize

Perspectives on Gender and Work, pages 9–22

that goal. In this chapter, I describe my experiences in becoming a feminist organization studies scholar, a process of becoming that is ongoing and continues to shape my research and teaching. For me, this is an engaged scholarship with the explicit feminist agenda of changing gendered power relations and intersectional gender inequalities in organizations and in society at large. Based on my experiences, I provide some advice to early career scholars, and end with an agenda of the hot topics for future research.

The daughter of parents who coupled an equal division of power to a traditional division of labor, I have been interested in gender relations ever since I can remember. I like to think I was born a feminist, although that makes me wonder how my parents managed that exactly with their fourth child. The lack of women authority figures in society puzzled me from a very young age. I vividly remember my first contact with the women's movement in the first year of high school, when the senior female students went on a strike on March 8th, International Women's Day in the early 1980s. This introduced me to the second feminist wave, and I was immediately won for the agenda of women's liberation, ending the violence against women, attention for the body, reproductive rights, and labor market inequalities. After having read whatever feminist classics and novels I could lay my hands on in high school, my choice for my university studies in political science was motivated by the possibility to include women studies courses, as they were called, in the program. When the one expert lecturer in women studies did not get her contract renewed during my first year, I became part of an active group of women students striving to influence the curriculum to increase the attention for gender inequality. Spurred by the feminist adage "the personal is political," we created our own courses, compiling reading lists of contemporary feminist work, and writing papers that we got graded by progressive faculty members. Political economy was my favorite course, as it introduced me to the relation between capitalism and patriarchy (Hartmann, 1979), and I became especially interested in the gendered division of labor in organizations. Organizations are certainly part of the problem of gender inequality, but they have the potential to be part of the solution. I, thus, took up a second study in business administration alongside political science to better understand how gender processes work at the level of organizations. This background equipped me with a political take on management and organizations and a sensitivity for the power processes that are the raison d'être of feminist theories. My master's thesis supervisor convinced me that I should pursue a PhD and made me an offer I could not refuse: to work interdisciplinary at the crossroads of gender studies, political science, and management and organization studies.

So, in the beginning of the 1990s, I embarked on a PhD in a business school. The topic of my dissertation was the production and reproduction of gender inequalities in organizations, and I was particularly interested in the coexistence of an ideology of equality and persistent gender inequalities, which became a red thread through my work all along. Supervised by two men with a background in organizational sociology, I reached out to the one specialized professor in women and work who worked at another university in the Netherlands and brought her on the supervisory team. The dominant framing of the research problem of gender at work at the time was *women in management.* While an important part, the focus on the representation, behavior, and leadership styles of women in management jobs was only part of the story of gender at work. Gender does not equal "women" and does certainly not equal "problem" in organizations. It became clear that new knowledge and new conceptual and analytical tools needed to be developed to understand and change the complex and multifaceted place and functioning of gender in organizations. Having branched out to academia in the 1980s and 1990s, the women's movement gained ground in universities and started to transform feminist activism into various strands of feminist theories in different disciplines. These were exciting times: Feminist theories blossomed and the field started to develop internationally, with specialized conferences and journals (such as *Gender, Work and Organization,* which started in 1994) providing platforms for academic discussion and networking, and developing the new knowledge so direly needed.

Looking for theoretical inspiration, I came across the work of sociologist Joan Acker, the first author to explicitly articulate a systematic feminist theory of gender in organizations (laid out in two highly cited publications in *Gender & Society* [Acker, 1990]), and a book chapter (Acker, 1992). As these were the pre-Google times, I must have found the book with her 1992 chapter while browsing the women studies shelves of the university library. This was exactly what I had been looking for and I was so thrilled to have found this feminist combination of gender, power, and organization. It helped me articulate ideas about a gender subtext underlying contemporary organizations and processes of organizing. Furthermore, it was so important to find a reputed scholar out there doing this kind of feminist work, even if she was on the other side of the ocean, as the strangeness of being a feminist in a business school sometimes got to me. Around the same time, I encountered the work of organization theorists Marta Calás and Linda Smircich, who wrote a series of papers "using the f-word" to explicitly address the social and ethical consequences of organizational knowledge (Calás & Smircich, 1992). Their critical work on the production of knowledge in the field of organization theory invoked poststructuralist feminism to deconstruct leadership, showing the importance and even the seduction of the structure masculinity/femininity in organizations (Calás & Smircich, 1991). This was an approach I wanted to know more of, and I visited them in Amherst after completing my PhD manuscript. They were finalizing their influential overview of how multiple strands of feminist theory inform and contribute to organization theories (Calás & Smircich, 1996). This chapter introduced me (and many, many others) to the cross-disciplinary richness of multiple feminisms and the similarities and differences in the political agendas for organizational change in these different strands.

Finding this unapologetic feminist work helped me both develop and legitimize my research agenda. Now, if people asked (which happened regularly, and still does to this day in my business school context) when I would finally take up a proper scientific research subject and do away with the scary political and feminist radicalism, I could point at these laurelled feminists. They proved that there could be a future, a career even, in academia for feminist scholars, and that there was no need to tone it down to a less controversial and more palatable or mainstream research subject. My research trip to Amherst especially helped me build connections and collaborations with colleagues across the globe with similar interests, which proved an invaluable network of academic friendships, support, and collaborations over the years.

Trying to find others who do the academic work that you want to do and who do it from perspectives that you value, and connecting to them in whatever way you can (virtual or in real life, at conferences, or by research visits) is my number one tip for early career scholars. Even though academics are busy people, nothing beats the pleasure of these connections with the like-minded, especially for those working in contexts where those like-minded are far and between. Although there is a constant dilemma for feminist scholars between seeking inspiration inside the community, and enlighten the outside world with a feminist perspective, it is the inside inspiration that energizes feminist scholars, drives the field forward, and enables the development of new knowledge and ideas for change.

A FEMINIST IN THE BUSINESS SCHOOL

During my PhD, I realized that I lost my heart to academic work. I loved and love all aspects of the research process; from delving deep into the literature, articulating a research question, getting into the field to collect empirical material, getting to ask respondents and informants curious questions about constructions of gender and its intersections at work, doing the analysis (and again, and again), and especially the creative process of writing it all up and then rewriting it. I also enjoyed teaching and the opportunity to work with both young and mature students, stimulate their intellectual development, and motivate them to think critically about topics that are all too often taken for granted (such as gendered power relations). The combination of research and teaching that makes the core of academic work, the relative autonomy to decide upon my research agenda, the obvious relevance of feminist organization studies and the pile of questions that remained about gender in organizations after my PhD, made me want to embark on an academic career.

The business school employed me as an assistant professor in gender and culture, and I started studying the policies regulating attention for gender in organizations, connecting to the growing feminist organization studies. This first brought me to the field of HRM (human resource management) as a core place to think about the relations between organizations and personnel. However, the HRM literature tended to have a stronger focus on the management, representing human resources as an abstract, generic, and undifferentiated category (Benschop, 2001). Even in organizations that have formal HRM policies in place to advance gender equality and manage diversity, inequalities continue to exist along gender and diversity lines. There is abundant evidence that many HR practices such as recruitment and selection, appraisal and reward, career management, talent management, and development have and continue to have different effects for different categories of personnel. With the "ideal worker" (Acker, 1992) underlying many of these practices remaining a White, middle-class, able-bodied, heterosexual, cis-gender man of a certain age, I realized that formal policies are not a promising path to deliver meaningful change towards gender equality and diversity any time soon. I also realized that more attention was needed for the impact of informal organization processes, such as unwritten rules and informal networks, on the reproduction of inequalities. I, therefore, changed focus to organizational change, trying to get to a better understanding of how inequalities can be so persistent and why change is so difficult to achieve, and how this could be remedied by both formal and informal organization processes.

This was quite an exotic research agenda in the business school, but not in the wider university that has a strong history as an emancipation university. I benefited enormously from my affiliation to the strong Interfaculty Institute for Gender Studies that brought gender studies scholars from all disciplines together. The interdisciplinary work done there introduced me to new theories, concepts and insights, and helped me to develop two core skills in the politics of academia. The first one was to get my feminist work published in the management and organization studies journals that were seen as relevant in my department. The second one was to make the necessary connections to the consecutive research programs of my department. I got really skilled in identifying the gender and diversity questions in those programs, although admittedly the profile of my business school with its focus on social processes of organizing, and the responsibility of organizations for social, environmental, and economic goals made it easy for me to do so.

These are my second and third pieces of advice for young scholars: Find out what matters in your department and deliver the best you can do in that field. This may often boil down to getting published as publications remain a cornerstone of contemporary academic work, and they are the entrance into the research grants that have become the second cornerstone. There are always opportunities to get feminist, interdisciplinary work published in management and organization journals, and all journals feature this kind of work from time to time, in special issues or in regular issues. Even when experienced colleagues tell you that it cannot be done with these kinds of radical, political, or feminist topics, and advice against it, stand your ground as there are plenty editors and reviewers who do see the merit of this work and can assess it accordingly. As a third tip, use your creative thinking to identify the connections between what you find to be important research questions and research program in your school or department. The benefits of gender and diversity research is that it requires just a tiny bit of imagination to connect it to all kinds of management and organization theories and questions, whether in the area of strategy, marketing, organizational behavior, organization design, change, entrepreneurship, leadership, or innovation. Making these connections is more than a political skill, it provides you the opportunity to belong and remain unique at the same time, the core ingredients of inclusion (Shore et al., 2011) that matters for academics as well as for any other occupational group.

EXPLAINING THE SLOW PACE OF CHANGE

Looking back on my journey in this field of feminist organization studies, I am most proud of a combination of insights about the complexity of organizational change towards gender equality, diversity, and inclusion. The building blocks are to be found in different papers that report on different studies over the years, studies in which I was lucky to collaborate with my favorite colleagues. I discuss them here in the chronological order in which they were developed.

The first building block is the idea of organizational change towards gender equality resembling the work of Sisyphus' sisters; gradually building the will and resources to work towards gender equality, but inevitably making very slow progress because it needs to be a collaborative effort of many stakeholders with their own agendas and interests (Benschop & Verloo, 2006). Mieke Verloo and I conducted a series of participatory research projects on gender mainstreaming targeting the HRM policies and practices in organizations in the Flemish public sector. Stepping out of the ivory tower of research and analysis and the experience of actually trying to accomplish change was a real eye-opener. The—admittedly ambitious —goal for this research, that was commissioned by the Emancipation Department of the Ministry of the Flemish Community, was gender mainstreaming: transforming organizational processes and practices by eliminating gender biases in existing routines, involving the regular actors in this transformation process (Council of Europe, 1998). We had to collaborate with the all-male leadership of the Ministry and negotiate the goals of the feminist intervention project, and we found that participatory action research necessarily means compromise around the diverging interests and micro-politics of different stakeholders. While we managed to involve more civil servants to work towards gender equality, and changed discourses about employees to include a wider variety of workers, changing the practices proved difficult and feminist analyses met with a lot of resistance. It made us realize that change projects require the collaboration of gender experts and organizational experts, of researchers and practitioners both. The projects showed us how gender equality work, in a way, resembles Sisyphus' labor: repetitive hard work that does not lead anywhere. Inspired by the Greek myth of Sisyphus who was punished by the gods and condemned to push a heavy rock up a mountain only to have it roll down again by the end of the day, we added the nonexistent sisters to the myth to claim that they were slightly smarter which helps them to make some progress in gathering the resources for change.

The second building block is the fine-grained analysis of how deeply intertwined gender practices are with everyday organizational practices, which demonstrates the complexity of the multilevel and multifaceted changes needed. I have done most work in this area on recruitment and selection processes that could be key processes for organizational change toward equality, diversity, and inclusion, but instead, routinely produce gendered, classed, and racialized inequalities. Regulating the entry and promotion in organizations, recruitment, and selection processes are sites of organizational power and politics that are influenced by both formal and informal organization processes , such as recruitment protocols and informal recommendations. Struggles over the normative meanings of work, workers, and success become manifest here and impact decisions about prospective organization, members, and careers. In various studies into recruitment and selection for top positions in academia and in the public sector, in collaboration with Marieke van den Brink, we have shown how gender is practiced in all elements of the recruitment and selection process. Who gets to take part in selection decisions, which criteria are used to base decisions on, and how these criteria are applied to different candidates by different evaluators, gender practices are to be found in each of these steps and phases (Van den Brink & Benschop, 2012a, 2018). For top positions, both within and outside academia, the discourse emphasizes excellence—the highest achievement of performance. We noticed how the excellent candidate has to be a proverbial sheep with five legs, which illustrates that there are always multiple criteria at stake (Van den Brink & Benschop, 2012a). Those criteria are not neutral standards of meritocracy that can be measured precisely and objectively, but rather social constructions of qualifications in which structures of inequality based on gender, race, and class are reproduced. Researchers have shown how the criteria that are used to assess academic excellence (i.e., journal rankings, citation indexes, grant applications, student evaluations, letters of reference, network connections) are systematically reproducing gender inequalities (Boring, 2017; Bornmann, Mutz, & Daniel, 2007; Dutt, Pfaff, Bernstein, Dillard, & Block, 2016; Laudel, 2006; MacNell, Driscoll, & Hunt, 2015; Moss-Racusin, Dovidio, Brescoll, Graham, & Handelsman, 2012; Nkomo, 2009; Özbilgin, 2009; Van der Lee & Ellemers, 2015). In addition, candidates typically do not excel at each and every qualification, which gives even more room to the micro-politics of committee members negotiating the importance of criteria and applying them differently to candidates. Gatekeepers of excellence are predominantly men who routinely mobilize masculinity to the effect that they privilege men candidates and disadvantage women candidates (Van den Brink & Benschop, 2014). Changing recruitment and selection processes to avoid the reproduction of inequalities is not an easy task, and our research shows that attempts to strive for transparency of criteria and increase the accountability of committee members have hitherto had limited effects against the ubiquity of gender practices (Van den Brink, Benschop, & Jansen, 2010). Nevertheless, the awareness of the gendered practices in recruitment and selection is becoming more and more widespread, and specialized trainings and tool kits for committees to avoid them are increasingly popular (see for instance Dennissen, Herschberg, Benschop, & Van den Brink, 2017). There are examples of departments whose members can only sit on selection committees after they have followed such gender awareness training.

The third building block combines the former two and concerns the slow progress of change explaining it by the complex interplay between those interventions that seek to improve equality (equality practices) and the organizational practices that produce inequalities (inequality practices). Invoking another animal metaphor, we argue that gender inequality resembles a seven-headed dragon, a multitude of faces in different social contexts (Van den Brink & Benschop, 2012b). Universities have a long track record of policies and measures to appoint more women professors, yet such gender equality practices have limited effects. Many measures set out to "fix the women" through training or mentoring them (Ely & Meyerson, 2000), but making women candidates behave more like assertive and accomplished men candidates is bound to fail. This is due to gender inequality practices, for instance that the women that do behave like men are not considered likeable, and the women that don't are not seen as competent enough. There are many different gender inequality practices that have to do with the explicit and implicit ideals about academics, the priority of academic careers over other things in life and the greediness of academic work, such as the idea that academic success requires a more than full-time devotion and cannot be combined with motherhood, or that special chairs for women help to solve the bias of men scouts supporting men candidates. We found how gender equality practices become intertwined with gender inequality practices, in the sense that they become covered, changed, and even hijacked by the inequality practices. The protocol of including women committee members, for instance, is hijacked when external women are appointed and committee meetings are held without their presence. The effective countering of gender equality practices by gender inequality practices explains why change is so slow. This implies that the design of effective equality practices should anticipate many unforeseen counter effects and requires the forging of as many sharp swords as there are heads of the dragon.

The fourth and final building block is the most recent one and refers to the slow pace of organizational change explained by the influence of postfeminist gender regimes on the popular gender equality interventions in organizations. The postfeminist gender regime is characterized by a false notion of modernity promoting the view that gender equality is achieved, as women and men now have equal opportunities, make their own career choices, and are equally responsible for managing their own careers. Postfeminism is a complex set of discourses around gender, feminism, and femininity that is deeply entangled with neoliberalism, promoting a selective take-up and restricted implementation of feminist values that emphasize the agency, choice, and empowerment of individual women in all spheres of life (Lewis, Benschop, & Simpson, 2017). This discourse of freedom of choice; autonomy; and agency, entrepreneurialism, and empowerment emphasizes the self-improvement of individual women, at the expense of a political agenda seeking to improve organizations and society (Ferguson, 2010). Postfeminist subjectivities require extensive self-surveillance, self-monitoring, self-discipline, and continuous makeover of bodies and souls to produce the confident, resilient, and empowered modus of successful femininities and masculinities (Gill, 2008). The influence of the postfeminist gender regime in organizations manifests itself in the preferences for interventions that aim to "fix the women," such as management development programs, training, mentoring, and networks (Benschop, Van den Brink, Holgersson, & Wahl, 2015). Many women are keen to participate in these management development and training programs as they are used to broader cultural appeals of self-improvement and makeover, for instance in women's magazines (Gill, 2007). Such interventions implicitly or explicitly build on postfeminist ideas of women as malleable subjects, stressing their responsibility for their own careers. Importantly, such interventions do little to problematize the "rules of the game" that presuppose unencumbered workers (Acker 1992), the gendered systems of upward career mobility, or the masculine construction of leadership. The effect of this postfeminist gender regime is that women's choices are problematized, and interventions are geared to women's assimilation into existing structures and cultures. It keeps the problematization of these structures and cultures off the agenda, leaving the current processes of dividing, organizing, and valuing work and workers intact. The insight that a postfeminist discourse hinders equality interventions from targeting organization processes helps explain the slow progress toward gender equality.

Summarizing, these four building blocks explain the complexity of organizational change towards gender equality, diversity, and inclusion. They highlight that different stakeholders are needed to effectuate change and how their divergent beliefs about gender relations and gender equality impact the scope of interventions possible and the pace of change. This is related to the counterforce of postfeminist discourses about gender that advocate and prioritize interventions geared to fixing the women instead of changing organization processes. In addition, the slow change has to do with how deeply gendered the formal and informal organizational practices are that regulate the entry and evaluation of organization members and routinely reproduce inequalities. Finally, in the design of interventions, more consideration should go to the incorporation of counter effects produced by the continuous intertwinement of equality and inequality practices.

WHAT LIES AHEAD

Elsewhere (Benschop, 2016), I quite recently developed a research agenda for gender in organizations consisting of three hot topics for the future: intersections of gender, keeping track of inequalities in global capitalism, and organizational change that I shortly summarize here.

The first theme refers to the intersections of gender with equally salient social categories of race, ethnicity, class, age, (dis)ability, sexuality, and religion. Originating in Black feminist thought, the notion of intersectionality stresses the simultaneity of multiple social categories, which is crucial to analyze manifestations of inequality in their full complexity. Intersectionality found its way to organization studies rather late, but is now increasingly accepted as impacting identities, institutional and social practices in organizations (Crenshaw, 1997; Holvino, 2010; Rodriguez, Holvino, Fletcher, & Nkomo, 2016). Intersectionality calls for a different conceptualization of gender (Cho, Crenshaw, & McCall, 2013) that highlights the relative relevance of gender in relation to other categories of difference that matter in the patterns of privilege and disadvantage in organizations. Thinking about organizational masculinities and femininities in the plural (Budgeon, 2014) can be a productive way to destabilize the traditional norms and ideas about gender at work. Yet, this plurality still emphasizes gender as a core category, and there is a need for further conceptual development to be able to express relations between social categories without having to mention all those categories separately every time (Bowleg, 2008).

The second theme concerns keeping track of the social inequalities that organizations in global capitalism produce in tasks, jobs, opportunities, careers, professions, sectors, countries, regions, and cultures. Sophisticated thinking about the production of social inequalities is a core strength of feminist organization studies. New ways of organizing in globalized organizations bring about less stability and job security, and more flexible and precarious work (Armano & Murgia, 2013). Keeping track of how the systemic dimensions of contemporary global capitalism produce inequalities at the intersections of gender, race, ethnicity, class, religion, sexuality, age, and (dis)ability, provides the knowledge needed to change these inequalities. Linking macro developments in the global economy to organizational employment trends and to micro work orientations and experiences, feminist organization studies is uniquely positioned to identify, map, and analyze new and existing inequalities and develop the political, cultural and economic arguments for capitalism critique.

The third and last theme on the research agenda, building on the two prior themes, is organizational change, more precisely, the development of evidence-based knowledge about effective interventions that take into account the intersectionality of inequalities in organizations. Research into the effects of interventions on gender and diversity is scarce, compared to research documenting inequalities, and existing work has been inconclusive in its explanations of the limited change (Kalev & Deutsch, 2018; Nishii, Khattab, Shemla, & Paluch, 2018). One promising route is to develop an intersectional approach to interventions, so far uncharted territory for the study of equality interventions. Yet, this approach can help to develop new knowledge about the effects that interventions designed for one group can have on other groups. We currently work to develop *intersectional equality* as a normative goal and framework to direct decisions about equality in organizations. Intersectional equality requires that individuals and groups can develop the capabilities that they value and that organizations provide the context and environment to develop these capabilities, ensuring that both the development of individual capabilities and the values that individuals form do not reproduce social inequalities (Woods, Benschop, Van den Brink, & Verloo, 2019).

Coming to the end of this chapter, I observe how the field of gender in organizations has matured over the past 30 years. Not all scholars active in the field feel comfortable with the label I prefer: feminist organization studies. But I find it important that there is space for us who do want to identify with the more political and radical aims and questions, and work from an agenda of change. There are many other research themes, besides the ones I highlighted in this section, and other scholars from different locations will highlight the need to study different themes. But their common denominator is the need for critical questioning of the place and function of gender in all its complexities in organizations. We can have fruitful discussions about that now, at any of the gender streams and divisions in general management and organizations conferences, or at specialized conferences. And so I end with a final piece of advice for young scholars that is admittedly a bit self-serving: Come to the conferences and help shape the debate in the new and innovative ways that come with those working at the forefront of the field.

REFERENCES

Acker, J. (1990). Hierarchies, jobs, bodies: A theory of gendered organizations. *Gender and Society, 4*(2), 139–158.

Acker, J. (1992). Gendering organizational theory. In A. J. Mills & P. Tancred (Eds.), *Gendering organizational analysis* (pp. 248–260). Newbury Park: SAGE.

Armano, E., & Murgia, A. (2013). The precariousnesses of young knowledge workers: A subject-oriented approach. *Global Discourse, 3*(3/4), 486–501.

Benschop, Y. (2001). Pride, prejudice and performance: Relations between HRM, diversity and performance. *The International Journal of Human Resource Management, 12*(7), 1166–1181.

Benschop, Y. (2016). Well-trodden paths and roads less traveled: research directions for gender in management and organization. B. Czarniawska (Ed.), *A Research Agenda for Management and Organization* (pp. 59–69). Cheltenham, England: Edward Elgar.

Benschop, Y., Van den Brink, M., Holgersson, C., & Wahl, A. (2015). Future challenges for diversity management in organizations. In R. Bendl, I. Bleijenbergh, E. Henttonen, & A. J. Mills (Eds.), *The Oxford Handbook of Diversity Studies in Organization and Management* (pp. 553–573). Oxford, England: Oxford University Press

Benschop, Y., & Verloo, M. (2006). Sisyphus' sisters: Can gender mainstreaming escape the genderedness of organizations? *Journal of Gender Studies, 15*(1), 19–33.

Boring, A. (2017). Gender biases in student evaluations of teaching. *Journal of Public Economics, 145*(C), 27–41.

Bornmann, L., Mutz, R., & Daniel, H.-D. (2007). Gender differences in grant peer review: A meta-analysis. *Journal of Informetrics, 1*(3), 226–238.

Bowleg, L. (2008). When Black+ lesbian+ woman≠ Black lesbian woman: The methodological challenges of qualitative and quantitative intersectionality research. *Sex roles, 59*(5/6), 312–325.

Budgeon, S. (2014). The dynamics of gender hegemony: Femininities, masculinities and social change. *Sociology, 48*(2), 317–334.

Calás, M., & Smircich, L. (1991). Voicing seduction to silence leadership. *Organization studies, 12*(4), 567–601.

Calás, M., & Smircich, L. (1992). Using the "F" word: Feminist theories and the social consequences of organizational research. In A. J. Mills & P. Tancred (Eds.), *Gendering organizational analysis* (pp. 222–234). London: SAGE.

Calás, M., & Smircich, L. (1996). From 'The Woman's' point of view: Feminist approaches to organization studies. In S. Clegg, C. Hardy, & W. Nord (Eds.), *Handbook of Organization Studies* (pp. 218–257). London: SAGE.

Cho, S., Crenshaw, K. W., & McCall, L. (2013). Toward a field of intersectionality studies: Theory, applications, and praxis. *Signs, 38*(4), 785–810.

Council of Europe. (1998). *Gender mainstreaming. Conceptual framework, methodology and presentation of good practices.* Strasbourg, France: Council of Europe

Crenshaw, K. (1997). Intersectionality and identity politics: Learning from violence against women of colour. In M. L. Shanley & U. Narayan (Eds.), *Reconstructing political theory.* Oxford, England: Polity Press.

Dennissen, M., Herschberg, C., Benschop, Y., & Van den Brink, M. (2017). *Toolkit for organizing reflexive working groups for selection committee members.* Retrieved from http://garciaproject.eu/wp-content/uploads/2017/01/GARCIA_working_papers_n.19.pdf

Dutt, K., Pfaff, D. L., Bernstein, A. F., Dillard, J. S., & Block, C. J. (2016). Gender differences in recommendation letters for postdoctoral fellowships in geoscience. *Nature Geoscience, 9*(11), 805.

Ely, R. J., & Meyerson, D. E. (2000). Advancing gender equity in organizations: The challenge and importance of maintaining a gender narrative. *Organization, 7*(4), 589–608.

Ferguson, M. L. (2010). Choice feminism and the fear of politics. *Perspectives on politics, 8*(01), 247–253.

Gill, R. (2007). *Gender and the Media.* Cambridge, England: Polity.

Gill, R. (2008). Culture and subjectivity in neoliberal and postfeminist times. *Subjectivity, 25*(1), 432–445.

Hartmann, H. I. (1979). The unhappy marriage of Marxism and feminism: Towards a more progressive union. *Capital & Class, 3*(2), 1–33.

Holvino, E. (2010). Intersections: The Simultaneity of Race, Gender and Class in Organization Studies. *Gender Work and Organization, 17*(3), 248–277. https://doi.org/10.1111/j.1468-0432.2008.00400.x

Kalev, A., & Deutsch, G. (2018). Gender Inequality and Workplace Organizations: Understanding Reproduction and Change. In B. Risman, C. Froyum, & W. Scarborough (Eds.), *Handbook of the Sociology of Gender* (pp. 257–269): Cham, Switzerland: Springer.

Laudel, G. (2006). The 'quality myth': Promoting and hindering conditions for acquiring research funds. *Higher Education, 52*(3), 375–403.

Lewis, P., Benschop, Y., & Simpson, R. (2017). Postfeminism, Gender and Organization. *Gender, Work, & Organization, 24*(3), 213–225.

MacNell, L., Driscoll, A., & Hunt, A. N. (2015). What's in a name: Exposing gender bias in student ratings of teaching. *Innovative Higher Education, 40*(4), 291–303.

Moss-Racusin, C. A., Dovidio, J. F., Brescoll, V. L., Graham, M. J., & Handelsman, J. J. (2012). Science faculty's subtle gender biases favor male students, *109*(41), 16474–16479.

Nishii, L. H., Khattab, J., Shemla, M., & Paluch, R. M. (2018). A multi-level process model for understanding diversity practice effectiveness. *Academy of Management Annals, 12*(1), 37–82.

Nkomo, S. M. (2009). The seductive power of academic journal rankings: Challenges of searching for the otherwise. *Academy of Management Learning and Education, 8*(1), 106–121.

Özbilgin, M. (2009). From journal rankings to making sense of the world. *Academy of Management Learning and Education, 8*(1), 113–121.

Rodriguez, J. K., Holvino, E., Fletcher, J. K., & Nkomo, S. M. (2016). The theory and praxis of intersectionality in work and organisations: Where do we go from here? *Gender, Work, & Organization, 23*(3), 201–222.

Shore, L. M., Randel, A. E., Chung, B. G., Dean, M. A., Ehrhart, K. H., & Singh, G. (2011). Inclusion and diversity in work groups: A review and model for future research. *Journal of Management, 37*(4), 1262–1289. https://doi.org/10.1177/0149206310385943

Van den Brink, M., & Benschop, Y. (2012a). Gender practices in the construction of academic excellence: Sheep with five legs. *Organization, 19*(4), 507–524.

Van den Brink, M., & Benschop, Y. (2012b). Slaying the seven-headed dragon: The quest for gender change in academia. *Gender Work and Organization, 19*(1), 71–92. https://doi.org/10.1111/j.1468-0432.2011.00566.x

Van den Brink, M., & Benschop, Y. (2014). Gender in academic networking: The role of gatekeepers in professorial recruitment. *Journal of Management Studies, 51*(3), 460–492.

Van den Brink, M., & Benschop, Y. (2018). Gender interventions in the dutch police force: Resistance as a tool for change? *Journal of Change Management, 18*(3), 181–197.

Van den Brink, M., Benschop, Y., & Jansen, W. (2010). Transparency in academic recruitment: A problematic tool for gender equality? *Organization studies, 31*(11), 1459–1483.

Van der Lee, R., & Ellemers, N. (2015). Gender contributes to personal research funding success in The Netherlands. *Proceedings of the National Academy of Sciences, 112*(40), 12349–12353.

Woods, D., Benschop, Y., Van den Brink, M., & Verloo, M. (2019, August). *Intersectional equality.* Paper presented at the Academy of Management Meetings, Boston, MA.

CHAPTER 3

I DIDN'T EVEN KNOW I WAS SEXUALLY HARASSED

One Scholar's Journey to Learning More About Why Sexual Harassment Occurs

Mindy E. Bergman
Texas A&M University

I was sexually harassed at work in college.

Twenty-five years after the fact, this is a difficult sentence to write. At the time it happened, I couldn't have written it because I didn't know that I was being sexually harassed. I only knew that I didn't like the way I was treated and I wanted it to stop. But it didn't seem like something to complain about. No one intervened and stopped the harassment because it never occurred to me to complain. I am still friends with my bosses from those days, so I know that if I had reported, they would have done something.

Here's what happened. I was a resident advisor (RA). I was assigned to a floor in a large residence hall, where there were 22 RAs and around 1,200 residents. RAs lived in the residence halls with our "clients" (the residents), held office hours in the small offices attached to our rooms for a few hours

Perspectives on Gender and Work, pages 23–30

each week, staffed the main office a few hours each week, and created programming and events to promote well-being and community among our residents. Additionally, we had some safety and security responsibilities, such as reporting to maintenance when there were problems in common areas, checking on resident well-being, and making some resources (like the community vacuum cleaner) available as needed.

One of our major tasks was to be on duty a few nights each month. Being on duty included staffing the main office in the evening, doing rounds (walking through the building to ensure that the building was safe and secure and that students were following rules), and being on call throughout the night in response to situations. We served duty nights in pairs. My first semester as an RA, our director paired the novices (including me) with a veteran (in my case, "Ed"—not his real name) for most of our duty nights. Ed was my harasser. Ed and I sat in the office together and walked the halls on rounds together. Most nights (10–15 over the course of 4 months, lasting upwards of 6 hours per shift), Ed would make me walk ahead of him and would comment on how my body moved while I walked, using lascivious words and telling me how much he loved to see my booty move.

Being an RA is weird. You live with your clients and coworkers. You sleep mere feet away from them. You eat together regularly. In some residence halls, you shower next to them. The extent to which the public and private overlap is extensive. Rowdy banter was common in our workplace among the RAs. We went drinking together. We watched TV together, played sports together, studied together, went grocery shopping together. Some of us dated each other; some got married after graduation. Being harassed while I was on duty seemed like an extreme version of asking a coworker who just walked into the office if they were going to shower before dinner or asking a coworker who said that they had just woken up from a nap if they had dreamed about you.

Back then, I couldn't articulate the difference (even though it felt different) between this banter and what Ed did. As I've been writing this chapter, I have tried to figure out what it was then versus what I know now. Why did the rowdy banter in a small group of coworkers not feel like sexual harassment (SH) to me (but, looking back, maybe it did to some other coworkers), but when I was alone with this man, who was a veteran worker and who was easily 8 inches taller and 75 pounds heavier than me, it was? Was it his relative power? His size? His race? (I will note that he is Black whereas I am White.) He was attractive, smart, clearly going places after graduation. Other men I worked with were much the same, but with this particular man, in this particular situation, my safety felt tenuous. I think the most critical reasons why this was different were (a) when we were on duty, some difficult situations arose; I was supposed to be able to rely on him, and he didn't act like he cared about my safety and well-being; (b) he was supposed to be training me to be an equal, and instead he treated me like an object; (c) unlike conversations with coworkers in the cafeteria or at a party, I could not leave the situation; and (d) we were alone, for hours.

HOW I CAME TO UNDERSTAND THAT I HAD BEEN TARGETED, OR MY DEVELOPMENT AS A SCHOLAR

It's funny that it took so long for me to label my experience as sexual harassment. Even after I became a sexual harassment researcher, trained in one of the most sophisticated and prolific sexual harassment research labs in the world, even after I earned my PhD, even after I published numerous papers on SH and other forms of harassment, it didn't really sink in that I had been a target too. When the #MeToo movement took social media by storm in Fall 2017, I posted #MeToo because of this. Frankly, at that point, it had only been a few years that I had been able to label my experiences as harassment. For context, I graduated from college in 1996 and have been reliably and regularly labeling my experiences as sexual harassment—without hedges, without caveats—since around 2014.

I finished graduate school (in 2001) as a superbly trained psychologist, with a strong set of methodological skills and a clear set of questions about how individual behavior (e.g., sexual harassment) is influenced by group norms (e.g., organizational climate) and stereotypes (e.g., job-gender context), and how that individual behavior can influence the well-being of others (e.g., job attitudes and psychological symptoms in sexual harassment targets). What I lacked was a sophisticated understanding of how those group norms are not produced just by the people within the organization but by society as a whole and how some individuals and societies benefit from the continuation of these norms.

My thinking about sexual harassment and the workplace evolved through many pathways. The work of industrial-organizational (IO) psychologists who integrated gender studies with IO psychology (e.g., Berdahl, 2007; Cortina, 2008) started me down this road. My ideas about race, sex, power, and intersectionality were influenced by hearing talks from luminaries in race and diversity in organizations like Kimberlee Crenshaw, Myrtle Bell, Christine Stanley, and Kecia Thomas. I got to know scholars across my department, college, and university through the service I do, especially in the areas of undergraduate education and climate/diversity/ inclusion. I learned quite a lot from colleagues and friends engaged in women's and gender studies, Black Studies, and sociology. I also began teaching a course called Psychological Aspects of Human Sexuality that, in the parlance of APA Code of Ethics, was at the boundary of my area of competence when I began teaching it.

Through these experiences, I learned more about how my picture of sexual harassment was incomplete by being too narrowly focused on individuals and small groups and not informed by historical and contemporary views of power, sex, race, and hierarchy. Here is a list of phrases that I did not know when I left graduate school and which I have learned (and, occasionally, pretended I understood until I had a chance to look them up later) from these many smart and generous colleagues: hegemonic masculinity, critical race theory, critical feminist theory, rape culture, toxic masculinity, white supremacy, sociosexual hierarchy. I am sure there were many others. Learning about these topics developed my understanding of sexual harassment as well as my understanding of why it is easy to overlook some sexually harassing experiences, like mine. Before I learned about topics like rape culture and hegemonic masculinity, it did not occur to me that I had been taught in both subtle and outrageous ways that there are societal expectations about accommodating men's sociosexual behavior as okay even when it crosses women's boundaries. That helped explain how I couldn't label my own SH experiences as such.

My early writings on harassment and discrimination reflect this lack of knowledge about the broader sociosexual structures. These early papers have titles like "Structural Equation Models of Sexual Harassment: Longitudinal Explorations and Cross-Sectional Generalizations" (Glomb, Munson, Hulin, Bergman, & Drasgow, 1999), "Test of the Cross-Cultural Generalizability of a Model of Sexual Harassment" (Wasti, Bergman, Glomb, & Drasgow, 2000), or "Sexual Harassment Severity: Assessing Situation and Personal Determinants and Outcomes" (Langhout et al., 2005). Don't get me wrong—I am proud of these papers and the contributions they've made to our collective understanding of sexual harassment and its causes and consequences. But from the vantage point of another 15 years' experience, I can see what is missing in this work: a discussion of the broader societal factors that cause organizations to be structured as they are, that lead individuals to approach the world with a particular lens, and that indicate the stubbornness of the problems of harassment and discrimination are unlikely to be resolved by individual-level interventions. Also missing is a critical evaluation of our field and its underlying assumptions, which directs researchers to a narrow set of questions and to suggest a narrow set of interventions.

THE PAPERS I AM MOST PROUD OF

As I further developed as a scholar and thinker through the experiences described above, I began to critique the perspective of IO psychology in its attempts to improve diversity and inclusion and reduce SH and other forms of harassment and discrimination. This has resulted in a series of commentaries and focal papers in *Industrial-Organizational Psychology: Perspectives on Science and Practice.* I have written about how training is likely to have little real effect on sexual harassment in the workplace, so we should also use other tools that we have as IO psychologists (Hernandez, Bergman, & Liu, 2020), and we should consider the larger societal and organizational power structures when working to mitigate harassment (Bergman, 2019). I've done parallel work in gender equity and STEM, describing how an individual-level focus misses the important societal-level factors that push and pull people in and out of STEM fields (Miner, Walker, Jean, Bergman, & Kaunas, 2018). I've argued that using performance criteria that are currently established for jobs that are producing negative societal outcomes (i.e., policing) to select people only perpetuates a negative societal cycle, and we need to refocus our efforts on revising these criteria—and then all of our systems—to reduce police shootings of Black and Brown men in the United States (Bergman, Walker, & Jean, 2016). I have noted that concerns about so-called reverse discrimination seem to suggest that "bias that favors minorities is somehow worse than bias that favors majority members" (Bergman & Salter, 2013, p. 443). I have analyzed the samples used in IO psychology research and questioned whether our field's knowledge base is tainted by classism (Bergman & Jean, 2016).

As a group, these papers and others (Diaz & Bergman, 2013; Thompson, Bergman, Culbertson, & Huffman, 2013) have tried to broaden the discussion about harassment and discrimination in IO psychology beyond a focus on the individual. This work goes well beyond SH and reflects the concerns I have developed about intersectional systems of oppression. These papers criticize IO psychology's approach to diversity and mistreatment. These papers encourage (I hope!) IO psychology to consider societal injustice and inequality, how they are reproduced in work and educational organizations, and what we can do to disrupt these cycles and create better, more just organizations.

None of my work in *Industrial-Organizational Psychology: Perspectives on Science and Practice* is what anyone would call traditional IO psychology, attempting to achieve the elusive ideal of a multi-wave survey data from 13 sites of a regional bank examining seven highly correlated dependent variables. But I think it's important, probably my most important work. We cannot move forward and solve the problems of harassment and discrimination if we premise our work on individual actors affected by local group norms who are mistreating others. We need to dig into the fundamental social systems that underlie our behavior and our organizations in order to make real change. That's the message I have been trying to send.

LOOKING BACK, LOOKING FORWARD

Those are all reflections of a 46-year-old woman, with considerable knowledge on the topic, reflecting on the experiences of her 20-year-old self and my growth and development as a scholar and a person in the years in between. Did being harassed in college nudge me into sexual harassment and diversity research? Maybe. There is a good chance I would have ended up doing research on difference and diversity, inequality and mistreatment, regardless of what happened to me as a first-time organizational employee. Being a religious minority, having finely calibrated equity sensitivity, and being a bit of a hothead were also a good recipe for finding this area of research and diving in.

Being mistreated—sexually harassed—at work has given me insights into targets' behaviors that maybe other scholars who haven't been harassed (if there are any) might not have. There were times that I played into Ed's degrading talk, exaggerating how I walked in the hopes that I could play the whole thing off as a joke and we could move on to something else. There were times that I ignored him or pretended I couldn't hear him. Occasionally, I tried to make him walk in front of me, although that never lasted. I would regularly offer to trade duty nights with others who had a conflict arise with their schedule. I didn't tell a friend or keep a contemporaneous journal. I didn't cry daily or avoid the perpetrator. I was 19–20 years old and had only heard of sexual harassment from watching Anita Hill testify at the Senate confirmation hearings for now Supreme Court Justice Clarence Thomas. What she said happened to her didn't look like anything that happened to me.

My experiences make me ask why so few people are able to label their experiences as sexual harassment. I know I am not alone in being unable to label my experiences when they happened, and I even struggled to do so after developing expertise. My experiences also make me ask about perpetrator behaviors and cognitions, in the moment and later—even much later. I wonder sometimes if Ed ever thinks about me. If he does, he probably thought he was flirting. He would deny that he had perpetrated SH, but would acknowledge his behaviors. The literatures on rape culture and toxic masculinity have insights on why this would happen, and it makes me think about what kinds of interventions we can make—in the workplace, in schools, in society—that would cause people to reframe their understanding of these behaviors to recognize the harm that they could cause.

My experiences and my expertise make me worry about what our youngest workers, new to the workforce, are learning about how they should expect to be treated throughout their careers. I worry about the carryover from their negative workplace experiences to their education. I worry that they early select-out of some careers because of what they experience in their first jobs. I wonder where and how we can effectively intervene in order to reduce these experiences and increase both school/career functioning and, more importantly, mental health.

So what questions do I think we need to address in harassment and discrimination? We need to know what the perpetrators are thinking. We need to know what we need to do to intervene in organizations and in societies to reduce the interpersonal violence that is predicated on people's demography. We need to rethink organizational structures and how they normalize some kinds of people and careers and marginalize others. We need to do research on firing people who perpetrate harassment to see what effect it has on the rest of the workgroup and organization. In my office, I have a sign that reads "There is no abusive 'genius' who could not be replaced by someone who isn't sh**ty." I'd love to see that research program.

As a scholar of a certain age (oh, wait, I told you 46), I also want to note that I started linking the workplace, society, and IO psychology recently, but that was only because I wasn't a mature enough scholar to do so earlier. I lacked the knowledge to even see my own harassment! I want to encourage young scholars who are wondering where IO fits into the story of social justice and societal change to just jump in and get started. Do not take the fact that we aren't studying something as a sign that we can't or shouldn't. Get us started.

REFERENCES

Berdahl, J. L. (2007). Harassment based on sex: Protecting social status in the context of gender hierarchy. *Academy of Management Review, 32*(2), 641–658.

Bergman, M. E. (2019). Ending harassment is more about changing power structures than about training. *Industrial-Organizational Psychology: Perspectives on Science and Practice, 12*(1), 42–47.

Bergman, M. E., & Jean, V. A. (2016). Where have all the workers gone? *Industrial and Organizational Psychology: Perspectives on Science and Practice, 9*(1), 84–113. http://dx.doi.org/10.1017/iop.2015.70

Bergman, M. E., & Salter, P. (2013). Backlash! What it is and what we can do to avoid it. *Industrial and Organizational Psychology: Perspectives on Science and Practice, 6*(4), 442–450.

Bergman, M. E., Walker, J. M., & Jean, V. A. (2016). A simple solution to policing problems: Women! *Industrial and Organizational Psychology: Perspectives on Science and Practice, 9*(3), 590–597.

Cortina, L. M. (2008). Unseen injustice: Incivility as modern discrimination in organizations. *Academy of Management Review, 33*(1), 55–75.

Diaz, I., & Bergman, M. E. (2013). It's not us, it's you: Why isn't research on minority workers appearing in our "top-tier" journals? *Industrial and Organizational Psychology: Perspectives on Science and Practice, 6*(1), 70–75. https://doi.org/10.1111/iops.12010

Glomb, T. M., Munson, L. J., Hulin, C. L., Bergman, M. E., & Drasgow, F. (1999). Structural equation models of sexual harassment: Longitudinal explorations and cross-sectional generalizations. *Journal of Applied Psychology, 84*(1), 14–28.

Hernandez, T. R., Bergman, M. E., & Liu, S. N. C. (2020). Why is training the only answer? *Industrial and Organizational Psychology, 13*(2), 147–153.

Langhout, R. D., Bergman, M. E., Cortina, L. M., Fitzgerald, L. F., Drasgow, F., & Williams, J. H. (2005). Sexual harassment severity: Assessing situational and personal determinants and outcomes. *Journal of Applied Social Psychology, 35*(5), 975–1007.

Miner, K. N., Walker, J. M., Jean, V. A., Bergman, M. E., & Kaunas, C. (2018). From "her" problem to "our" problem: Using an individual lens vs. a social-structural lens to understand gender inequity in STEM. *Industrial and Organizational Psychology: Perspectives on Science and Practice, 11*(2), 267–290. https://doi.org/10.1017/iop.2018.7

Thompson, R. J., Bergman, M. E., Culbertson, S. S., & Huffman, A. H. (2013). Yes, we're fishing – in rough waters for hard-to-find fish. *Industrial and Organizational Psychology: Perspectives on Science and Practice, 6*(1), 61–65. https://doi.org/10.1111/iops.12008

Wasti, S. A., Bergman, M. E., Glomb, T. M., & Drasgow, F. (2000). Test of the cross-cultural generalizability of a model of sexual harassment. *Journal of Applied Psychology, 85*(5), 766–778.

CHAPTER 4

MEN, GENDER, AND SECOND-ORDER BIAS

A Reflection

Martin N. Davidson
University of Virginia

Nearly a decade ago, I was approached by scholars at Catalyst to contribute blog posts to a new site called MARC (Men Advocating for Real Change). The vision for MARC was to serve as an online community that would empower and inspire more men to work toward building more inclusive workplaces. As a result of this work, I found myself exploring the dynamics of male resistance to both gender equity awareness and to the concrete change that can emerge from that awareness. As I reflected on the opportunity to contribute, I saw myself then—as I do now—as a man reasonably conscious and aware of gender dynamics and the persistent inequities that result from them. I was invested in studying the literature—and adding to it modestly—wherever I could. Moreover, I found myself both critical of men who blatantly exhibited biased behavior, whether conscious or unconscious. I embraced a strong commitment to supporting behavior change in these men whenever I could. What I failed to appreciate was the way

Perspectives on Gender and Work, pages 31–37

in which the positive work I engaged in, including my writing for MARC, masked my persistent contribution to gender inequity. A decade's worth of perspective leads me to offer this reflection on what I call second-order diversity bias, the patterns of thought and behavior in men that reinforce gender inequity *after* a man becomes "enlightened." In the spirit of the invitation to contribute to this special volume on gender and work, I share my thinking on how I, as a cisgender man, make sense of my experiences and behaviors in a gendered world with the hope that my stories spark insight and conversation for anyone reading along.

EXPLORING MALE PRIVILEGE. AGAIN.

When I embarked on my task of writing blog posts for MARC, I was relatively unaware of the dual persona I was enacting. Despite a narrative I had constructed for myself of relative skillfulness with my gender bias, I continued to enact microaggressions toward friends and colleagues, both women and men. I supported many of my women colleagues in their professional development, yet I failed to take critical stands on behalf of some of them when I could have. I justified my inaction at these watershed moments by reminding myself of all the good I had done, and was continuing to do, to support gender equity. I reminded myself of the many instances where I had supported and mentored women leading to professional success. I remained always ready and available to lend a helpful ear to any colleague seeking advice. I used this historical evidence, most of which was accurate, to support my narrative of being a "good guy." But by invoking these stories, I supported myself to maintain the relative comfort of my male privilege and dominance. I took myself out of the continuing work of identifying and interrupting biased behavior. I failed to remember that the beneficial outcomes of male privilege never really end, that they are reinforced relentlessly. And I was not willing to scrutinize and counter them.

At first, I did not fully grasp the nature of this apparent incongruity between my self-image and my behavior. It was just baffling and debilitating. The subtlety and insidiousness of privilege is well documented (e.g., Pratto & Stewart, 2012). I began to deepen my understanding of the phenomenon when my colleague Heather Wishik and I undertook a qualitative examination of dominance, commonly known as privilege (Wishik & Davidson, 2012). We sought to better understand the experience of holding dominant identities and the underlying structure of dominance. We argued that one can enact a dominant identity along a continuum of skillfulness. At one end point of that continuum, people who hold dominant or privileged group identities are relatively unconscious of privilege and are vulnerable to enacting conscious and unconscious bias and harm. At the other end of the continuum, these individuals are aware and open to the presence of internalized and behavioral bias as a consequence of the dominant identity they hold. These individuals are able to embrace and engage that dominant identity in ways that produce generative relationships and that reduces bias and inequity. With this general framing of privilege and dominance in hand, I have been able to think more deeply about how a man—how I—could be simultaneously a gender equity advocate and assailant.

SECOND-ORDER GENDER BIAS

Second-order gender bias is a subtle means by which gender inequity is perpetuated. By second-order strategies, I reference a concept Ray Friedman and I wrote about several years ago in which we theorized about why diversity conflicts in organizations remained so persistent (Friedman & Davidson, 2001). We argued that first-order conflicts were sparked by unambiguous biases and inequities visited upon marginalized group members and perceived as minimally impactful to dominant group members. For example, gender discrimination deprives women of equal access to critical developmental opportunities and promotions. This first-order conflict spawns a solution: implement a high potential "fast track" promotion process for women. When men learn of the new fast-track process, they react with calls of "reverse discrimination." Now a second-order conflict emerges. A debate ensues on whether fast tracks are fair to men or not. The debate sparks resistance from men, and women are outraged at the men's pushback. Second-order conflicts are generated by remedies or responses to first-order conflicts and often create identity threats for both marginalized and dominant group members. Typically, second-order diversity conflicts are complex and morally controversial. In this example, the fast-track program is weakened or tabled in response to this second-order conflict, and progress toward advancing women equitably is thwarted. Second-order conflict usually serves to divert attention and resources away from addressing the fundamental first-order conflict and the status quo reigns (Davidson & Proudford, 2008).

But this type of dynamic is not restricted to intergroup dynamics. At the individual level, a parallel process can occur. A man who commits himself to attacking gender inequality decides to attend gender awareness workshops, learn more about feminist theory, and speak on behalf of women colleagues at work who he observes are being discounted or ignored. These are all admirable steps for him to take and all indicative of a first-order response to his awareness of gender inequity. At this point, he begins to feel confident that he is a capable male ally. He develops an ego-enhancing narrative that he's one of the good guys, that he is increasingly immune to enacting gender bias. And when he does exhibit biased behavior (as he absolutely will at some point) his self-image as a capable ally motivates him to discount his bias. In fact, the more egregious the biased behavior, the more its impact is harmful to women, the stronger his motivation to reject that bias becomes. After all, a good guy could *never* behave so inappropriately. This is the essence of second-order bias.

In retrospect, I have seen myself enact this kind of second-order bias. It is particularly difficult to spot and to combat. Nevertheless, there are ways to overcome it, to transform the narrative from one that reinforces defensiveness to one that fosters personal change.

WAYS TO INTERRUPT SECOND-ORDER BIAS

Mindfulness Practice

There is an emerging body of theoretical and practical insight on how to mitigate gender bias. Most people seek concrete action-oriented solutions, embracing steps for redesigning systems all the way to scripts and language to use when a bias shows itself. I have found that the work of interrupting this second-order bias is more subtle and probably resistant to simpler, concrete action steps. Enacting this kind of bias utilizes psychologically sophisticated routines to perpetuate itself. Disrupting these routines may require more complex strategies and tactics.

One possible approach is to engage in mindfulness practice. Several years ago, I read an article on sexual misconduct in which actor Minnie Driver offered a scathing critique of men—one man in particular, actor Matt Damon—who attempted to categorize the different behaviors that constitute sexual abuse (Helmore, 2017). In an interview with ABC News, Damon said alleged sexual misconduct by powerful men involved "a spectrum of behavior," discussing his perception of the impact of various kinds of sexual transgressions. In her comments after that interview, Driver countered that whether the behavior was verbal taunting or casual touching or rape, men cannot understand what abuse is like on a daily level and therefore, should not attempt to differentiate or explain sexual misconduct against women. I recall my defensive reaction while reading Driver's comments: What was she talking about? I agreed wholeheartedly that as a man, I could not understand the experience of being the target of constant sexual abuse the way women are in a heteronormative environment. But I rejected the position that I could not and should not analyze and comment on the phenomenon. Indeed, I reasoned, as men, we have a responsibility to engage this way if we are serious about trying to change the toxic status quo. She was just wrong, I concluded. In addition, the article noted that she used to date Damon. *That's* part of what motivated this whole thing, I surmised. She didn't like her ex commenting on this. I wondered if this was a veiled attack on him. Bad relationships can lead people to be bitter toward one another. There was quite a show going on in my head.

But while I was being annoyed and sanctimonious and sexist, I was *simultaneously* aware that I was having this string of reactions. I was being mindful about my bias. Simply put, mindfulness is the practice of bringing awareness to what one is directly experiencing via one's senses or one's state of mind. It can sound esoteric, but it is actually important in very practical ways. A growing body of research points to a variety of physical, emotional, and psychological benefits to cultivating a practice of mindfulness (Papies, Pronk, Keesman, & Barsalou, 2015; Van Doesum, Van Lange, & Van Lange, 2013). Far too little attention has been paid to how mindfulness can be an asset in interrupting bias. Because I became aware of my reactions, I was able to reflect on and analyze those reactions, learn from them, and ultimately, change my behavior.

Immersion

Building on the practice of mindfulness, a subsequent strategy that men can undertake to counter second-order bias is to immerse oneself in a counter-normative gendered context. A counter-normative space is not just an environment in which women are in the numerical majority. Rather, it is a space that intentionally privileges women's experiences. Typically, entry into these spaces is only available through invitation and men's roles in the space are somewhat prescribed. My experience of immersion in a gender counter-normative space was an invitation to teach in a women's leadership development program. I served as the only male faculty member on a team of three faculty. All participants were women enrolled in a week-long program. I recall being jokingly introduced by my colleague who led the program as the "token male." It was a funny and unsettling moment to hear myself described that way and, as the week unfolded, I really decided to pay attention to my role in the program.

Just before I taught my first session in the program, I had an email exchange with a female colleague about women's experience in organizations. We were lamenting the fact that in her organization, the focus of diversity that year was on increasing the representation of people of color because, at about 25–30% representation, the company determined it had "taken care" of the gender issues. My colleague and I were agreeing that it is common for organizations to think that because a near critical mass of women have been recruited to a company, that it has solved its gender problems. Frequently, this creates a cadre of disaffected women who are part of this "satisfied" minority. As I worked with the women in the program, I began to understand more deeply the frustration of their experience being "check marked"—having assumptions made that they were content with their experience as women in the organization—while actually experiencing ongoing marginalization.

But my experience in this counter-normative context also provided insight into my own ongoing learning as a "good guy." For example, I quickly realized that my experience and expertise in diversity did not spare me from the ongoing sense of awkwardness and defensiveness I felt at times when I was with the group. I felt ignorant when I heard of women's negative experiences, the magnitude and complexity of which I was largely clueless. It wasn't that I did not know that women such as those in the programs struggled to succeed—I have read the research. Rather the experience of being in context began to break down the shielding and defensiveness that was part of my second-order bias. The visceral experience of being *present* with the women is what mattered. Even as I wandered mentally, struggling to muster narratives that would explain why these women had different experiences than I had in our respective professional journeys, being present in the context continued to pull me back to the reality of their stories and to the healing they experienced as a result of being in the program.

I also noted how presence in this context fostered deeper insight into my intersectional experience. At times, I could not help but center my racial identity as a Black man. I noted that the stories the women shared often mirrored my racial experience. The parallels were compelling, and there was something for me to learn in this regard. But I quickly realized that frequently, I retreated to a racial analysis as a way of shielding myself from the discomfort of the women's stories. As a man, I had the privilege of softening the impact of their words with the "comfort" of my experience of struggle. Because I was in this context, however, I discovered that the more I could set aside the familiarity of seeing myself only racially, the more I could actually hear and understand what the women in the room—both participants and my own colleagues—were telling me about their lives. I was able to practice being less absorbed by my own experience of marginalization and instead be more open to understanding their life experiences. This is part of what it means to engage constructively with one's second-order bias.

LESSONS

There is something in the writing of an essay like this that feels well worn. I find the crafting and reiteration of experiences of privilege and dominance tiring, especially when I am mining my own privilege. But I am continuing to appreciate the necessity of constantly confronting dominant identity experiences, pushing through discomfort and reticence, and moving toward insight. I suspect that beyond second-order gender bias, there are additional "orders" of bias awaiting scrutiny and remedy. The confrontation is strenuous and the appeal of resting in the comfort and obliviousness of privilege is compelling. I continue to search for new ways to remain connected to the work it takes to alter the status quo. I try to remind myself that it is not just about me. It's not even about just helping women. It's about manifesting organizations and communities and societies that are right. Just right.

REFERENCES

Davidson, M. N., & Proudford, K. L. (2008). Cycles of resistance: How dominants and subordinants collude to undermine diversity efforts in organizations. In K. M. Thomas (Ed.), *Diversity resistance in organizations.* (pp. 249–272). New York, NY: Taylor & Francis.

Friedman, R. A., & Davidson, M. N. (2001). Managing diversity and second-order conflict. *International Journal of Conflict Management, 12*(2), 132–153.

Helmore, E. (2017, December 17). Minnie driver: Men like Matt Damon 'cannot understand what abuse is like'. *The Guardian.* Retrieved from www.theguardian.com/film/2017/dec/16/minnie-driver-matt-damon-men-cannot-understand-abuse?utm_source=esp&utm_medium=Email&utm_campaign=GU%2BToday%2BUSA%2B-%2BCollections%2B2017&utm_term=257011&subid=17768429&CMP=GT_US_collection

Papies, E. K., Pronk, T. M., Keesman, M., & Barsalou, L. W. (2015). The benefits of simply observing: Mindful attention modulates the link between motivation and behavior. *Journal of Personality and Social Psychology, 108*(1), 148–170. https://doi.org/10.1037/a0038032

Pratto, F., & Stewart, A. L. (2012). Group dominance and the half-blindness of privilege. *Journal of Social Issues, 68*(1), 28–45. https://doi.org/10.1111/j.1540-4560.2011.01734.x

Van Doesum, N. J., Van Lange, D. A. W., & Van Lange, P. A. M. (2013). Social mindfulness: Skill and will to navigate the social world. *Journal of Personality and Social Psychology, 105*(1), 86–103. https://doi.org/10.1037/a0032540

Wishik, H., & Davidson, M. (2012). *A model of grounded identity management* (Unpublished manuscript). University of Virginia, Darden Graduate School of Business.

CHAPTER 5

RELUCTANTLY LEARNING TO APPRECIATE THE IMPORTANCE OF GENDER

Nancy DiTomaso
Rutgers Business School—Newark and New Brunswick

I did not go to graduate school to study gender. Far from it. I came of age in the 1950s, graduated from high school in the midst of the civil rights movement, and then arrived at graduate school at the end of the 1960s in the middle of the Vietnam War. I was interested in how jobs were being replaced by automation, how the caste system of race was being challenged by social movements and urban riots, and how global capitalism was causing upheaval all over the world. I wanted to do research on power and politics and stratification and inequality, in other words, serious issues, not on gender, which I perceived to be a pigeonhole that would constrain me.

Like the social movements of the 1960s, I did not see gender as a major issue, and frankly, I did not fully understand why there was a need for a women's movement. Betty Friedan's book (1963), *The Feminine Mystique,* was published the same year as the first urban riot and the year that President John F. Kennedy was assassinated. It was also a year before the Civil

Perspectives on Gender and Work, pages 39–55

Rights Act was passed and the War on Poverty was launched under President Lyndon Johnson. Friedan helped create the National Organization for Women in 1966 during the height of the civil rights movement, the Vietnam War, the space race, and the Cold War. In this historical context, a movement that focused primarily on the malaise of White, middle class women who did not feel fulfilled in their lives was not something that resonated with me. I had grown up in a working-class family, in which my mother and the women with whom I was closest worked outside the home for pay, and in the family, they made primary decisions and enacted leadership roles. It never occurred to me that I would not be working at a paid job, nor did I think of myself as having a secondary role or a back seat in any of my endeavors. I was not concerned about being constrained by the "feminine mystique," and I did not feel that I needed a women's movement to encourage my professional ambitions.

It is not, of course, that I was unaware of gender issues. I was keenly aware of them. In high school and college, I was sexually harassed in almost every job that I held, including by the undergraduate dean for whom I worked during my senior year of college. I was startled that after he called me into his office to give me a token graduation gift that he then picked me up and kissed me. On my drive home one night, my car was purposely hit on a dark and deserted street by a man who then tried to rape me and threatened to kill me. When I finally got home and my parents called the police, the policeman made insinuating remarks suggesting that it was my fault. And male colleagues at work thought that because I talked my way out of the situation that it was a bit amusing, even though the man had beat me with his fists. The detective who handled the case later told me that I should not ruin the man's life by pressing charges, because he had a wife and three children. So, indeed, I understood gender issues.

My working-class family did not encourage me to go to college despite my being a very good student. Paying for college was on my own. To earn money, I worked full time as a secretary (because of course, I could type) for 2 years while attending a local college four nights a week. My desire to go to a "real" university, though, finally led me to transfer to Ohio State. It was there that I learned about graduate school, while working for the lecherous dean. I initially planned only to get a master's and then to teach high school, but once in graduate school, I reformulated my plans. While sexual harassment was always a threat and continued in nonacademic summer jobs, my conscious strategy for deflecting potential harassment from male faculty members was to talk up my religious faith and to play the role of a daughter, rather than a coequal. That had the downsides of potentially not being taken seriously, but it also made me off limits for some faculty who seemed to have ambiguous relationships with other female graduate students.

There were very few women faculty at that time, and interestingly, one of the most prominent ones in the department studied romantic relationships. The women's movement was just then getting underway, initially as an outgrowth of the other social movements of the period. One experience I recall seemed very strange to me. Other women graduate students wanted to call a meeting to set rules about turn-taking while speaking in meetings of students and faculty. Because I had never had any difficulty speaking up or speaking out, once again, I did not understand why there was an issue or a need. As I recall, the rules were never adopted and the organization of women graduate students did not get off the ground, although many of the women students were joining consciousness raising groups and turning their research attention to women's issues. At that time, the focus was on women and not more broadly on gender.

It was in my first academic job in a sociology department where I began to see more clearly how gender played a role in who was valued on the faculty and how people got rewarded. The situation was somewhat more complex, though, than the way it is sometimes portrayed. It turns out that I was hired in this job because my graduate school adviser lobbied heavily with the incoming department chair and another good friend on the faculty. My advisor's friend, a senior male faculty member, appointed himself as my mentor (for which I was grateful), but when he left the university soon after I joined, he literally turned the responsibility for me over to another senior male faculty member. The new mentor turned out to be extremely helpful in my career because he closely edited a number of my papers and in doing so, taught me how to write. But the relationship was also ambiguous because he started giving me very expensive presents and inviting me to lunch or dinner alone with him. I finessed the situation as best I could, and the relationship turned into a lifelong friendship and nothing more.

Several junior women faculty in the department did not get tenure, and when the time came for me to be evaluated, I did not get tenure either. Looking back, I can now admit that I probably did not understand how to structure my academic career. But I also looked at the faculty directory for the university and saw that across the university there were 83 couples, with almost all of the women on the faculty either married to or sleeping with a male faculty member. Many of these women were in lecturer positions, not in tenure track jobs. One of the exceptions was a senior woman in my department who had been hired to head up a women's studies program. She was not especially supportive of me, in part, because I did not do research on women. She told me that my work was just too complicated because it required the reader to think. Although I had no intention of actually following through, I ended up filing an Equal Employment Opportunity Commission (EEOC) complaint against the department because I wanted it on the record in case other women faced issues subsequently.

I still remember walking up the stairs to my office when the department chair, who was clearly a misogynist, opened the letter from the EEOC. He let out a loud cry of dismay.

One of the advantages of my first academic position, though, was that because it was a prominent university, well-known academics were always coming to town and often requested or asked to give seminars at our department. Partly because of that, I gained a great deal of visibility in the field. In addition, with the help of various friends and mentors, I started taking on leadership roles in professional organizations, even as an untenured faculty member. As one person mentioned along the way, people clearly knew me, they liked me, and they thought I did good work. Hence, I was able to get another job at a significant salary increase when I left this first job. On the job market, however, I had several strange experiences when after the interview more than one department chair or dean told me that I was "head and shoulders" above other candidates, and therefore, they could not hire me. In one case, the recruitment chair told me that salary increases at the school were pooled and that if they hired me, I would get all of their raises. In another case, the dean had already offered the job to someone else before I was interviewed. These were experiences that helped me understand in a way different from my initial presumptions that an academic environment can be very competitive and that people are not necessarily rewarded for merit.

Through a circuitous route, I finally ended up in my current position where I have been for over 35 years, now as a distinguished professor. Over the years, I have served at each rank and have also taken on administrative positions as department chair, PhD director, and vice dean for faculty and research. Unlike previous positions, at the outset, the senior male faculty members encouraged me and supported my promotions, and I was also a favorite of the dean who hired me, it seems, because he put me on a number of committees where I gained visibility across the school. I also had a good relationship with the campus provost. Even so, there were a number of important incidents where gender dynamics came into play. The two other women who were in the department when I was hired did not get tenure, so I was left as the only woman in my department and one of only a handful in our school of about 120 faculty members.

Once tenured and as an associate professor, I became department chair. Immediately after I took on the chair's role, untenured male faculty members started treating me differently. They became very deferential and obsequious in interactions with me, and yet behind my back, one or two of the junior men aligned themselves with the dean against me. It turns out after talking with female friends in similar roles across the country that my experience was not a unique one. Prominent women faculty at major universities with whom I discussed the situation reported that they, too, had similar experiences of junior men plotting against them, and sometimes succeeding. Interestingly, at this time, senior male faculty members in the school were allied with me against the dean, but in retrospect, I finally understood that I was out in front as the spokesperson, while they remained in the background urging me on. One of the senior male faculty members called me every night for several years to complain about the dean. Others did so fairly regularly. My husband thought it was a very strange situation, as did I, but I did not know how to put a stop to it diplomatically.

In my role as department chair (at different times) and later as vice dean, I was instrumental in our department and the school hiring more women faculty members and faculty members of color. Doing so was often an uphill battle for which I had to maneuver around obstacles. In one case, I played a role as department chair, with the support of the provost, to tell the department members who really wanted to hire a male faculty member that they could not get permission to do so unless they also hired a female candidate, which they finally agreed to do. This was back in the days when guidelines about affirmative action still mattered, and the provost was upset that our school kept getting cited for underutilization, meaning they were not hiring enough women. Interestingly, I had to tell the female faculty candidate hired at this time to ask for a better deal, because the male candidate had done so, and I wanted to create as much equity as possible. At present, our department is about half female, but it was a long time in the making.

As a senior, tenured faculty member, I soon became a spokesperson for women's issues in the department and the school. Although my research has not primarily been on gender issues, my colleagues often interpret my work as focusing on gender, presumably because they assume that a woman faculty member who studies diversity and inequality will be concerned mostly about gender issues. In a sense, this situation is precisely the pigeonhole I was trying to avoid early in my career that has now become part of my reputation, although I now see it as a credential rather than a constraint.

RESEARCH ON GENDER

The first paper I wrote specifically on gender issues (DiTomaso, 1989)—more than a decade after finishing my degree—appeared as a chapter in an edited book on *The Sexuality in Organizations* (Hearn, Burrell, Sheppard, & Tancred-Sheriff, 1989). The paper was developed inadvertently as part of a different study when conversations with women at a large manufacturing firm about labor force issues uncovered a constant theme about sexual harassment on the job. It was especially poignant because these were jobs that paid enough for women to support themselves and their families, and yet, they constantly felt vulnerable and uncomfortable. As one said, the guys at work would never behave the same way outside of work. Although only a chapter in a somewhat obscure book, this paper became one of my most cited works. Subsequently, I was asked to be part of an all-academy symposium at the 1994 Academy of Management meetings on sexuality and organizations. I did a presentation entitled, "The CEO's Second Wife," which was about the trophy wives of powerful and rich men. The presentation highlighted issues of sexual discrimination, sexual harassment, and the gendering of organizations. Because it was an all-academy symposium, it was scheduled for a large ballroom that probably could have accommodated 1,000 or more people. I think there were probably 20 people in attendance, which undoubtedly reflected that AOM members at the time were not entirely comfortable with acknowledging the relevance of sexuality to the workplace, nor with showing their interest in such topics at a professional meeting.

I did not do additional writing on gender issues until several years later collecting data for a large survey on diversity among scientists and engineers. The focus of the study was initially on citizenship, but of course, it also addressed issues of race/ethnicity and gender as well. Because of this study and some of the work that followed from it (Cordero, DiTomaso, & Farris, 1996; DiTomaso & Farris, 1992a, 1992b; DiTomaso, Farris, & Cordero, 1993; Post, DiTomaso, Farris, & Cordero, 2009; Post, DiTomaso, Lowe, Farris, & Cordero, 2009), I ended up attending many conferences on women in science, engineering, and math, and I became somewhat of an expert on that issue as well. About the same time, I also had an article published in *Academy of Management Journal* (Barnum, Liden, & DiTomaso, 1995) from the data I had collected earlier on the labor force.

Overall, my research has focused on issues of diversity and inequality more generally, with perhaps more research on race and ethnic differences than on gender differences. The height of my academic achievement, in my view, is the book on which I worked for 20 years, *The American Non-Dilemma: Racial Inequality Without Racism* (DiTomaso, 2013). The book won the C. Wright Mills Award and came in second for the Academy of Management Terry Book award. It also won several other awards and received a great deal of media attention. The main premise of the book is that scholars and the media have focused so much on discrimination against and racism toward minorities as explanations for racial inequality that we have missed that the primary dynamic that reproduces racial inequality is that Whites help other Whites, especially to get jobs that pay a living wage and that provide important benefits. My argument is not just another iteration of arguing that there is White privilege, because I argue that the ultimate White privilege is that Whites do not have to be racists to benefit from racial inequality. Instead, they gain significant advantages by receiving favoritism, preference, and help from other Whites, and these dynamics are reinforced by the extreme segregation of neighborhoods and schools in most of the

United States. The argument, of course, could be extended to men helping other men as well as to other dimensions of diversity. In a subsequent article (DiTomaso, 2015), I endeavored to make my argument more general and to place it within the context of the ongoing research on diversity. I specifically contrast my argument about favoritism and advantage with discussions within the diversity literature on anti-racism and prejudice reduction, implicit bias, microaggressions, the need for mentors, and White privilege.

My book is based on interviews with Whites between the ages of 25–55 in three parts of the country—New Jersey, Ohio, and Tennessee—on their educational and job histories, as well as their views of inequality and public policy. Because I interviewed both men and women and both working class and middle class people, I gathered a lot of information about gender issues that for purposes of length and focus did not receive much attention in the book. For example, although I found that for about 70% of the jobs my interviewees obtained over their lifetimes they got help from family, friends, or acquaintances to get the job—which is what I mean by Whites helping other Whites—that for men the average was 75% of jobs, while for women the average was 60% of jobs. While both numbers are high, I interpreted the difference as having to do with women's jobs not paying a living wage as often as men's jobs. Hence, for women especially, there is less at stake and less need to call on help from friends when one job is as good or bad as another.

Because men's jobs pay more, I also found in my interviews, but did not discuss in the book, that most adult women were dependent on their relationships with the men in their lives in order to live a decent life. In other words, many women are only one divorce away from a completely changed economic situation, and often after a divorce or other personal challenge, finding a new mate is often what makes the difference in the kind of life a woman and her children can live. Those who remain single are more likely to have financial difficulty and are able to offer much less to their children, if any, in terms of opportunity. Because I only interviewed White women for this book, I did not address the complexities of nonwhite women in this regard.

Perhaps one extreme example of this kind of dependence is that I interviewed a woman who described herself as a trophy wife, and indeed she was. She had had a long-term affair with the CEO of a major company and eventually convinced him to leave his wife to marry her. When he died, she inherited his money, but she was sued by her husband's daughter over the estate. The wife won the lawsuit, as she said, because she had a better lawyer. And she subsequently married the lawyer, who had also left his wife for her. When I asked her, as I did of all of my interviewees, if she deserved the kind of life that she was now leading, she said that yes, of course, because she had given up her youth and had given up having children of her own for these relationships. As she said, there was no other route to her having the same kind of lifestyle.

When she was working for the company whose CEO she married, she said that they would not give her a better job and would not pay her more, so she chose the only path available to her to have the kind of lifestyle that she thought was warranted for her. I found her, surprisingly, to be a very likable person and one with ostensibly good values about people and public policy. It was not what I had anticipated in my earlier commentary on trophy wives.

Despite not focusing primarily on gender issues in my research, as it turns out, I ended up developing a course entitled Women Leading in Business, which I have now been teaching for over a decade. The course is part of a program on women's leadership in our undergraduate program, and I agreed to develop the course because I knew that there was no one else on our faculty who had better grounding than I had in the research on gender. Surprisingly, although my university had identified gender as a key research theme and even though we have a number of centers and institutes that address gender issues, I found only one doctoral-level course that addressed issues of gender and work. There were several programs on women's leadership outside the business school, but the course associated with these programs drew from historical work in the humanities, not from the social sciences or management. Mine, therefore, became one of the few courses in the university covering this material. I initially gathered syllabi from women I knew across the country or from programs on women's leadership at other schools.

The course was initially a mix of research on gender and leadership, although over time, as my department has developed a more explicit focus on leadership, the course has become more about the impact of gender on behavior in organizations. The course includes three major themes: understanding yourself, understanding how to influence and collaborate with others, and understanding what leadership is for, namely, to create a better future through innovation. In every section of this class that I have taught, I have had at least a few men, and every semester, one or more of the men try to dominant the class by being both outspoken (because class participation counts for the grade) and as outlined in a book about gender inequality, also by "calling on themselves" (Sadker & Sadker, 1994). That is, even in a course focusing on women's leadership, men who are a minority in the class often take center stage and women in the class often let them do so. Of course, I try to manage the participation to make access equitable, but it is a challenge every semester.

ADVICE FOR YOUNG SCHOLARS

Throughout my career, it has been very helpful to be actively involved in professional organizations that have afforded me the opportunity to meet and get to know many major scholars in my areas of study in both sociology and management. As I think about it, though, my closest connections have been with women, both peers and graduate students. I did not purposely choose this mix. I have collaborated on research with men many times throughout my career, but those with whom I maintain ongoing contact and to whom I turn when I have career or research questions are women. Perhaps I am an example of someone who has benefited from both instrumental and social support (Ibarra, 1992, 1997), that is, those who can collaborate on research and those who can talk about the research process and my role in it. In my case, getting to know people in the profession, in my university outside of my school, and in my school outside of my department all assisted in my career development and supplemented any ties that I had with those in my department.

Many give advice to develop networks and find people who can mentor you along the way, even better if one can find a sponsor (Hewlett, 2013). It is important for young scholars to know, however, that despite the terminology of "instrumental" networks, that such networks are not developed instrumentally. I never set out to get to know someone for the sole purpose of how they could help my career. Instead, I actively pursued my scholarship, regularly submitted my work and presented at professional meetings, took on many voluntary service responsibilities, and tried to be a good citizen along the way. I have always responded to those who have reached out to me, and I tried to be helpful when I could. In my case, and I assume in most, successful networking and finding mentors or sponsors came out of engagement and doing what I was supposed to do in my career.

When you present on panels, when you attend conferences, when you take on service responsibilities and serve on committees, you have the opportunity to follow through on commitments, to show that you add value, and to become visible to people who otherwise might not know of your work. That is how I developed my networks and the support that I have had throughout my career. It helps that I attended a graduate school with a large cohort of students, many of whom became movers and shakers in the field and that by regularly attending professional conferences, I could stay in touch with my friends. At conferences, I also found, although again it was not intentional, that it also helps to speak up and have something meaningful to say. On committees, it makes a difference if you take initiative and follow through. At social occasions, it helps to mingle. One can be more directed, for example, by reaching out to people whose work you admire and sending them a note to tell them, sending copies of your work to people whom you think might find it of interest, and purposefully attending a session with a presentation by someone you would like to meet. These kinds of activities can help, but relationships that matter usually grow out of the work that you do, more than strategic behavior.

At some point while serving as department chair, I was asked to serve on a panel at the Academy of Management meetings about how to be productive in research while serving in an administrative role. I did not necessarily think of being department chair as administration, but I did give the question some thought and came up with the following. Most of my advice is likely to be helpful to all academics, whether in administrative positions or not. My advice generally follows the recommendations that Arthur Stinchcombe (1986) wrote about decades ago when he discussed the malady he called "getting hung up." You need to recognize and acknowledge the emotional dimensions of doing research and deal with the challenges the same way you would deal with any emotionally charged situation. That includes talking with others, developing a network for social support, and doing things to reduce stress like exercise, healthy eating, and getting enough sleep.

Stinchcombe (1986) advises that you should also always work on more than one thing at a time, often at different stages of development. If one project stalls, you can turn to others and keep your work moving forward while trying to figure out what you need to do to make progress on the stalled project. It also helps to have co-authors who can both help you do the work and who can hold you to account by their own deadlines. Most important in this regard, is not to let things sit while trying to perfect them. To be successful, one has to "keep the paper moving," meaning that you need to submit your work for feedback, and if you get critical comments and if revisions are requested, you should follow through with the revisions and resubmit. If there are obvious things that you know need to be corrected or added to your manuscript, then by all means keep working on it, but if you are not sure how to improve it, then get it under review, perhaps after seeking advice from a close friend or colleague. If you receive especially difficult reviews, it is acceptable to let them sit for a week or two while you gather the emotional energy to face it, but do not allow yourself to be enervated by it. After you have calmed down from your initial reaction to the feedback, take a deep breath, read the feedback again, and then begin a plan for how you will address it. If you can find a group of friends who will regularly read your work and give you feedback, that is a fortunate situation, but of course, if you have such friends, they will expect you to reciprocate, so be sure that you are able to invest the time to give advice as well as get it.

While most of this advice is quite predictable and nothing new for those who have had good support through graduate school, there is one additional recommendation that I included on that AOM panel about how to be research productive while doing administration. That is, I believe it is a learned skill to be able to transition from one thing to another without downtime. I think it is partly a mindset that one can choose to adopt and practice. For example, I find that I can answer an email, deal with a phone call, write a letter of recommendation, and work on a paper at the same time, moving from one to the other as needed. One strategy I have used to facilitate this skill when working on a paper is to always write myself a note about what comes next when I need to stop writing to do something else. I also tend to create and revise a running outline as I go along so I have a general idea about what the structure of my argument is and how it will flow. That makes it easier to get back into a paper even when interrupted and even when there is a need to step away for some period of time. Although I like to start writing and keep at it until I am finished, I have never found that I have to have uninterrupted time to write. One has to learn to write when you can, not when you wish.

Perhaps it is the same mindset that has guided my thinking about issues with regard to work and family. While there is an extensive literature on work–family conflict and the difficulties of managing family responsibilities while giving sufficient time to work tasks, I have not seen these issues in the same way. Having family responsibilities is a lot more work than not having family responsibilities, but having a family also provides significant benefits that can make both work and life easier all around. Having a spouse or significant other usually means someone to help with the bills and the chores, so at a very basic level, it is helpful to share your life with someone else. Engagement with your family also helps keep things in perspective. The setbacks in writing and publishing and the petty politics that often characterize academic workplaces are much easier to face if you understand them within the larger picture. There were times when my children were little that I felt exhausted, and it seemed that I could never sit down; yet my children provided a means of satisfaction and served to release tension and stress. Even cooking and cleaning were ways to take my mind off of the challenges of a writing project, that is, ways to not get hung up. And further, it is enjoyable to do things with a spouse and with children—to watch them grow, to experience their excitement and help them learn about life and the world around them. Seeing things through the eyes of children is clearly a way to keep one grounded and full of anticipation.

At the same time, I think it is important to remind those at earlier stages of their careers that with the time demands of graduate school and then the tenure process, there is no good time to have a family. But that also means that there is no bad time to have a family. One should not let your career determine when you should marry or have children. You should do so when it makes sense in your life. Of course, there will be constraints and you will have less flexibility than you had before. But those things can be managed, and as I said, there are benefits with family responsibilities as well as costs. As is the case with your career, it helps to have a support system, either relatives or neighbors. Having children, though, also helps you build a support system, because other parents can provide significant information about ways to get things done. Especially if you have your children in childcare or in school, that becomes a conduit to learning about what is available in your neighborhood and how to manage things cooperatively. There were many times when I felt panic about childcare arrangements or schedule conflicts around major events for my children. But, with a great deal of effort and help from family and friends, I managed. There are many more options available now than there were when I had my children.

Perhaps most importantly, I am convinced that my children are far better off for my having had a real career without compromising my own ambitions for theirs. There were times when they were very young when I felt guilty about leaving the house or missing an event, but by the time they were in adolescence and more interested in their own lives than time with me, they also told me how much they appreciated my career and the opportunities that it afforded them. As I tell the students in my class on Women Leading in Business, with the current divorce rate and the possibilities of significant health emergencies, it is important that women plan their lives so that they can always support themselves and not assume that they can count on someone else to pay their bills.

THE FUTURE OF GENDER RESEARCH

An important shift has occurred for women compared to men over the last several decades that changes what should be of concern in ongoing research on gender. Women overtook men in terms of college completion rates, controlling for family background and test scores, by the early 1990s, and the proportion of women achieving degrees at every level has accelerated ever since, both in the United States and in most of the rest of the world (Diprete & Buchmann, 2013; Goldin, Katz, & Kuziemko, 2006). That means that since the advent of the women's movement and perhaps even predating it, women have been preparing themselves for success in the paid labor force, although they still trail in degrees obtained in engineering and the hard sciences. But in graduate schools and in the professions, women are an increasing proportion of graduates, making obstacles to their upward mobility harder to justify. In business fields, women represent about 40% of the doctoral degrees granted, with a somewhat higher proportion in management and organization behavior than in other fields (Flynn, Haynes, & Kilgour, 2015). Women also represent almost 40% of assistant professors hired, but only about a third of associate professors and just over 20% of full professors (AACSB, 2019). Hence, there is still a lag with regard to promotion and tenure, but less so than in the past. In other words, the lessons of diversity should affect business schools in the same way that they have for other industries (including accounting firms, by the way). If schools do not hire and promote women closer to their proportion among available candidates, then they will not have anyone to hire or they will have to significantly reduce the quality of their workforces. At the very least, they will have less legitimacy with important constituents.

These shifts, however, as is the case for gender dynamics within management positions in general, have more to do with White women than with all women. White women have benefited more from the new opportunities in the paid labor force than is the case for other women or for minority men (Stainback & Tomaskovic-Devey, 2012). Thus, addressing issues of intersectionality is still a forefront issue for studies of gender, and it needs to receive more attention than it has been given within the field of management (Crenshaw, 1989). While most of this research follows Crenshaw's lead of examining the intersection of race, class, and gender, too much has conceived of this intersection in terms of poor, minority, women, rather than advantaged, majority women. The research evidence is rather clear, although not highlighted sufficiently, that the challenges and opportunities for White women are not the same as for Black, Hispanic, and Asian women. The problems often discussed within the research on gender dynamics in management are really issues of concern primarily about educated, White women, and the solutions often presented, will help White women more than others. For example, the recommendations about the benefits of gender-blindness suggest that such advice does not work the same way for race/ethnic-blindness (Martin & Phillips, 2017). These variations in the dynamics of diversity need to be sorted out by more nuanced research on gender and on other dimensions as well.

I think one of the best articulations of these issues is in a recent article by Ridgeway and Krecheli-Katz (2013) on the "binds" and "freedoms" that vary by the race/ethnicity of women and men. They review the literature that finds that the "double bind," for example, that is often discussed with regard to women in leadership roles (Ibarra, Ely, & Kolb, 2013; Rudman, 2001) is experienced by White women in a way that is quite distinct from the experiences of Black and Asian women. Ridgeway and Krecheli-Katz (2013) also review the literature to show that while it may be more difficult for Black women to reach leadership positions, when they do, they may have more "freedom" to show agentic behavior than is the case for White women. I especially like their notion that those who are "off diagonal" in terms of normative statuses will have a different experience both in terms of binds and freedoms than those who fit the normative prototypes more closely.

Another cutting edge that has become, at this point, almost mainstream is the growing research on the effects of women on boards (Post & Byron, 2015; Post, Rahman, & McQuillen, 2015). The importance of this research is that it provides a window toward what the future may entail. As more countries are mandating greater representation of women at the board level, the research tends to suggest that this will affect the representation of women at the executive level, the managerial level, and otherwise in the labor force (Stainback, Kleiner, & Skaggs, 2016). The combination of women being represented more appropriately at the top, combined with women now obtaining a majority of degrees across most fields, suggests future opportunities for women to assume leadership roles that in the past would have been unthinkable.

Women's opportunities are also likely to improve in the future because of the changing dynamics of population trends across most of the developed world (Frey, 2018). Couples are marrying later and many are choosing not to have children, contributing to a decline in the already declining birth rate among native-born populations. Those countries that allow immigration from elsewhere are likely to thrive (Goldin, Pitt, Nabarro, & Boyle, 2018), but unfortunately, at present, the politics of immigration have been leading to restrictions. Women's opportunities are likely to increase because in most developed countries there are fewer people available to take on many important jobs, but women are also likely to be constrained if immigration is restricted because women in the paid labor force depend extensively on the services provided by immigrant women (Hochschild, 2000).

A related issue is that gender studies must go global. Traditionally there has been a split between the research done in the United States primarily on educated, White women and the research in the rest of the social sciences and humanities that has focused more on poor, minority women. But there has also been a split between research that tends to fall under the rubric of "development research" on women in the non-Western world and the research that we have generally thought of as the heart of gender studies. Increasingly, these realms of research need to be integrated and seen in the context of each other because they are interrelated. Women in the United States and in the broader developed world have benefited from the services of women elsewhere, and even at a national security level, women in the developed world cannot live in peace if women elsewhere are not able to do so.

Finally, in terms of the future of gender research, we probably need to make clear that understanding gender is not so much a credential as it is prerequisite for successful career outcomes. Neither universities nor companies hire women because they have great understanding of gender dynamics. They hire them instead to do a job, whether that is publishing their research on gender or other topics or because they can increase sales, reputation, or financial performance. Women academics, as well as women managers outside the university, need to understand what gender research is about, namely, to help women become more effective in the contributions that they can make and understanding the circumstances that can be leveraged to assist them in this regard. Organizations want to foster good relationships among people in their workforces, but they mostly want those in their workforces to perform effectively at whatever it is that makes the organizations successful. That is the purpose of gender research and what should drive those who want to make contributions in the field.

CONCLUSIONS

Gender research is serious research to the extent that it encompasses the whole spectrum of humanity and does so in a way that has the prospect of improving both performance and well-being for women and men of all backgrounds and social circumstances. Women are not the only ones who have a gender. Further, gender cannot be isolated from other statuses that define who we are as people and what challenges and opportunities we face with what consequences. Gender is a complex topic that has implications at all levels of analysis and that has both structural and institutional dimensions as well as interpersonal ones. The experience of being a woman in the paid labor force, including within academia, has changed over my lifetime, so what I experienced is not an automatic guide to what women today are likely to experience in their careers. But there are hopefully some insights and lessons to be learned by my reflections on what has occurred over the course of my career, especially in terms of what has changed as I initially tried to avoid and later had to finally confront the issues of gender in my work and in my career. I look forward to the next generation of research on gender studies and to the implications of what we yet need to learn about how women and men can work together productively and in collaboration. Women of all backgrounds need to join men of all backgrounds in leadership roles across institutions and countries, and men need to welcome the contributions that women can make on behalf of us all.

REFERENCES

AACSB. (2019). *2019 Business School Data Guide.* Retrieved from https://bized.aacsb.edu/articles/2018/06/aacsb-2018-business-school-data-guide

Barnum, P., Liden, R. C., & DiTomaso, N. (1995). Double jeopardy for women and minority workers: Pay differences with age. *Academy of Management Journal, 38*(3), 863–880.

Cordero, R., DiTomaso, N., & Farris, G. F. (1996). Gender and race/ethnic composition of technical work groups: Relationship to creative productivity and morale. *Journal of Engineering and Technology Management, 13*(3/4), 205–221.

Crenshaw, K. (1989). Demarginalizing the intersection of race and sex: A Black feminist critique of antidiscrimination doctrine, feminist theory and antiracist politics. *University of Chicago Legal Forum, 1989*(1), 139–167.

Diprete, T. S., & Buchmann, C. (2013). *The rise of women: The growing gender gap in education and what it means for American schools.* New York, NY: Russell Sage Foundation.

DiTomaso, N. (1989). Sexuality in the workplace: Discrimination and harassment. In J. Hearn, G. Burrell, D. Sheppard, & P. Tancred-Sheriff (Eds.), *The sexuality of organizations* (pp. 71–90). London, England: SAGE.

DiTomaso, N. (2013). *The American non-dilemma: Racial inequality without racism.* New York, NY: Russell Sage Foundation.

DiTomaso, N. (2015). Racism and discrimination versus advantage and favoritism: Bias for versus bias against. *Research in Organizational Behavior, 35,* 57–77.

DiTomaso, N., & Farris, G. F. (1992a). Diversity and performance in R&D. *IEEE Spectrum, 29*(6), 21–24.

DiTomaso, N., & Farris, G. F. (1992b). Work and career issues for women scientists in industrial research and development in the U.S. *Berlin Journal of Sociology, July,* 91–102.

DiTomaso, N., Farris, G. F., & Cordero, R. (1993). Diversity in the technical workforce: Rethinking the management of scientists and engineers. *Journal of Engineering and Technology Management, 10*(1/2), 101–127.

Flynn, P. M., Haynes, K., & Kilgour, M. A. (2015). *Integrating gender equality into business and management education: Lessons learned and challenges remaining.* New York, NY: Routledge.

Frey, W. H. (2018). *Diversity explosion: How new racial demographics are remaking America.* Washington, DC: Brookings Institute Press.

Friedan, B. (1963). *The feminine mystique.* New York, NY: Norton.

Goldin, C., Katz, L. F., & Kuziemko, I. (2006). The homecoming of American college women: The reversal of the college gender gap. *Journal of Economic Perspectives,* 20(4), 133–156.

Goldin, I., Pitt, A., Nabarro, B., & Boyle, K. (2018). Migration and the economy: Economic realities, social impacts, and political choices. New York, NY: Citi GPS: Global Perspectives & Solutions.

Hearn, J., Burrell, G., Sheppard, D., & Tancred-Sheriff, P. (1989). *The sexuality in organizations.* London, England: SAGE.

Hewlett, S. A. (2013). *Forget a mentor, find a sponsor: The new way to fast-track your career.* Boston, MA: Harvard Business Review Press.

Hochschild, A. R. (2000). The nanny chain. *The American Prospect, 11*(2), 1–4.

Ibarra, H. (1992). Homophily and differential returns: Sex differences in network structures and access in an advertising firm. *Administrative Science Quarterly, 37,* 422–438.

Ibarra, H. (1997). Paving an alternative route: Gender differences in managerial networks. *Social Psychology Quarterly, 60*(1), 91–102.

Ibarra, H., Ely, R., & Kolb, D. M. (2013). Women rising: The unseen barriers. *Harvard Business Review, September,* 60–66. Retrieved from https://hbr.org/2013/09/women-rising-the-unseen-barriers

Martin, A., & Phillips, K. W. (2017). What "blindness" to gender differences helps women see and do: Implications for confidence, agency, and action in male-dominated environments. *Organizational Behavior and Human Decision Processes, 142,* 28–44.

Post, C., & Byron, K. (2015). Women on boards and firm financial performance: A meta-analysis. *Academy of Management Journal, 58*(5), 1546–1571.

Post, C., DiTomaso, N., Farris, G. F., & Cordero, R. (2009). Work–family conflict and turnover intentions among scientists and engineers working in R&D. *Journal of Business and Psychology, 24*(1), 19–32.

Post, C., DiTomaso, N., Lowe, S. R., Farris, G. F., & Cordero, R. (2009). A few good women: Gender differences in evaluations of promotability in industrial research and development. *Journal of Managerial Psychology, 23*(4), 348–371.

Post, C., Rahman, N., & McQuillen, C. (2015). From Board composition to corporate environmental performance through sustainability-themed alliances. *Journal of Business Ethics, 130*(2), 423–435.

Ridgeway, C. L., & Kricheli-Katz, T. (2013). Intersecting cultural beliefs in social relations: Gender, race, and class binds and freedoms. *Gender and Society, 27*(3), 294–318.

Rudman, L. A., & Glick, P. (2001). Prescriptive gender stereotypes and backlash toward agentic women. *Journal of Social Issues, 57*(4), 743–762.

Sadker, M., & Sadker, D. (1994). *Failing at fairness: How America's schools cheat girls.* New York, NY: Touchstone.

Stainback, K., Kleiner, S., & Skaggs, S. (2016). Women in power: Undoing and redoing the gendered organization. *Gender & Society, 30*(1), 109–135.

Stainback, K., & Tomaskovic-Devey, D. (2012). *Documenting desegregation: Racial and gender segregation in private-sector employment since the Civil Rights Act.* New York, NY: Russell Sage Foundation.

Stinchcombe, A. L. (Ed.). (1986). On getting "hung up" and other assorted illnesses. In *Stratification and organization: Selected papers* (pp. 271–281). Cambridge, England: Cambridge University Press.

CHAPTER 6

CONFESSIONS OF AN ACCIDENTAL TOURIST

My Journey as a Gender Researcher

John F. Dovidio
Yale University

Growing up in a working-class community outside of Boston, I came to understand intergroup relations among people of different races and ethnicities at an early age—well before I received my PhD. Our city was clearly segregated residentially—a Black section, a Jewish section, and another section, where I lived, with largely first- and second-generation Americans of Italian and Irish descent. Race and ethnicity organized our social lives. In sports, teams were largely based on where people lived and symbolized competition between ethnic and racial groups. Moreover, there was a clear social pecking order. I understood it; I did not question it. My friend Tony once asked me, "Jack, why do the Irish keep picking on us Italians?" We identified as victims of discrimination. But then Tony added, "After all, we're not Black." We also were victimizers.

Of course, gender also mattered in significant and cross-cutting ways. It shaped our roles, aspirations, attitudes, and beliefs. However, it took me a

Perspectives on Gender and Work, pages 57–74

long time to recognize the pervasiveness of gender bias and its unique intergroup qualities. There was no singular "aha" moment. As an academic, my interests in gender bias developed slowly (and surprisingly inconsistently), stimulated by learning that what I knew about intergroup relations and biases based on race, ethnicity, and immigration status did not fully apply to gender bias. I stumbled awkwardly into the area of gender. I am an accidental tourist in the study of gender relations.

Although I could see other forms of intergroup relations with clarity, I had blinders that prevented me from fully perceiving sexism. My personal experiences, the social and political climate during formative times of my career, and the state of psychological research and theory during my professional training all played a role. In terms of my personal experiences, intergroup divides based on race and ethnicity were easy for me to discern. We lived in different places, went to different schools, and had different groups of friends. Boundaries were palpable. That was not the case for gender. From the time I was born, I lived in a household with women. Through preadolescence, I played with both girls and boys in my neighborhood. In high school and college, I dated girls. I did not see girls and, later, young women as the "other," and I certainly did not consciously consider my social world as "us" (men) versus "them" (women). I thought of women in a very personalized way, quite differently than the way I thought about members of racial or ethnic groups other than my own. In addition, in my narrowly construed view of gender relations as interpersonal relations, I did not view myself as a member of a socially privileged group. But, of course, that is exactly how members of privileged groups perceive the social world.

I also grew up in a very complex political environment with respect to gender. On the one hand, the women's movement had full momentum. It brought attention to the collective disadvantage of women and the importance of pursuing equal rights for women. I wholeheartedly endorsed giving individual women equal opportunity and treating women fairly. On the other hand, I still had difficulty recognizing the truly collective nature of the women's movement. I was not alone; America as a whole was having difficulty embracing that, too. Coming on the heels of monumental civil rights legislation in the mid- to late-1960s to ensure racial equality, the Equal Rights Amendment, which was a proposed Constitutional amendment that would guarantee equal rights regardless of sex, was submitted to states for ratification in 1972. The amendment still has not received support from enough states to be ratified.

My professional training as an intergroup researcher was similarly skewed. Throughout my career, Gordon Allport's (1954) book, *The Nature of Prejudice*, has had a profound influence, not only on me but also on the field as a whole. It is a seminal text that foreshadowed, and probably stimulated, major developments in the study of intergroup relations, such as social cognitive and social identity influences. However, despite his consideration of a wide range of prejudices related to race, ethnicity, and religion, Allport mentioned women as targets of bias only once (on pp. 33–34). Moreover, his classic definition of prejudice as "an antipathy based on faulty and inflexible generalization" (p. 9) drew the field's attention to certain types of intergroup relations but further away from the phenomenon of gender bias, which is, as Eagly and Diekman (2005) observed, "a prejudice that targets about half of the population . . . whose nature poses a critical challenge to defining prejudice as antipathy" (p. 20). Although there was a rapidly accumulating literature on gender (including work on sexism) for decades, it was not until the mid-1990s (40 years after Allport's book and 2 decades into my professional career) that research on sexism and intergroup relations became closely aligned.

I have been a slow learner in the study of gender relations, and my understanding of this topic has evolved in a nonlinear way. I did have ideas that were guided by gender-related theories, but gender was typically a secondary factor in my thinking. It was often a variable of convenience, representing a readily available way to study relations between individuals and between groups that are meaningful to students in an otherwise markedly nondiverse introductory psychology participant pool. Thus, across my research career I regularly conducted "gender research" in a way that was not primarily designed to understand gender relations.

Over time, though, I came to realize that I regularly gravitated to gender-related research not simply out of convenience but from a core interest. I saw gender relations as central in their own right for understanding group processes and intergroup relations. The differences and similarities that gender relations have in relation to other kinds of individual and group identities (e.g., race, ethnicity) shed new light on the integrated dynamics of intragroup and intergroup processes. Although gender, traditionally studied in terms of people who identify as a woman or a man, represents one of the most socially significant forms of social categorization that defines an intergroup boundary, the desire for close relationships between men and women and the interdependence between women and men at personal, group, and societal levels qualifies gender relations as a fundamental *intra*group phenomenon.

SOME OF MY GENDER-RELATED RESEARCH

In this section, I discuss examples of the intragroup and intergroup perspectives I adopted in my research concerning gender. Within each of these sections, I present concrete examples of the research that I have pursued in the earlier and more recent stages of my career and identify the threads that connect them. I then describe how these seemingly discrete lines of research suggest a more comprehensive and integrated view of group processes and intergroup relations.

Gender From an Intragroup Perspective

Groups are more than a collection of individuals. They represent the coordinated activity of individuals that enables us to accomplish more than we could through independent efforts. Groups also satisfy our psychological needs for understanding, belonging, self-worth, and symbolic immortality (Correll & Park, 2005). We are, in our essence, social animals.

Groups empower us but also exert power over us. Structure is a defining element of a group (e.g., as compared to the simultaneous presence of individuals), and there are a number of forces that tend to maintain and reinforce this structure. Studies of a range of animal societies, including human groups, demonstrate the critical value of differentiated roles to effective group functioning. Within groups, individuals are differentiated not only by having different responsibilities and specializations (horizontal differentiation) compared to others but also within a dominance or power hierarchy (vertical differentiation). Groups with members who have well-defined, accepted, and complementary roles are better able to manage scarce resources and to respond more quickly and effectively to unexpected challenges.

This is where gender becomes directly relevant. For most (although certainly all) species and across most (but not all) human societies, male members occupy the highest level of the dominance hierarchy (Wood & Eagly, 2002). Much of my initial research on intragroup processes, which included work on visual dominance behavior and on objectification, investigated the subtle ways that the higher status of men compared to women is communicated and perpetuated.

The Look of Power: Visual Dominance Behavior

Nonverbal behavior, which often occurs spontaneously and with limited awareness and control, reflects expectations based on traditional power structures in society and also communicates and reinforces power relations between women and men on a daily basis. The research that I pursued early in my career on social power and nonverbal behavior involved close collaborations with Steve Ellyson, Clifford Brown, and Caroline Keating.

We focused largely on visual behavior as a nonverbal power display. In general, the amount of time a person looks at another individual depends significantly on whether the person is speaking or listening. Speaking is a cognitively challenging task, made even more demanding when people are anxious about others' evaluations of them. Listening allows for and acknowledges the influence of another person. Generally, people look at another person less when they are speaking (around 40% of the time) than when they are listening (approximately 60% of the time).

However, within this general pattern, power matters. People who occupy higher positions in a power hierarchy are more confident and are less cognitively challenged when speaking. Thus, high-power persons tend to look more at an interaction partner (about 50–60% of the time) than do low-power individuals (about 25–35% of the time). Because looking while listening reflects interest and conveys respect, humans who are relatively low in power devote high levels of visual attention while listening (about 60–75% of the time) to a higher-power interaction partners, whereas higher-power individuals look while listening to their partners at a lower level (about 40–50% of the time). The visual dominance ratio is a reliable nonverbal power display that represents the percentage of time a person looks while speaking divided by the amount of time they look while listening. People who have more power by virtue of their military rank, social status associated with their role in a situation, or the greater knowledge for completing a task display higher visual dominance ratios, typically around 1.00, than do those in the same situation who are relatively low in power, who show visual dominance ratios of about 0.65. Although people are not usually consciously aware of their visual dominance ratio, those who display a higher ratio give the impression to others that they are more in control, feel more confident and powerful, and ultimately are more influential in their interactions.

In a series of studies, my colleagues and I studied how and when power differences are communicated nonverbally, particularly with respect to the visual dominance ratio, between women and men. Guided by work in sociology (see Ridgeway, 2014), we hypothesized that when power roles are well-defined, women and men would exhibit similar visual dominance ratios reflective of their high- or low-power role. However, because gender is a general status cue in society, linked to greater power and influence of men, we predicted that in mixed-gender interactions in which situationally relevant power roles are absent, men would assume the higher-power position nonverbally whereas women would adopt a lower-power role.

We tested this set of hypotheses across a number of experiments examining the visual behavior of men and women while varying situationally relevant power in terms of (a) high- and low-power roles of an evaluator and person being evaluated; (b) possession of relatively high, relatively low, or equivalently moderate personal expertise on a task; and (c) assignment of tasks traditionally seen as masculine, feminine, or gender-neutral. Female and male college students were brought together to work on a series of problem-solving tasks. During these interactions, we videotaped participants, later coded these interactions for how much the participants looked at the other person while they were speaking and listening, and then computed the visual dominance ratios (percent looking while speaking divided by percent looking while listening).

As summarized in Table 6.1, across studies there was a consistent pattern of findings. As expected, when occupying the position of relatively high power, women and men displayed high visual dominance rations; when they were low in relative power, both exhibited low visual dominance ratios. However, there were consistent gender differences in the absence of structurally designated power. In mixed-gender interactions, when no evaluator role was assigned, when participants had equivalently moderate expertise, or when a task was gender-neutral, the male participant displayed high power nonverbally while the female participant exhibited low power nonverbally. In the study involving the gender-association of the task, we found similar effects for other behaviors. For instance, for the topic that was not gender-linked, male participants initiated speech more often and spoke longer than did female participants.

One interpretation of these findings is that women's relatively low visual dominance ratio may not necessarily reflect an acquiescence to subordinate status; rather, it may reflect a strategic response by women to avoid the particularly negative responses that often occur from men when they overtly challenge men's power and status. Instead, women may be shifting to indirect strategies to achieve power and have influence. However, such shifts in power displays may be occurring more spontaneously because expressions of high-power displays often automatically elicit submissive displays from others. In our research, women who exhibited a low visual dominance ratio were also less assertive in their discussions with men and, when judged by independent observers as well as by their male partner, were seen as being low in influence. As noted earlier, nonverbal power displays not only reflect

TABLE 6.1 Visual Dominance Ratios (percent looking while speaking divided by percent looking while listening) for Men and Women Relatively High or Low in Power or in Unstructured (control) Conditions in Mixed-Gender Interactions

Study	Independent Variable	Participant	Power Position		
			High	Control	Low
Dovidio, Ellyson, Keating, Heltman, & Brown (1988, Study 2)	Role (Reward) Power	Man	1.08	1.23	0.84
		Woman	1.20	0.70	0.61
Dovidio, Ellyson, Keating, Heltman, & Brown (1988, Study 1)	Personal Expertise	Man	0.98	0.89	0.60
		Woman	1.03	0.53	0.54
Dovidio, Brown, Keating, Heltman, & Ellyson (1988, Study 2)	Task Gender Association	Man	1.78	1.02	0.27
		Woman	1.24	0.46	0.26

immediate and larger structural differences in social power between men and women, they also reinforce and perpetuate power differences. This has continued to be a theme I pursued in my research.

Interacting Like a Body: A Study of Sexual Objectification

About a decade later, with my graduate student at the time, Tamar Saguy, my colleagues, Diane Quinn and Felicia Pratto, and I considered another aspect of the power of visual behavior—specifically, "the gaze." In this research (Saguy, Quinn, Dovidio, & Pratto, 2010), we studied how leading women to believe that others were viewing their body (vs. viewing their face or not seeing them) affected their feelings of sexual objectification and ultimately their engagement in a social exchange. Sexual objectification is an experience that occurs when people feel that they are viewed by another person as a mere body that exists for the pleasure and use of others. This treatment targets women more often than men and occurs through media portrayals that routinely focus on women's bodies as well as through interpersonal interactions that include comments about or gazes at women's bodies. Sexual objectification has both immediate and longer-term negative impacts on women's psychological well-being.

We led female and male participants to believe they were interacting with a male or female partner through a closed-circuit device in one of three communication conditions: (a) body ("from the neck down"), in which participants' bodily appearance was made salient by having them believe that only their bodies were visible in the interaction; (b) face ("from the neck up"), in which participants believed that only their faces were visible in the interaction; or (c) audio (in which participants believed that they were only heard and not seen). Ostensibly as a prelude to their interaction, we asked participants to introduce themselves to their partner. We then timed participants' oral introductions. Our hypothesis was that women would talk less when objectified, particularly when interacting with men.

The results of this study revealed distinct effects in the condition in which women believed that they were interacting with a male partner in which only their bodies could be viewed in the interaction. Compared to the five other conditions in this experiment (the three conditions involving a male participant and the face and audio conditions for female participants), women felt most anxious in this condition and spent the least time talking. This pattern of results suggests that women talk less when objectified because they attempt to align their behavior with what they assume is expected of them as sexual objects—deferent to a man. This behavioral submissiveness, in turn, can further restrict their full and respectful contributions to society and from achieving the social status that women deserve.

The studies I have described in this section illustrate how exposure to another's nonverbal behavior—visual dominance and direct gaze—not only directly affect relations between a particular woman and man but also have a cumulative effect on the lives of women and men generally. These generalized effects qualify gender relations as a core intergroup phenomenon, as well as an intragroup process.

Gender From an Intergroup Perspective

Research in the study of intergroup relations emphasizes that how individuals categorize people into groups based on distinguishing characteristics has profound psychological and social consequences. For instance, when people are categorized into groups, differences among members of the group (within-group differences) tend to be minimized, and distinctions between members of different categories (between-group differences) tend to be exaggerated. In the United States, three of the most important social categories, which are automatically activated when we encounter a person, are race, age, and gender. Moreover, people spontaneously distinguish between people who are members of their own group, the ingroup, and others who are members of another group, an outgroup, and people favor ingroup over outgroup members in their evaluations, feelings, and generosity. Also, people tend to compete with and discriminate against other groups to create or maintain an advantage for the ingroup.

Intergroup bias is often antithetical to the principles of civil societies that emphasize equality and fairness as core values, however. In these societies, in which overt discrimination is normatively and/or legally unacceptable, bias is commonly expressed in subtle and indirect ways. At a societal level, for example, system-justifying beliefs, such as meritocracy, often portray the unfair advantages enjoyed by members of dominant groups as legitimate, which motivates people—both members of the dominant and marginalized groups—to adopt attitudes and engage in behaviors that support the status quo (Jost, Gaucher, & Stern, 2015).

Subtle bias also operates on an individual level—how a member of one group behaves toward members of another group. Much of my work, conducted over 40 years with my dissertation advisor and primary research collaborator, Samuel Gaertner, has focused on a particular form of subtle bias—aversive racism. The aversive racism framework posits that intergroup discrimination is particularly likely to occur (a) under conditions that challenge the traditional power structure; (b) when people can rationalize their actions that ultimately disadvantage another group on the basis of some factor other than on the basis of the person's group membership; and (c) in forms, such as seemingly positive actions (e.g., paternalistic helping), that enhance the relative status of the ingroup in the long-run but do not appear on the surface to have harmful intent. The aversive racism framework was originally developed to help understand why and how Blacks were treated unfairly by Whites in the United States despite strong prevailing egalitarian norms and far-reaching federal laws against racial discrimination. Since its original formulation, the aversive racism framework has been applied to biases toward a range of groups, including women (see Dovidio, Gaertner, & Pearson, 2017, for a review). I highlight three examples of my research, conducted at different periods in my career, on bias against women and discussed through the lens of aversive racism.

Subtle Bias Against Blacks and Women

In an early line of research conducted in collaboration with Sam Gaertner, we investigated how spontaneously helpful participants were to another person as a function of their perceived status relationship. In one version of the research, we examined how White participants would respond to a White or Black male partner (Dovidio & Gaertner, 1981); in another version of the research, we investigated how White male and female participants would behave toward a White male or female partner (Dovidio & Gaertner, 1983). In both studies, participants received information that, based on previous testing, they had performed better or worse than their partner in the session on a test that assessed their intellectual ability related to the task at hand. Participants were then informed that they would be either the supervisor (high status or subordinate (low status) on the experimental task, and the partner would assume the other role. The dependent measure in the study was spontaneous helping of the other person. As they were preparing to begin the task, the partner (a confederate) "accidentally" knocked over a container of pencils; we measured whether or not the participant chose to help the confederate pick up the pencils.

Our hypothesis was that participants would respond in ways related to the legitimacy of the status relationship with the partner, being more helpful when they perceived their relations in the task as more legitimate (i.e., when their relative ability corresponded to their relative status on the task). In the race study (Dovidio & Gaertner, 1981), this is what we found when the partner was White. The results were different when the partner was Black. When the partner was Black, only the partner status (supervisor vs. subordinate) mattered. In the traditional status relationship between Whites and Blacks in the United States, Whites have disproportionately occupied positions of greater prestige and power. As a consequence, White participants responded to Black supervisors in the study, regardless of the ability of the partner, as if the status relationship was illegitimate.

In the study in which we varied the gender of the White confederate partner (Dovidio & Gaertner, 1983), because women in the United States have traditionally occupied positions of less prestige and influence than men, we obtained an analogous pattern of results. Replicating the previous study, when the partner was a (White) male student, participants helped more often when their positions of status legitimately corresponded to their relative ability than when they did not correspond. However, when the partner was a (White) female student, the results were similar to the condition in which the partner was Black in the previous study: Participants (both men and women) were less spontaneously helpful to the female supervisor than to the female subordinate, even when her higher ability would normally legitimize her higher status.

Bias Against Women in Academic Science

I was aware that, despite evidence of significant and persistent disparities between men in women in science, technology, engineering, and mathematics (STEM fields), some scholars held the position that gender discrimination does not exist within academic science. For instance, Ceci and Williams (2011) stated that "recent and robust empiricism... fails to support assertions of discrimination in these domains" (p. 3157). To me, that conclusion seemed debatable.

I personally experienced the intensity of the debate about whether gender bias exists in science when I was co-conducting a workshop with Jo Handelsman, a prominent scholar and educator on issues relating to gender bias in STEM, with chairs and other leaders of science departments at a prestigious research university. The majority of faculty members attending the workshop were men, and they were generally sympathetic to the idea that bias existed in society in subtle as well as blatant forms. However, both the women and men in the group resisted the idea that gender could operate in the objective and intellectually sophisticated world of science. They dismissed the psychological evidence of bias because of the rational nature of science and scientists. However, rather than being "rational," their arguments were more "rationalizing." For example, without seeking actual evidence, they devoted considerable energy to explaining away women's complaints about inequitable distribution of laboratory space by arguing that any such differences were probably due to different research topics pursued by male and female science faculty members.

In a subsequent meeting with Jo Handelsman and Corinne Moss-Racusin, a postdoctoral associate working with us, I expressed my confusion and frustration at the response of the group of science leaders of the university. In the workshop, they seemed to understand the information presented about the role of rationalization in varied expressions of bias, but they could not accept that these processes could apply to the domain of science (and to them). Corinne then suggested that we test the question empirically. She took the lead in recruiting other experts on gender bias, Tori Brescoll and Mark Graham, and in designing and conducting an experiment. The study (Moss-Racusin, Dovidio, Brescoll, Graham, & Handelsman, 2012) was straightforward. In a randomized double-blind study, we contacted science faculty from research-intensive universities and asked them to rate the application materials of a student—who was randomly assigned either a male or female name—for a laboratory manager position.

We found that faculty participants rated the male applicant as significantly more competent and hireable than the female applicant, who had identical credentials. These participants also endorsed a higher starting salary and offered more career mentoring to the male applicant. The gender of the faculty participants did not affect responses, such that female and male faculty were equally likely to exhibit bias against the female student. Also, the faculty members reported that they liked the female applicant as much as the male applicant, but they saw the male applicant as more competent, which formed the basis of and justified their decisions favoring male over female applicants. The greater representation of men and women in science may have led to greater expectancies for the success of the male relative to the female applicant to produce stronger perceptions of competence. This finding thus again suggests how historical disparities between women and men can influence current perceptions in ways that rationalize decisions and actions that are actually forms of subtle bias that unfairly perpetuate gender disparities.

Third-Party Prejudice Accommodation

A recent line of work on gender bias, initiated by my PhD student at the time, Andrea Vial (also in collaboration with Tori Brescoll), identified another way that subtle bias against women can occur. Across over 10 studies (Vial, Brescoill, & Dovidio, 2019; Vial, Dovidio, & Brescoll, 2019), this research illuminates how "third-party prejudice accommodation," in which decision-makers accommodate the imagined or actual prejudice against women of relevant third parties, leads women as well as men to favor male over female job candidates. For example, in one study male and female participants were asked to select a person for the position of vice president (VP) of a company who would work closely with the male chief executive officer (CEO). In addition to reading brief files of a man and a woman who were equivalently well qualified for the job, participants in both the control and experimental conditions read background information about the CEO that was the same except for a few lines. In the experimental condition, these lines indicated that the CEO held traditional, conservative views about women, such as, "Gary [the CEO] believes that it is important for women to put families before careers." Consistent with the hypothesis that people accommodate to the prejudices of others, participants in the experimental condition who believed that the CEO *might* be biased against a female VP were significantly less likely to choose the female (compared to the male) candidate for the position than did participants in the control condition. Thus, third-party prejudice accommodation occurs even in the absence of explicit requests by the third party. It also affects both male and female participants in ways independent of their personal attitudes toward women and the gender stereotypes they hold.

The third-party prejudice accommodation effect occurs because people in decision-making roles typically desire to facilitate positive interpersonal relations and accomplish goals that are important for the groups with which they identify, even when the decision does not align with the decision maker's own beliefs and egalitarian attitudes. These decisions are made because people primarily value harmony with others and try to avoid actions that can potentially disrupt the smooth functioning of the organization. The consequence, though, is that people are allowing others' biases to shape their behavior in discriminatory ways. Third-party prejudice accommodation thus represents another subtle form of intergroup bias that may operate, often unintentionally, to restrict the opportunities and resources of women relative to men in society.

INTEGRATING INTRAGROUP AND INTERGROUP PERSPECTIVES ON GENDER RELATIONS: LOOKING AHEAD

My gender research, which has helped me come to see gender relations and bias as reflecting elements of both intragroup and intergroup processes, continues to lead my work in new directions. Efforts to understand the dynamics of gender relations offer valuable insights for integrating the disparate literatures on intragroup and intergroup processes more generally and suggest new perspectives on the nature of prejudice.

Rather than framing gender relations as a unique, exceptional form of group relations, it might instead be considered as a model of the dynamic interplay between intragroup processes and intergroup relations that likely characterizes complex societies. As noted earlier, several psychological forces (e.g., social categorization, social identity, and intergroup competition) generally promote bias and conflict between distinct groups in which relations are typically framed as zero-sum (when one group wins, the other necessarily loses). However, when groups (such as women and men) are strongly interdependent, open demonstrations of bias may be strongly inhibited or even prohibited. In such contexts of interdependence, overt bias and conflict violate basic principles of fairness and justice that bind the society together, and conflict between groups may undermine the society in ways that may commonly be viewed as detrimental to members of both groups. Direct exertions of power, particularly when applied in ways that appear unfair, also create negative reactions among the targets of such behavior, which over time increases resistance and ultimately erodes the resources of those in power.

The tension between intergroup forces that promote bias and the intragroup mechanisms that promote fairness may be reconciled through the expression of bias in subtle forms. Like blatant bias, subtle biases restrict the opportunities for social advancement of members of traditionally disadvantaged groups, but they do so in ways that may be less recognizable as unfair bias. The study of gender relations reflects the challenges faced by different but interdependent groups. These "lessons learned" in the study of gender relations are likely to be particularly valuable, both theoretically and practically, for understanding social dynamics in an increasingly multicultural social world in which the well-being of different groups are more intertwined, as well as in guiding the development of interventions to create more just societies.

ADVICE FOR GENDER RESEARCHERS

It is essential to adhere to the conventional standards for grounding research in theory and to adopt best practices for establishing the validity and replicability of research findings. The science needs to be sound. However, it is also important to be expansive and inclusive in perspective. Fight the tendency to dismiss or to obscure unexpected or disconfirming findings. Instead, acknowledge and embrace them; learn from them.

My perspective on unexpected findings has changed over the years. I originally found them, at the minimum, to be a nuisance and largely to indicate a research failure. I now think differently. I have learned that my participants are smarter than I am. I base my predictions on a body of existing literature, derive logical extensions of current theory in small and systematic steps, and test my ideas in conventional ways. My participants experience none of those constraints, and their behavior is reality. So, when they behave in ways that disconfirm my hypotheses and/or challenge the conclusion for which I hope to advocate, I remind myself that they are "right," and I am "wrong." That is not a bad thing. Working to understand why participants behave in ways that I do not expect liberates me to think more creatively and in discontinuous ways that are theoretically novel and better represent the world the way it actually is. Indeed, my interest in gender really originated from the fact that while it had effects similar to other kinds of relations (e.g., interracial, interethnic) that I studied, gender relations often showed different, unanticipated effects.

So my advice here is, on the one hand, to be a theory-based researcher who follows best practices methodologically but, on the other hand, to be a scholar who listens to what the data are telling you and to be open to discovery—even if it challenges conventional theory or the kinds of arguments you wish to make from your research. Allow yourself to wander in scholarly ways that help you see your research in a different light and appreciate unexpected or nonconforming findings as an invitation for new insights.

Beyond what questions we choose to study, how we choose to pursue a research career also matters substantially. The great part of our profession, which we need to always keep in mind, is that success is *not* zero-sum. If someone else publishes, it does not mean that I will publish less. In fact, it can be just the opposite. Stimulating others to publish more, for example through mentoring or collaboration, can also lead us to have more scholarly impact. Collaboration has been the most rewarding aspect of my scholarly career. Thus far, I have published papers with 450 different co-authors. My colleagues in research have stimulated, challenged, educated, and truly enlightened me; they have made me a better researcher and person. They have led me on the journey into gender research. If our goal is really to make a lasting scientific contribution, the best way to achieve this objective is to support and collaborate with others in their research, which produces a cascading impact on scientific knowledge through others. Such efforts, which are mutually rewarding, are also exceptionally valuable to the field more generally because it can move the discipline to be more inclusive, respectful, and inviting to diverse scholars who bring new insights into human psychology and gender relations.

FUTURE "HOT TOPICS" IN GENDER RESEARCH

The future "hot topics" that I see in the area of gender research are good examples of the value of looking at key issues in a new light. Gender research has traditionally characterized sex and gender as dichotomous and, in some ways, fixed dimensions. For example, sex has long been thought about as being male or female, determined at birth. People still tend to gravitate to an "either/or" perspective with women/feminine on one side and men/masculine on the other. Current "hot topics" in gender research question such a simplified view in a number of ways. I present three examples of more complex conceptualizations of gender that will likely stimulate lines of new inquiry: (a) intersectionality, (b) in-between groups, and (c) nonbinary identities.

Intersectionality

Within social psychology, despite widespread recognition that people have multiple identities, research continues to focus primarily on simple categorization—categorization based on a single dichotomous dimension (e.g., Black vs. White, citizen vs. immigrant, man vs. woman). However, people can experience and display multiple identities simultaneously that represent intersectional identities, which are multiple, conjoined identities (e.g., as a Black woman).

The study of intersectionality, which is a prominent topic in other fields (e.g., sociology) and continues to gain momentum within psychology (Purdie-Vaughns & Eibach, 2008), potentially considers the responses of perceivers, the nature of the intersectional identity, and the experience of individuals with an intersectional identity. Perceivers have more difficulty categorizing and processing information about people who have intersectional identities than single-dimension identities (Chen & Hamilton, 2012) and question the loyalty of people who express dual identities (Kunst, Thomsen, & Dovidio, 2019). Whereas some forms of intersectional identity are widely acknowledged and thus may be seen as valid social categories in their own right (e.g., businesswoman, Black athlete), others are more difficult for people to process (e.g., Jewish athlete) either because of less exposure or because there are elements of the constituent identities that seem incompatible. In addition, the experience of people with intersectional identities can be quite different. For example, Ghavami and Peplau (2013) found that the most common traits associated with Latinx people were "poor" and "have many children," while those associated with women were "emotional" and "caring." However, Latinas, members of the intersectional identity involving ethnicity and gender, were characterized quite differently than either of those categories: Latinas were primarily stereotyped as "feisty" and "curvy." Because men and women are rarely seen solely in terms of their gender, research on intersectionality is likely a particularly fertile area for future gender research.

In-Between Groups

Related to, but conceptually distinct from, the study intersectional identities is an emerging literature on "in-between," or intermediate groups—groups with members whose identities have elements of two different groups that perceivers have difficulty reconciling. There is, for example, a vibrant literature on the experiences of biracial and bicultural individuals related to their social adjustment and adaptability (Albuja, Sanchez, & Gaither, 2019). Research on in-between groups also considers how people respond to individuals whom they perceive as having an in-between identity. For example, members of some in-between groups, such as people with a bisexual identity, may be seen as being inauthentic and stigmatized additionally because of the difficulty people have in acknowledging the validity of such entities (Burke

& LaFrance, 2018). However, these responses can be shaped significantly by history or culture. For instance, work on hypodescent in the United States reveals that biracial individuals are typically attributed by perceivers the status of the socially subordinate group (e.g., of Blacks for Black-White biracial individuals; Ho, Sidanius, Levin, & Banaji, 2011).

Nonbinary Identities

I still know many people who regularly use the phrase "the opposite sex," communicating the view that people are one or the other sex. I was taught to use sex to refer to the biological classification of individuals as a woman or a man, and to apply the term gender to a person's social orientation. However, we need to rethink these oversimplified conventions. Indeed, scholarly interest is already moving in that direction, and future research will go even further in understanding and normalizing nonbinary and fluid self-descriptions relating to gender. Much of the recent media attention, political discourse, and empirical interest in psychology has crystallized around the topic of transgender individuals. The term "transgender" (or "trans") is used to describe people whose gender identity (i.e., their fundamental sense of self as woman or man, or something else) does not match their assigned sex (i.e., the sex assigned to them at birth). This topic is of pressing importance practically: The number of adults who report being transgender is increasing and, on average, people have more negative feelings toward transgender individuals than cisgender (i.e., non-transgender) persons, including gay men and lesbians and oppose basic rights for transgender individuals (see Wittlin, Dovidio, LaFrance, & Burke, 2018).

While considerable current attention focuses on transgender identity, work on this topic represents only an initial step theoretically and empirically into an exciting, broader study of nonbinary and fluid identities related to gender. Traditional views propagated in psychology, other disciplines (e.g., biology), politics, law, media, and public discourse conceived of gender, sex, and sexuality in binary ways, but there is now expanding awareness of the error in such oversimplification and the consequences for science and society. This more systematic consideration of nonbinary and fluid identities opens the door to new research questions and opportunities. For instance, because language profoundly shapes the way we think about others and what we view as normative, understanding the impact on both the individuals who prefer to be referred to as "they" or "them" as compared to "he" or "she" and how others respond to them can illuminate the dynamics of gender in novel ways. Such research can transform how the field understands social categorization and essentialism, gender bias, and influences on mental health and social and political change.

CONCLUSION

In this chapter, I have recounted how I became a gender researcher. I described myself as an accidental tourist because so much of my journey has been unplanned and so much of my experience has been opportunistic. I have contributed in some ways, which I described in this chapter, but also, as I hope I also communicated, I gained a lot more—new scientific and personal insights about gender, as well as new perspectives on the field of intergroup relations more generally. My daily and intimate experiences with gender relations made me feel like I already had expertise in this area. It was a truly misguided perception; I now realize not only how little I truly knew but also how much of what I thought I understood was not correct. The opportunities I have had as a scholar to wander into this area has significantly changed my theoretical perspectives and redirected my empirical pursuits. It has been a transformative journey, one that I wholeheartedly encourage others to pursue.

REFERENCES

Albuja, A. F., Sanchez, D. T., & Gaither, S. E. (2019). Identity denied: Comparing American or White identity denial and psychological health outcomes among bicultural and biracial people. *Personality and Social Psychology Bulletin, 45*(3), 416–430.

Allport, G. W. (1954). *The nature of prejudice.* Cambridge, MA: Addison-Wesley.

Burke, S. E., & LaFrance, M. (2018). Perceptions of instability and choice across sexual orientation groups. *Group Processes & Intergroup Relations, 21*(2), 257–279.

Ceci, S. J., & Williams, W. M. (2011). Understanding current causes of women's underrepresentation in science. *Proceedings of the National Academy of Science, 108*(8), 3157–3162.

Chen, J. M., & Hamilton, D. L. (2012). Natural ambiguities: Racial categorization of multiracial individuals. *Journal of Experimental Social Psychology, 48,* 152–164.

Correll, J., & Park, B. (2005). A model of the ingroup as a social resource. *Personality and Social Psychology Review, 9*(4), 341–359.

Dovidio, J. F., Brown, C. E., Keating, C. F., Heltman, K., & Ellyson, S. L. (1988). Power displays between women and men in discussions of gender-linked tasks: A multichannel study. *Journal of Personality and Social Psychology, 55*(4), 580–587.

Dovidio, J. F., Ellyson, S. L., Keating, C. F., Heltman, K., & Brown, C. (1988). The effects of social power on visual displays of dominance between men and women. *Journal of Personality and Social Psychology, 54*(2), 233–242.

Dovidio, J. F., & Gaertner, S. L. (1981). The effects of race, status and ability on helping behavior. *Social Psychology Quarterly, 44*(3), 192–203.

Dovidio, J. F., & Gaertner, S. L. (1983). The effects of sex, status, and ability on helping behavior. *Journal of Applied Social Psychology, 13*(3), 191–205.

Dovidio, J. F., Gaertner, S. L., & Pearson, A. R. (2017). Aversive racism and contemporary bias. In C. G. Sibley & F. K. Barlow (Eds.), *The Cambridge handbook of the psychology of prejudice* (pp. 267–294). Cambridge, England: Cambridge University Press.

Eagly, A. H., & Diekman, A. B. (2005). What is the problem? Prejudice as an attitude-in-context. In J. F. Dovidio, P. Glick, & L. A. Rudman (Eds.), *On the nature of prejudice: Fifty years after Allport* (pp. 20–35). Malden, MA: Blackwell.

Ghavami, N., & Peplau, L. A. (2013). An intersectional analysis of gender and ethnic stereotypes: Testing three hypotheses. *Psychology of Women Quarterly, 37*(1), 113–127.

Ho, A. K., Sidanius, J., Levin, D. T., & Banaji, M. R. (2011). Evidence for hypodescent and racial hierarchy in the categorization and perception of biracial individuals. *Journal of Personality and Social Psychology, 100*(3), 492–506.

Jost, J., Gaucher, D., & Stern, C. (2015). "The world isn't fair": A system justification perspective on social stratification and inequality. In M. Mikulincer, P. R. Shaver, J. F. Dovidio, J. F., & J. A. Simpson (Eds.), *APA handbook of personality and social psychology* (Vol. 2; pp. 317–340). Washington, DC: APA.

Kunst, J. R., Thomsen, L., & Dovidio, J. F. (2019). Divided loyalties: Perceptions of disloyalty underpin bias toward dually-identified minority-group members. *Journal of Personality and Social Psychology, 117*(4), 807–838.

Moss-Racusin, C. A., Dovidio, J. F., Brescoll, V. L., Graham, M. J., & Handelsman, J. (2012). Science faculty's subtle gender biases favor male students. *Proceedings of the National Academy of Science, 109*(41), 16474–16479.

Purdie-Vaughns, V., & Eibach, R. P. (2008). Intersectional invisibility: The distinctive advantages and disadvantages of multiple subordinate group identities. *Sex Roles, 59*(5–6), 377–391.

Ridgeway, C. L. (2014). Why status matters for inequality. *American Sociological Review, 79,* 1–16.

Saguy, T., Quinn, D. M., Dovidio, J. F., & Pratto, F. (2010). Interacting like a body: Objectification can lead women to narrow their presence in social interactions. P*sychological Science, 21*(2), 178–182.

Vial, A., Brescoll, V. L., & Dovidio, J. F. (2019). Third-party prejudice accommodation increases gender discrimination. *Journal of Personality and Social Psychology, 117*(1), 73–98.

Vial, A., Dovidio, J. F., & Brescoll, V. L. (2019). Channeling others' biases to meet role demands. *Journal of Experimental Social Psychology, 82,* 47–63.

Wittlin, N. M., Dovidio, J. F., LaFrance, M., & Burke, S. E. (2018). About face: Memory for transgender versus cisgender targets' facial appearance. *Journal of Experimental Social Psychology, 78,* 77–92.

Wood, W., & Eagly, A. H. (2002). A cross-cultural analysis of the behavior of women and men: Implications for the origins of sex differences. *Psychological Bulletin, 128*(5), 699–727.

CHAPTER 7

MY LEARNING JOURNEY

Seven Turning Points in My Life as a Gender-and-Race Scholar

Robin J. Ely
Harvard University

My old friend, Bill Kahn, once said to me many years ago, "All learning takes place in the context of relationships." My quest to study gender and, later, race, as well as my research, attests to the wisdom of that statement. Over the course of my 40-plus-year learning journey, I have encountered a series of turning points, each punctuated by relationships with one or more key people who invested in me and taught me to see the social world—and myself—in new ways. At each turn, I had the opportunity to learn from and with amazing people, and that learning has profoundly shaped how I think about these topics as well as how I study and teach about them.

I didn't sit down intending to tell my story this way; it's just the way it unfolded as I wrote: turning points, seven of them to be exact—"the magical number seven"—the integer with the uncanny properties that pioneering cognitive psychologist George A. Miller famously wrote about back in 1956, the year I was born (see Miller, 1956). That coincidence seemed inanely

Perspectives on Gender and Work, pages 75–89

fitting, so I didn't overthink it; I just went with it: seven turning points in my life as a gender-and-race scholar.

TURNING POINT #1: MY FEMINIST AWAKENING

The first turning point was when I was 16 years old and invited to join a "women's consciousness raising" group by a woman in the next tiny rural town over from the tiny rural town where I grew up in Connecticut. She was the mother of some guy I vaguely knew in the high school class ahead of me. I actually have no idea how I ended up sitting in her living room in a circle of three or four of my 16-year-old girl friends. That is the first time I remember being introduced to feminism, so I guess I would call those meetings my "feminist awakening." That was in 1972. It was before *Roe v. Wade*. I know that, because I have a vivid memory of sitting in that living room discussing whether my friend would be taking the train or driving to New York City for her abortion—abortion was still illegal in Connecticut.

The first decision I made as a result of that awakening was to quit cheerleading, a sport that suddenly struck me as disconcertingly subservient.

TURNING POINT #2: MY INTELLECTUAL AWAKENING

From that point, I eventually made my way to Smith College—my second big turning point—by way of the University of New Hampshire (UNH), where I'd initially decided to go to school because I saw a cute guy in the admissions office and because it was such a pretty campus. Such was the stuff of my life decisions back then. But I found in that first year of college a second awakening—to the joy of learning and the transformational potential of ideas—and I was most engaged by what I was learning in my psychology courses. So, I went back to all the college course catalogues I'd collected the year before, and Smith's was among them.

I hadn't been much interested in Smith when I was applying to college. It was a women's college, and how could that possibly be fun (read: Not likely to see any cute guys roaming the campus!)? I had the catalogue because attending a "Smith tea" at neighboring Connecticut College my junior year of high school got me out of gym class. But I will admit that, by the end of that 90-minute introduction, I was somewhat intrigued. I loved the 80-year-old Smithie who sat at the edge of our circle and spoke so fondly of her years there. And I loved the *esprit de corps* that seemed to rise up among the young women pictured in the slides (slides shown from a projector, of course—no powerpoint back then!).

I tucked those images away until I picked up that catalogue again in my freshman year, turned to the psychology department courses, and found a wonderful array of so many more courses than were offered at UNH. So, I applied to Smith as a transfer student for my sophomore year, got in, and what happened there put me on a life course I could never have imagined.

Smith was a place where feminism, not to mention smart women, was taken for granted. And there, I became enamored of sociology. I took every course Estelle Disch—a super cool, fabulous young feminist sociologist—offered, and in her courses, I learned about inequality. And race and power and status and social class. I started losing interest in psychology, mostly turned off by the fact that to keep that major, I had to take the dreaded experimental psychology and, after that, statistics. But in the end, I decided that taking a double major, in sociology and psychology, would be worth it, and I plunged into those courses I thought surely I would hate.

The long and the short of it is this: I loved both of those psychology courses. Not least because experimental psych was taught by Jacquie Parsons (aka Jacquie Eccles, a feminist developmental psychologist who later left Smith and joined the faculty at University of Michigan, where she went on to publish prolifically studies about gender in young children). Jacquie's course wasn't all about rats (yes, we had our obligatory rat in the maze that we learned to condition to the bell); it was about people and the experimental study of people. I loved her course! And then I took statistics with Fletcher Blanchard, a social psychologist who studied race and gender, and, to my surprise, I loved statistics, too! And so, my interest in psychology was rekindled, and I graduated fully steeped in the macro structures of society *and* the micro structures of the social mind—the roots of the "meso" scholar I am today.

After a couple of years working for a "belt-way bandit" consulting firm in DC, and upon Ronald Reagan's election, which portended cuts in the kinds of defense and energy social science contracts I was working on, I decided to go to graduate school. I'd heard about this field called "organizational behavior" (OB), and that there was a program at Yale, where a couple of social psychologists—Richard Hackman and Vic Vroom—taught. I was intrigued, but my stats professor from Smith insisted that OB wasn't a "real field" for "real scholars" and that, if I were going to go to graduate school, I must get grounded in a discipline. The recency of my psych (versus soc) courses at Smith led me to apply to social psych programs. I also applied to Yale, which was secretly my first choice (secretly, because I was afraid of appearing "unscholarly").

I didn't get into Yale; I was wait-listed at Michigan and Stanford, and I got into the University of Texas. I had applied to Texas because I'd worked on a project at Smith for which I'd read *Masculinity and Femininity*, by Janet

Spence and Bob Helmreich, and they were both at Texas. So off to Austin I headed in my little Honda Civic, expecting to work with them.

Shortly after I started my PhD program there, however, I learned that Bob was no longer interested in gender (he had become completely enamored of People Express, that new-fangled airline that was meant to turn the industry upside down), and Janet was elected president of APA, which meant she spent most of her time in DC. By early October of my first year, I was panicking because, unlike my three first-year classmates, I wasn't yet running subjects and thus was woefully behind.

So, dejectedly, I went to Bill Swann's office one morning and told him I needed to run a study, any study, I didn't care which one, I just needed to be "running some subjects." He had a whole slew of ideas, being a young assistant professor at the time, gunning for tenure, so he outlined a few hypotheses he thought needed to be tested to further develop his theory of self-verification, and I picked one. It involved filling four experimental conditions with pretested subjects: certain and uncertain extroverts, and certain and uncertain introverts. Turns out, it's mighty hard to find "introverts" who are "certain" of their standing on that trait—and then get them to show up to the lab. I ran subjects for that study, and that study alone, for the next two years, until I finally filled that darn cell. (Turns out, my efforts were not for naught—we published the study in *JPSP*, Swann & Ely, 1986.)

That was in the mid-1980s, and to my mind, no one in the field of social psychology, let alone at Texas, was doing anything related to gender that was even remotely interesting. (Claude Steele wasn't yet on the scene.) I'd just read Rosabeth Moss Kanter's *Men and Women of the Corporation*, so I added "power," "opportunities," and "numbers" to my interest in "gender." But I was hamstrung by the only method I'd been taught: the laboratory experimental method. Try as I might to design a study I was actually interested in conducting, I consistently ended up wanting to test hypotheses involving 6- and 8-way interaction effects—obviously not feasible. And I couldn't possibly imagine how I might experimentally manipulate power as Kanter had conceptualized it. I knew there had to be an alternative method, and I wanted it to be one that would take me into the field—into organizations.

For 2 years, my disaffection with social psychology grew, and all the while Yale's OB program lurked in the back of my mind. So, I reapplied to Yale, and this time I was accepted. With the coursework for the PhD in social psych under my belt,[1] most notably my excellent training in statistics (training that turned out to serve me well in my first two jobs where teaching statistics became my bread-and-butter), I hit the road in my little Honda Civic once again, this time bound for New Haven: huge turning point number three.

TURNING POINT #3: DISCOVERING NEW METHODS AND THEORIES

Yale was amazing—and challenging—like all fantastic PhD programs should be. I went into the program thinking it would be my last attempt to become a social scientist; if Yale didn't work out, maybe I'd go get an MBA. Or something. I had no idea, really. But what I encountered in the OB program at Yale was beyond anything I could have imagined. I had left Texas in search of a research method that would allow me to study what I was interested in, but I never imagined that what I'd find would be not only a method but also a set of theories that would rock my world: clinical field methods and theories of systems psychodynamics—unconscious processes in organizations to be investigated by honoring people's emotions, including my own, as valid data about social systems.

Using clinical research methods and applying a systems psychodynamic lens, I learned to see how social systems, including groups, organizations, and institutions, shape and are shaped by members' emotional needs; how people's behavior in organizations has as much to do with managing their emotional needs and identities as with pursuing the organization's task; how these aspects of experience occur largely outside of people's conscious awareness; and how people are motivated—and the social systems within which they are embedded are set up—to keep it that way.

These new ideas and approaches turned me on to a whole new way of viewing gender—but not just gender, intergroup relations more generally. And not just intergroup relations, but intergroup relations as embedded within larger social systems, like organizations, industries, and societies more broadly. Wow: my psychology and sociology backgrounds brought together in an extraordinary, utterly compelling set of ideas that blew my mind.

Clay Alderfer and David Berg were my intellectual mentors. I hung on their every word and secretly sought their approval at every turn. I was not the darling of my program; in fact, I was pretty much *personae non grata* when it came to those guys, and that was a foreign experience for me. I don't think I could have stuck it out but for my women peers in the program: Herminia Ibarra, Paula Caproni, Maria Arias, Ellen Kossek, Sharon Rogolsky, Jill Kern, Jane Fountain—fabulous women, the unmarried of whom spent most of our time together, daily propping each other up as we stumbled, at times soared, stumbled again, and eventually sprinted, most of us, to the finish line of our PhDs.

This support group of women was the kernel that led me to my dissertation topic: the quality of relationships among professional women as a function of how much power women have in the social system. I realized that both my worst (in my job in DC) and my best (in undergraduate and graduate school) work relationships had been with women. So, what gives with the uniformly negative stereotype that women are catty, back-biting horrors—"mean girls grown up," "tripping the prom queen," fighting an "uncivil business war" (titles of books purporting to tell all about the nature of women's workplace relationships)? What gives, my Yale training suggested to me, is the distribution of power in the social system within which these relationships are embedded. When women lack power in a system, I hypothesized—when the system communicates to them that their gender is a liability—they are more likely to turn against each other; but when their gender isn't a liability, it can serve as a positive basis for identification. It's funny, because I'd never actually been in a system in which women didn't lack power. For most of my time at Yale, the OB faculty was all male, with a revolving door of women assistant professors, one or at most two, at any given point in time. But at least Yale was a place where that lack of power was acknowledged as a problem, and maybe that acknowledgment helped loosen the grip of women's powerlessness on our ability to connect deeply and supportively with one another.

I launched my dissertation research in 1987, testing my hypothesis in a study of women associates in law firms and operationalizing women's power as the proportion of women partners in the firm. I scoured the *National Association for Law Placement Directory* for firms in the Northeast that had "a lot" of women partners. "A lot" turned out to be 15%, a crazy high proportion in 1987. I found one in Connecticut, one in New York City, and two in DC, and I matched them to firms with only one or two women partners—plenty of those to choose from. The proportion of women associates was generally around 50%, even back then, so I interviewed randomly chosen women from each of the firms' associate ranks.

To write a "gender" dissertation that included only women was rare, and I probably only got away with it because no one on the OB faculty was paying much attention to me. Richard Hackman, who likely would have chaired my committee, had already left us for Harvard. (Though Richard was instrumental on my journey to becoming a gender scholar: When I announced to him one day that, to avoid the stigma of studying gender, I would hide my interest in a study of "power," he looked at me aghast and told me I would do no such thing. To hide my true interest would be to suppress my passion, he exhorted, and no good scholar ever came from a place of suppressed passion.) David Berg was going on sabbatical, and he wasn't tenured anyway, and much as I revered Clay Alderfer's mind, he and I had too contentious a relationship for him to be my chair. In the end, Vic Vroom, who had zero knowledge of gender and with whom I'd never even taken a course, kindly agreed to serve as my chair. When he looked at my study design and said, fine, just add a parallel condition with men, I turned to him with a curious eye: a parallel condition? What might that look like? Relationships among men associates in firms with few male partners? That clearly made no sense. He easily relented and, from then on, let me do my own thing.

In the end, my dissertation served me very well. Despite receiving low-but-still-passing ratings from the three official readers of my dissertation, I eventually—5 and 6 years after finishing my PhD—published two papers from the study, one in *Administrative Science Quarterly* (Ely, 1994) and one in *Academy of Management Journal* (Ely, 1995a), proof that the adage "a good dissertation is a done dissertation" held some truth. My dissertation had good bones, but it was far from publishable when I defended it.

By way of background, here is a thumbnail sketch of my major personal and professional moves from that point. My first job was at the Harvard Kennedy School (HKS), which I'd applied to more or less on a lark, having seen the job posted on some obscure bulletin board in the halls of Yale School of Organization and Management—a job in which I met my soulmate. Three years later we were married, and 3 years after that, in January 1996, I left that job and moved to New York City to accommodate my husband's long-time dream to enter the field of public education. He'd been offered the job of deputy chancellor for operations at the New York City Board of Ed, which was hard to pass up. I'd recently been promoted to untenured associate, but in those days, no one was getting promoted to tenure at the Kennedy School, so it was a relatively easy decision to leave. Plus, I was 6 months pregnant. I figured I'd get a visiting appointment somewhere later that summer, but at nine months pregnant, I found myself interviewing for a job that had opened up late in the market at Columbia's School of International and Public Affairs (SIPA). They were looking for someone who could teach "gender" and statistics. I fit the bill and spent 4 years gloriously happy at SIPA, which was never, from my perspective, more than a temporary job, as both my husband and I had a keen desire to eventually return to Boston. And return we did, in 2000, when I landed a visiting appointment at Harvard Business School; they hired me the next year and promoted me to tenure in 2007. In short, I had not followed a conventional path to tenure nor was it a path I'd planned or ever anticipated: I'd received my PhD in 1989 and didn't come up for tenure until 18 years later—proof to me that some good things are worth waiting for.

TURNING POINT #4: MY RACIAL CONSCIOUSNESS-RAISING AND DEEPENING UNDERSTANDING OF GENDER

Turning point number four happened at HKS, where I spent 7 years incubating insights from graduate school and expanding in earnest my scholarly development beyond gender to the broader field of intergroup relations, particularly race relations (in my research) and all manner of power-differentiated identity-group relations (in my teaching). Kicking off this turning point was my relationship with Pam Ellis, an African American and Native American (Nipmuc) woman who was assistant dean of students at HKS and who graciously invested huge amounts of time as well as psychic and emotional energy educating me about race. I'll never forget the day she dropped off an immense pile of books for me to take on my summer vacation—books by the likes of bell hooks, Gloria Anzaldua, Barbara Smith, Cherrie Moraga—which I devoured and which, together with years of deep, intimate, often difficult conversations with Pam, transformed me. I took these lessons into my classroom, which became a grand laboratory of experiential learning—for me and for my students—in a course I called Group Behavior and the Politics of Diversity (for lessons I learned teaching this course, see Ely, 1995b). Over the years, I co-taught the course with others who were critical to my development including, most notably, Ron David, a faculty colleague, and teaching assistants Frank (a.k.a. "Hill") Harper, Betsy Hasagawa, and Terry Bowman (all former students in the course). Each of us brought his or her identity fully to the teaching group and the classroom, and we learned an enormous amount from each other.

At the same time, I was working with David Thomas, my long-time dear friend and colleague from graduate school days, who was teaching at HBS and collaborating with me on a project that significantly propelled each of our careers forward and from which I began to develop an identity, not only as a gender scholar, but also as a race-and-diversity scholar (see Ely & Thomas, 2001; Ely, Padavic, & Thomas, 2012; Thomas & Ely, 1996). (For a brief essay on my collaboration with David, specifically, how our struggles over authorship-order helped us build deep and abiding trust across our race and gender differences, see Ely, 2011.)

Deb Meyerson also entered my life during my HKS years, as we embarked, along with Debbie Kolb, on an action-research project at The Body Shop, giving us our first opportunity to spell out and test a theory of gender in organizations and of how to eradicate gender inequality (see Ely & Meyerson, 2000). (I would—and will, if I can ever find the time—write that theory somewhat differently today, standing by our analysis of how gender inequality is baked deeply into the culture of most organizations, but proposing a different approach to change.)

It was an excellent ride, working with Deb, our last publication together being probably our favorite joint project, the culmination of our 19-month qualitative study of masculinity on two off-shore oil platforms. Among other adventures, that field study included our evacuation off one of the platforms on 9/11; being subsequently stuck in New Orleans for what seemed an eternity (but was just 3 days), halfway across the country from our respective families (my daughter had just started kindergarten the week before, Deb's three kids were all still in elementary school); and piecing together initial takeaways on the Greyhound bus we eventually took from Baton Rouge to

Dallas, where we each departed for opposite coasts on what I think were among the very first flights to take off after the terrorist attack.

We loved the paper we wrote from that project! It gave us insight into how the world could be different, how an organizational culture change that ostensibly had nothing to do with gender—it was part of the company's safety initiative—could unintentionally release men from societal imperatives for "manly" behavior, prompting them to let go of masculine-image concerns and to behave instead in counter-stereotypical—and more task-effective—ways. Finally, a paper of hope! Our love for that paper made the hell of a time we had trying to publish it in *ASQ* particularly heartbreaking. After three or four revisions for *ASQ* (I no longer recall the details), it was rejected, so we published it in *Research in Organizational Behavior,* where Art Brief, bless his heart, welcomed it with open arms (see Ely & Meyerson, 2010).

Literally 3 days after Deb and I toasted having hit send on the final version, she suffered a serious stroke leaving her to this day with speech aphasia, limited use of her right hand, and a limp. My stalwart research partner and dear friend was ultimately forced to end her academic career as she had known it. (Not that she's stopped her career, just transformed it into a different one—still writing books and now also running a nonprofit, having shifted her focus from advancing gender equality to supporting the work of stroke survivors and their caretakers. See Meyerson & Zuckerman, 2019.)

TURNING POINT #5: DISCOVERING THE EGO—AND ITS ANTIDOTE, PURPOSE

The story of how we found ourselves on those offshore oil platforms (see below) brings me to Turning Point 5 in my career development as a gender-and-race scholar: my introduction, through Deb's husband Steve, to Learning as Leadership, Inc. (LaL), a small leadership development organization in Sausalito, CA. From the principals, facilitators, and coaches of LaL, I came to see how, at the interpersonal level, struggles around gender and race inequality are battles between egos—those too easily threatened, fearful, shame-ridden parts of ourselves that erect barriers within us, blocking access to our own humanity and to true human connection with others. These insights were not inconsistent with my previous training, they were complementary, taking me deep into my own and others' psyche for a double click on identity threats (what we called "identity abrasions" in an *Harvard Business Review* article; see Ely, Meyerson, & Davidson, 2006).

What's the antidote? Purpose: In the battle between the part of our self that is deeply devoted to advancing a meaningful purpose, on the one hand, and the part of our self that is devoted to defending the puny but pugnacious little tyrant that is our ego, on the other, the puny, pugnacious little guy will win every time—unless we are vigilant to not let that happen. A meaningful purpose gives us the motivation to take our defensive self out of the driver seat and let our curious self take over: to investigate what we might learn about ourselves, the other, the situation that can give us a fuller picture of reality and a better handle on how best to move forward. When our ego is threatened, our view is narrowed: We make a caricature of the other, and in the process we make a caricature of ourselves—an insight I credit to my dear colleagues, Anne Morriss and Frances Frei (see Morriss, Ely, & Frei, 2011).

Fascinated by the prospect of applying these lessons from LaL to what we might learn about how to address inequality, I convened a small group of like-minded colleagues including, most notably for my development, Charles Behling, who was running the Program on Intergroup Relations at the University of Michigan, and Martin Davidson, whose perspectives on gender/race/diversity I had long found sympatico with mine. Together with my then research assistant, Laura Wernick, we embarked on LaL's "one-year-program," a series of four intensive seminars, ranging from 3 to 9 days each. One upshot of that collaboration was the *HBR* article I referenced above; another was a series of exercises we adapted from LaL to address intergroup inequality, which once again, enabled me to glean further insights from my teaching; and last, but most importantly, was a long and abiding friendship among Charles, Martin, the folks at LaL, and me.

My connection to LaL was generative in other ways as well. Through LaL, Deb and I had met the asset manager of one of the oil platforms we studied, Rick Fox, whose name I can share here because he agreed to be interviewed for an NPR Invisibilia episode that was based on Deb's and my article. I wrote a paper with Debra Rhode (Ely & Rhode, 2009), applying the lessons of LaL to women's leadership; and today, I am collaborating on a project with several colleagues to test those ideas in lab and field experiments. (Yes, I'm returning to the lab after all these years, and it is really a challenge for me—I simply no longer think methodologically like an experimental social psychologist! Luckily, members of my research team do.)

TURNING POINT #6: RETURN TO MY YALE ROOTS AND SYSTEMS PSYCHODYNAMICS

Turning Point 6 was my return to systems psychodynamics, prompted by the entry about 10 years ago of two young(er) psychodynamically trained scholars into the field of organizational behavior: Jennifer and Gianpiero Petriglieri, both at INSEAD. At this turning point, I joined a small group of like-minded colleagues, which convenes annually, to support one another in our efforts to publish organizational research informed by a systems-psychodynamic perspective and, more generally, to bring this perspective back into the mainstream of organizational research.

Systems psychodynamics enjoys a long and rich history in the field of organizational behavior, but lost its center of gravity in the United States when these elements of the OB programs at Yale and Wharton, which had become the principal purveyors of business-oriented scholarship within this tradition, were dismantled (in the case of Yale) or spun off into a separate entity (in the case of Wharton) in the late 1980s. The result has been a diaspora of clinically trained organizational scholars who have been profoundly influenced by this perspective but who, for lack of a community and publication outlets for this kind of thinking, have been using these insights largely privately to inform their work and, until very recently, have tended not to write or teach about them explicitly. In other words, these scholars had been more or less closeted for some 25 years, essentially halting the development of the next generation of scholars who might carry on and develop this work. For these reasons, I was thrilled when I happened upon the Petriglieris, new-generation scholars steeped in this tradition and, most importantly, actively developing it both in the classroom and as part of a vibrant research agenda now coming fully into its own.

As part of this effort, I am proud both to have been able to help develop, as a reviewer and editor at *ASQ*, a number of papers drawing on systems psychodynamics and to have recently published one of my own, with Irene Padavic and Erin Reid. In this paper, we advance systems-psychodynamic theory to explain why, despite countervailing evidence, men and women alike routinely invoke the "work–family narrative" to explain women's stalled advancement. The narrative goes something like this: High-level jobs require extremely long hours; women's devotion to family impedes their ability to put in the requisite hours, and their careers suffer as a result. Drawing on data from a consulting firm, we show how organizations use this narrative, together with unconscious psychological defense mechanisms that reinforce the belief in women's natural fitness for family and men's for work, as part of an unconscious "social defense" system. This system helps protect men from the disturbing emotions that arise from firms' demand for long work hours, lets firm leaders off the hook for women's failure to advance, and deflects attention away from firms' general culture of overwork, leaving women's thin representation at senior levels in place (see Ely & Padavic, 2020; Padavic, Ely, & Reid, 2020). For me, writing this chapter was a homecoming of sorts—a tribute to and honoring of my Yale roots. I think it represents my best thinking about gender to date. (But I'm fickle: My most recent paper is always the one I'm most in love with!)

TURNING POINT #7: BUILDING PERSONAL POWER THROUGH "SHADOW" WORK

The seventh and most recent turning point in my development as a gender-and-race scholar came with my participation over the past 2 years in a program called Journey to Completion, led by a Jungian-trained shaman, Norma Burton. Having studied for some 20 years with a Huichol shaman master, Norma guides a shamanic process in which one connects with one's "shadow" self—the disempowered parts of the self that grow from fear and shame—and transforms them into sources of personal power. I mention this turning point because, while it didn't give me insights into the workings of gender, race, or other forms of inequality, it is a process that is deeply about power—personal power. I have the sense that this experience will equip me in ways I can't yet even imagine as I finish out my scholarly journey over the next 20 years.

What this work has taught me is that we can have tons of great ideas, develop our minds forever, but if we don't cultivate our internal capacity to hold steady in the face of our demons—experiences that have carved into us beliefs about what to fear and the patterned ways we seek to protect ourselves from those fears—we cannot reach our full potential. This is a particularly important insight for me personally, as a long-time feminist who learned early about the devastating impact of power disparities on individuals, groups, the world. To this understanding of power I now add insights about how, when we cling to beliefs about our own powerlessness developed long ago and nurtured throughout our lives, we dramatically sell ourselves short. As a strong feminist, I was the last person I'd have suspected of having nevertheless colluded in pernicious ways with my own oppression: at times, letting myself be intimidated by those more powerful than I, not pushing harder for change, shrinking when I could have been enlarging myself in service to my purpose as a scholar—to advance structural equality by generating and disseminating knowledge.

CONCLUSION: MY ADVICE TO YOUNG SCHOLARS

As I look back over these turning points and the many people in my life who helped make them happen, I feel a great deal of gratitude. In the spirit of paying it forward, I offer the following advice to young scholars in the field. Some of it is on the loftier side, but I hope still actionable; some of it is more prosaic.

1. Find people who inspire you, people who see the world differently from how you see it: Honor them, connect deeply with them, and learn from them.

2. Find your power and ground yourself in it.
3. Study what your experience tells you is important, what it begs you to study, not what the field (or some old scholar like me) deems "hot."
4. Don't waste your time worrying about someone else "scooping" your ideas; if you follow my advice in (3) above, no one will—or could—write the paper you're writing.
5. When possible, cite the work of scholars in marginalized identity groups whose careers could use your support. As Pat Yancy Martin once pointed out to me, "Citations are a political act:" Mainstream scholars, who have larger, denser networks, are cited more often, a bias we should take care to rectify whenever we can.
6. When it comes to decisions around coauthorship, be true to yourself:
   a. If you can possibly resist the pressure to jump on the current bandwagon of scholars putting their name on every paper they've so much as glanced at, do. That trend cheapens true contributions and advantages those with more power.
   b. Have the difficult conversation about authorship, including author order, up front, and be willing to re-evaluate as the work unfolds; don't let feelings of inequity fester.
   c. Be generous when you can afford to be (as Deb Meyerson did with me, offering me first author on our 2000 *ROB*—a paper on which she could by all rights have claimed that position for herself—because she deemed it more important to me than to her, given our different job situations at the time).
   d. Coauthor with your best friends; it's more fun.
7. If you're going to study how "supply-side" factors (e.g., people's preferences) contribute to inequality, please, also examine how "demand-side" factors (e.g., biased attitudes, skewed opportunities) give rise to the supply side ones (for a critique of sex-difference research along these lines, see Ely & Padavic, 2007; Tinsley & Ely, 2018).
8. Learn how to write well; anything worth saying is worth saying clearly and succinctly. I learned this from Irene Padavic, my dear friend since Smith and coauthor on several papers; she learned it from Barbara Reskin, to whom we are both forever grateful.[2]

NOTES

1. I didn't bother to pick up the MA in social psych as that required writing a thesis.
2. This chapter violates many of Barbara's rules: For instance, it lacks proper topic sentences and contains many sentence fragments. But this is a chapter of an altogether different type, so I think it's okay.

REFERENCES

Ely, R. J. (1994). The effects of organizational demographics and social identity on relationships among professional women. *Administrative Science Quarterly, 39*(2), 203–238.

Ely, R. J. (1995a). The power in demography: Women's social constructions of gender identity at work. *Academy of Management Journal, 38*(3), 589–634.

Ely, R. J. (1995b). The role of dominant identity and experience in organizational work on diversity. In S. E. Jackson and M. N. Ruderman (Eds.), *Diversity in work teams: Research paradigms for a changing workplace* (pp. 161–186). Washington, DC: American Psychological Association.

Ely, R. J. (2011). Seeing and being seen across differences in race and gender. In C. A. Carlsen & J. E. Dutton. (Eds.), *Research alive: Exploring generative moments in doing qualitative research* (pp. 174–177). Copenhagen, Denmark: Copenhagen Business School Press.

Ely, R. J., & Meyerson, D. E. (2010). An organizational approach to undoing gender: The unlikely case of offshore oil platforms. *Research in Organizational Behavior, 30*(1), 3–34.

Ely, R. J., & Meyerson, D. E. (2000). Theories of gender: A new approach to organizational analysis and change. *Research in Organizational Behavior, 22*, 105–153.

Ely, R. J., Meyerson, D. E., & Davidson, M. (2006). Rethinking political correctness. *Harvard Business Review, 84*(9), 78–87.

Ely, R. J., & Padavic, I. (2007). A feminist analysis of organizational research on sex differences. *Academy of Management Review, 32*(4), 1121–1143.

Ely, R. J., & Padavic, I. (2020). What's really holding women back? It's not what most people think. *Harvard Business Review, 98*(2), 58–67.

Ely, R. J., Padavic, I., & Thomas, D. A. (2012). Racial diversity, racial asymmetries, and team learning environment: Effects on performance. *Organization Studies, 33*(3), 341–362.

Ely, R. J., & Rhode, D. L. (2009). Women and leadership: Defining the challenges. In N. Nohria & R. Khurana (Eds.), *Advancing leadership: Theory and practice* (pp. 377–410). Boston, MA: Harvard Business School Press.

Ely, R. J., & Thomas, D. A. (2001). Cultural diversity at work: The effects of diversity perspectives on work group processes and outcomes. *Administrative Science Quarterly, 46*(2), 229–273.

Meyerson, D. E., & Zuckerman, D. (2019). *Identity theft: Rediscovering ourselves after stroke*. Kansas City, MO: Andrews McMeel.

Miller, G. A. (1956). The magical number seven, plus or minus two: Some limits on our capacity for information processing. *The Psychological Review, 63*(2), 81–97.

Morriss, A., Ely, R. J., & Frei, F. (2011). Stop holding yourself back: Five ways people unwittingly sabotage their rise to leadership. *Harvard Business Review, 89*(1/2), 160–163.

Padavic, I., Ely, R. J., & Reid, E. M. (2020). Explaining the persistence of gender inequality: The work–family narrative as a social defense against the 24/7 work culture. *Administrative Science Quarterly, 65*(1), 61–111.

Swann, W. B., & Ely, R. J. (1984). A battle of wills: Self-verification versus behavioral confirmation. *Journal of Personality and Social Psychology, 46*(6), 1287–1302.

Thomas, D. A., & Ely, R. J. (1996). Making differences matter: A new paradigm for managing diversity. *Harvard Business Review, 74*(5), 79–90.

Tinsley, C. H., & Ely, R. J. (2018). What most people get wrong about men and women: Research shows the sexes aren't so different. *Harvard Business Review, 96*(3), 114–121.

CHAPTER 8

UNDERSTANDING THE LIVED EXPERIENCE OF WOMEN'S HEALTH AND WELL-BEING AT WORK

Allison S. Gabriel
University of Arizona

Since earning my PhD in industrial-organizational psychology from the University of Akron in 2013 and earning tenure at the University of Arizona in 2018, my research agenda and focus has taken what may be viewed by some as a dramatic twist. If you asked the 2013 freshly minted PhD version of me what my research interests were, I would have told you that my research broadly focused on emotions at work and employee well being. I was researching how employees regulated their emotions at work in the context of customer service exchanges (e.g., Gabriel, Daniels, Diefendorff, & Greguras, 2015; Gabriel & Diefendorff, 2015) or how people reacted to salient affective events, such as accomplishing direct and indirect patient care tasks in nursing (e.g., Gabriel, Diefendorff, & Erickson, 2011). I was also fascinated by understanding within-person processes, using methods

Perspectives on Gender and Work, pages 91–100

such as experience sampling (e.g., Beal, 2015) or continuous rating assessments (e.g., Ruef & Levenson, 2007) to examine my effects. Knowing what happened day-to-day or moment-to-moment was more intrinsically interesting to me than considering how aspects of the work environment operated statically, or "in general."

The 2019 associate professor version of me, however, has a slightly different story to tell. My research is still focused on emotions at work and employee well-being. However, after a serendipitous conversation with a close friend who was discussing her struggles finding time to pump breast milk at work and the stigma she felt she faced for doing so, I now find myself having a heightened focus on how these processes are occurring in relation to women's health at work. I'm talking about the "controversial," taboo topics that still may make people pause and say, as I've heard before, "Is that really a management topic?" Or, my favorite question, "Why should organizations really care about something that's a 'home issue?'" Specifically, since I began my time at the University of Arizona, I've taken interest in understanding how menstruation affects women's experiences at work day-to-day (Motro, Gabriel, & Ellis, 2019), and how women who are breastfeeding or pumping breast milk experience their work and family lives when they are working full time (Gabriel, Volpone, MacGowan, Butts, & Moran, 2019). This culminated most recently in an annual review piece that I am wildly proud of (Grandey, Gabriel, & King, 2020) that highlights how the "three Ms"—menstruation, motherhood, and menopause—have the potential to intersect with women's career trajectories at critical junctures.

To me, researching these issues is timely—it is hard to not go a day without seeing news coverage surrounding women's health. For instance, a story in November 2019 highlighted how a department store in Japan was considering having female employees wear badges when they were menstruating (Meredith, 2019). The badge included a logo of Seiri Chan—a symbol for menstruation—and was meant to be worn by women optionally as a way to evoke sympathy from coworkers. Although the goal was for women to receive added breaks and assistance when wearing the badge (which could have its own pitfalls: Jones, Clair, King, Humberd, & Arena, 2019), public outcry highlighted that it could increase harassment towards women. At the same time, in November of 2019, there was public discussion of new legislation in California aimed to better support women returning to work postpartum who want to continue breastfeeding and/or pumping (Krans, 2019). The law (SB-142) not only legislates for organizations to provide space for women to express breast milk, but requires a space close to women's work areas that has a chair and table/shelf to store breast pump parts, as well as electricity. The law also goes a step further, noting that there should be accessible running water and proper refrigerated storage. This runs in stark contrast to the many tales of women who struggle to find time and space at work to achieve this key aspect of motherhood (Gabriel et al., 2019; Joyce, 2017). As a final example (also from November 2019; there's a theme here), companies such as PricewaterhouseCoopers (PwC) are starting to recognize that women need added support during menopause, with discussion of how to build well-being policies to better support women at work (Mesure, 2019).

Yet, despite this added public discourse, discussion of women's health in the applied psychology and management literature is surprisingly quiet. This was the onus for our review piece on the three Ms noted above—we have papers about daily fluctuations in pain at work (Christian, Eisenkraft, & Kapadia, 2015) or the allostatic load model and employee health (Ganster & Rosen, 2013), yet we see little discussion surrounding how women's health (a) predictably fluctuates over the course of careers, (b) has the potential to violate what have been deemed prototypical norms of being an "ideal employee" (Acker, 1990; Jones, 2017), and (c) can be supported in ways that are not undermining. Thus, it appears as though a classic scientist-practitioner gap may be opening up when it comes to women's health at work; in this case, organizations are beginning to develop policies to support women, but we (organizational scholars) are not researching what these types of support may or may not look like day-to-day.

Because of this, I want to highlight recent findings I am most excited about from our work on breastfeeding. I then want to provide some insights into topics related to women's health for the future, and advice I have for those considering pursuing research on these topics.

BREASTFEEDING AT WORK: IMPORTANT FINDINGS AND PRACTICAL RECOMMENDATIONS

Our research on breastfeeding and pumping at work on a day-to-day basis (Gabriel et al., 2019) will likely be the paper I am most proud of over the course of my career. This is not to discredit my other work, or the coauthors I have from other projects. Rather, I have not yet been part of a project where—as I was writing it—I knew I was speaking directly to the "lived experience" (e.g., Weiss & Rupp, 2011) of several working mothers in organizations today. Our research started with a simple question: What are the challenges women face when they return to work full time postpartum but want to continue breastfeeding for their baby (or babies)? However, over the course of the peer-review process, our paper evolved to also address the following important question: What *benefits* emerge when breastfeeding and work blend together successfully? We viewed breastfeeding as encompassing three groups of women: those who exclusively breastfed at home and at work (e.g., go to an on-site or close-by day care; return home to feed their child); those who did a combination of breastfeeding and pumping (e.g., breastfeeding at home and pumping breast milk while at work); and those who exclusively pumped breast milk. Because of this, when I describe our findings below (and why I think they are cool!) I use the term *breastfeeding* to encompass all three of these groups of women.

Our paper was mixed methods (my first one, actually) and began with a qualitative study of 38 women who described their daily experiences working full-time and breastfeeding. From these interviews, it became apparent to my colleagues and I that breastfeeding could be a source of strain *and* a source of enrichment. This was really interesting, as theory related to the work–family literature that we were drawing from suggested that breastfeeding should be largely problematic (i.e., a family role demand spilling into the work domain; Greenhaus & Beutell, 1985). Yet, women were empowered! Several noted that when breastfeeding at work went well, they felt accomplished. Because of this, we designed an experience sampling study, tracking the daily experiences of 106 women over 15 workdays. Although there are several parts to this study, we primarily wanted to know if breastfeeding interference (i.e., breastfeeding interfering with work on a daily basis) and breastfeeding enrichment (i.e., breastfeeding generating feelings of accomplishment that could benefit the work role) had unique effects of women's affect (i.e., feelings of fatigue/depression and calm/contentment) and outcomes in both role domains daily. This is the part of the paper I loved the most—we included work goal progress *and* breastfeeding goal progress, conceptualized as the amount of breastmilk women reported producing at work on a daily basis controlling for the amount of breastmilk they planned to produce and the amount of time they spent breastfeeding/pumping. When I first told individuals outside my author team that we were going to include this variable, we got a lot of varied reactions. Some people thought it was cool; some people thought it was too tangential and not "work relevant enough." We, of course, landed in the "this is *really* cool camp," and I have to say that my impression is that this variable was the one reviewers loved most from the start. Baked in here is an important lesson to be learned: If you're going to do a paper on breastfeeding (or any of the three Ms), make the paper *really* amount breastfeeding. We as a team knew from the start that if we were going to do a paper on breastfeeding, we were actually going to study breastfeeding-relevant outcomes.

Our experience sampling results painted important theoretical and practical implications. I personally believe this to be the most important finding—breastfeeding interference increased daily feelings of depression and fatigue, which in turn reduced work goal progress and women's breastfeeding goal progress; however, the effects reversed for breastfeeding enrichment, with enrichment reducing these negative affective experiences, leading to benefits tied to work and breastfeeding. Thus, this is not a matter of breastfeeding "distracting" women from work or pumping breaks being time away that hinders goal progress; rather, time spent succeeding in blended work–family roles (i.e., breastfeeding at work) has the potential to create success across role domains. Theoretically, we helped identify that role domains can in fact blend together when a family role demand (i.e., breastfeeding) is entirely integrated into the work role. Practically, we also helped show that organizations should ensure that women have the time they need to engage in this blended experience successfully and that framing time spent breastfeeding as a "break" or a distraction is going to do more harm than good for women and the broader organization.

WOMEN'S HEALTH AT WORK: WHAT'S NEXT FOR ME?

Most of my upcoming research on women's health is still related to breastfeeding at work. For instance, we have an on-going project that builds on Gabriel et al. (2019) where we seek to determine which types of support are most beneficial for women to balance work and family (e.g., Volpone, Gabriel, Campbell, MacGowan, & Moran, 2019). More specifically, we use fuzzy set analysis to help determine which configurations of support—combining both structural forms of support (e.g., formal practices aimed at helping breastfeeding women) and informal forms of support (e.g., social support, psychological safety)—are most impactful. Our results highlight that psychological safety tied to breastfeeding within one's workgroup is most important, in addition to experiencing a lack of breastfeeding stigma from coworkers. Our hope is that this work continues to build on women's personal experiences tied to breastfeeding at work, and further highlights that having a break room for pumping may not be enough; rather, the social environment surrounding breastfeeding and/or pumping at work plays a major role.

Beyond this work, I would personally like to expand upon the stigma associated with breastfeeding at work, albeit in the opposite direction—what happens when women do *not* breastfeed or pump and this information is communicated to others? The "breast is best" narrative is incredibly powerful and being pushed consistently in the U.S. healthcare system. But, as someone who is currently expecting, I've been doing some additional reading about breastfeeding. Of course, there are benefits to women, children, and organizations when women breastfeed (see Gabriel et al., 2019, for a brief review). However, upon reading *Cribsheet* by Brown University economist Emily Oster (2019), the science behind breastfeeding benefits is not as definitive as one would hope. Studies on breastfeeding are often confounded with factors that can contribute to whether children reap health and cognitive benefits (e.g., socioeconomic status). Thus, it is plausible that making the choice to formula feed will be just fine (I at least hope this is the case, as I was a formula-fed baby and I think I ended up okay!). Because of this, I see two questions that need to be examined. First, which types of stigma associated with breastfeeding are more or less problematic for women at work—women breastfeeding/pumping, or women formula feeding? How do these choices when communicated affect coworkers' perceptions of the working mother, and how can any problematic perceptions be corrected? Second, how do women cope with the stigma associated with either breastfeeding or formula feeding? My intuitive hunch is that both carry the potential for a hefty psychological toll for women, and as someone who is about to enter into babyhood with the hope to breastfeed but (ideally) the grace to adjust expectations should my body and baby not be responsive to my best-laid plans, what are the tactics women use to cope with this process, and how does that spill into the work environment when they reenter the workplace? The terms *mommy guilt* and *mommy shaming* are so present when preparing to for a baby; the organizational psychologist in me would like to somehow take my own experience—whatever it may be—and learn from it in a way to help others who are juggling this new family role and wanting to come back to work.

Outside of breastfeeding, there are a number of women's health issues that did not get enough attention in our review of the three Ms, largely due to space-related constraints. For instance, issues associated with infertility, miscarriage, and even the choice to not have children are all important aspects of the motherhood experience that are not well understood. How do these experiences shape women's identities both at work and at home as they adjust their own expectations in light of these important, often heartbreaking, challenges? Likewise, when it comes to studying menstruation, there are several severe medical conditions (e.g., premenstrual dysphoric disorder [PMDD]; endometriosis; polycystic ovarian syndrome) that could affect this monthly fluctuation for women. In Motro et al. (2019), we focused only on women with typical cycles who did not have these conditions, nor were on any type of hormonal contraception. Yet, these are real medical issues that are recurring, incredibly painful, and likely pose a challenge for women on a month-to-month basis. Although I am unsure of the theoretical rationale for studying these (which would naturally come up in the review process; see below), practically, I feel compelled to understand how we can better help women who suffer from these conditions.

WOMEN'S HEALTH AT WORK: WHAT'S NEXT FOR YOU?

One interesting question I've received at conferences is whether I think it is risky to have my doctoral students working on research related to the three

Ms. My answer is always a quick (and, perhaps a bit nervous), "Goodness, I sure hope not!" My hope is that our publications on breastfeeding and the three Ms more generally have helped pave the way for our journals being more receptive to topics that were once deemed distal to organizations. And, it seems as though our top journals are expanding their scope, with a recent call for papers for a special research forum at *Academy of Management Journal* on topics important outside our field but potentially understudied at work (which, I would argue, women's health fits squarely within). That being said, here are three big take-away points I have for scholars thinking about entering this area.

First, be prepared to answer the "theoretical contribution" question that often comes up during the review process. This may sound obvious, but I was actually caught off guard a bit by the theoretical questions that were sent our way when publishing our breastfeeding paper. Even though our topic was novel, we had the problem in our initial submission of being phenomenon-driven versus challenging current theory associated with the work–family literature in particular. Luckily, we had a review team who was highly constructive and helped guide us down the road that got us to discussing blended work–family experiences. But, this was something that also came up in our experience sampling work on menstruation (Motro et al., 2019), meaning it is likely to be a consistent issue to consider when entering this domain. As highlighted above, there is value in tackling problems that are practically important to women's health, and I hope our field's blending of occupational health topics can mitigate some of the issues in answering the always frustrating reviewer question: "Why is this important?" But, I say this as a warning to be cognizant of the battle that could ensue, particularly as journals focus on theory development.

Second, be careful when studying these topics to not victim blame. When writing our breastfeeding paper, we had moments where we were afraid that the ultimate message could get twisted into women somehow harming organizations by needing time away to pump (this was mostly a concern before we expanded to have the two pathways that I detailed above). This is largely a concern for when the media picks up this kind of work, as it is attractive to potentially run a headline that is controversial. But, as you are writing, make sure you think about how the words can potentially get twisted. Is the message that women's health-related issues "get in the way" at work? (No!) Or, is the message that women's health is a naturally occurring and fluctuating aspect of their work and nonwork lives that needs to be discussed holistically and authentically in organizations? (Yes!) Keeping these thoughts in mind can be really helpful. When publishing our work on menstruation, for instance, we were asked why we were not interested in having an outcome variable that was counter to our focal outcome of helping (e.g., including a juxtaposing marker related to counterproductive work behavior). We intentionally made this choice for the reason noted above—we were unwilling to publish a paper that ran the risk of saying "women who experience menstrual pain may have an increased likelihood of engaging in [insert negative work behavior here]," even though our effects demonstrate that menstruation is only likely to create a temporary change in coworker interactions 3–4 days per month on average. Our message therefore was to offer support and the opportunity for flexible work and respites—something that can be applied to support all individuals suffering from transient forms of pain (e.g., Christian et al., 2015). Had we included a "dark" outcome variable, I have concerns over how the take-away message could have been construed.

Third, and finally, if you can incorporate cool physiological markers, please go for it. The hormonal fluctuations associated with the three Ms are *so cool*, and in my prior research, I wish we had breast milk samples available to us, or actual hormonal markers tied to menstruation. If you have the opportunity to engage in cross-disciplinary work that can facilitate the appropriate capturing and analyzing of this kind of data, please do so (as an example of such work, see Yang, Bauer, Johnson, Groer, & Salomon, 2014). We actually note in our breastfeeding publication that future research should consider the composition of breast milk in relation to work stress, as research in the medical sciences has demonstrated that immunity increasing antibodies in breast milk (e.g., immunoglobulin A) may be hindered by stress and strain (Kawano & Emori, 2015). As more and more grant agencies and schools weigh the importance of cross-disciplinary research, I hope that these types of collaborations surrounding women's health can flourish and thrive. I know I will certainly be cheering for them as I see them develop.

ACKNOWLEDGMENTS

I'd like to thank Eden King, Mikki Hebl, and Quinetta Roberson for inviting me to be a part of this wonderful book, and our baby girl, ECR, for the little kicks and jabs as I finished writing this during the third trimester.

REFERENCES

Acker, J. (1990). Hierarchies, jobs, bodies: A theory of gendered organizations. *Gender & Society, 4*(2), 139–158.

Beal, D. J. (2015). ESM 2.0: State of the art and future potential of experience sampling methods in organizational research. *Annual Review of Organizational Psychology and Organizational Behavior, 2*(1), 383–407.

Christian, M. S., Eisenkraft, N., & Kapadia, C. (2015). Dynamic associations among somatic complaints, human energy, and discretionary behaviors: Experiences with pain fluctuations at work. *Administrative Science Quarterly, 60*(1), 66–102.

Gabriel, A. S., Daniels, M. A., Diefendorff, J. M., & Greguras, G. J. (2015). Emotional labor actors: A latent profile analysis of emotional labor strategies. *Journal of Applied Psychology, 100*(3), 863–879.

Gabriel, A. S., & Diefendorff, J. M. (2015). Emotional labor dynamics: A momentary approach. *Academy of Management Journal, 58*(6), 1804–1825.

Gabriel, A. S., Diefendorff, J. M., & Erickson, R. J. (2011). The relations of daily task accomplishment satisfaction with changes in affect: A multilevel study in nurses. *Journal of Applied Psychology, 96*(5), 1095–1104.

Gabriel, A. S., Volpone, S. D., MacGowan, R. L., Butts, M. M., & Moran, C. M. (2019). When work and family blend together: Examining the daily experiences of breastfeeding mothers at work. *Academy of Management Journal.* Advance online publication.

Ganster, D. C., & Rosen, C. C. (2013). Work stress and employee health: A multidisciplinary review. *Journal of Management, 39*(5), 1085–1122.

Grandey, A. A., Gabriel, A. S., & King, E. B. (2019). Tackling taboo topics: A review of the Three Ms in working women's lives. *Journal of Management.* Advance online publication.

Greenhaus, J. H., & Beutell, N. J. (1985). Sources of conflict between work and family roles. *Academy of Management Review, 10*(1), 76–88.

Jones, K. P. (2017). To tell or not to tell? Examining the role of discrimination in the pregnancy disclosure process at work. *Journal of Occupational Health Psychology, 22*(2), 239–250.

Jones, K. P., Clair, J., King, E. B., Humberd, B., & Arena, D. F. (2019) How help during pregnancy can undermine self-efficacy and increase postpartum intentions to quit. *Personnel Psychology.* Advance online publication.

Joyce, A. (2017, August 3). Workplaces must give moms space to pump breast milk. Women share what it's really like. *The Washington Post.* Retrieved from https://www.washingtonpost.com/graphics/2017/lifestyle/on-parenting/mothers-experiences-pumping-at-work/?utm_term=.752162434219

Kawano, A., & Emori, Y. (2015). The relationship between maternal postpartum psychological state and breast milk secretory immunoglobulin A level. *Journal of the American Psychiatric Nurses Association, 21*(1), 23–30.

Krans, B. (2019, November 25). California's moms get stronger support for workplace lactation. *Los Angeles Daily News.* Retrieved from https://www.dailynews.com/2019/11/25/californias-moms-get-stronger-support-for-workplace-lactation/

Meredith, S. (2019, November 29). Japanese department store 'reconsidering' plan for staff to wear menstruation badges. *CNBC.* Retrieved from https://www.cnbc.com/2019/11/29/period-badges-japanese-store-reconsidering-plan-after-public-backlash.html

Mesure, S. (2019, November 18). The stigma around menopause fades as women seek change at work. *Financial Times.* Retrieved from https://www.ft.com/content/311504fa-04a2-11ea-a958-5e9b7282cbd1

Motro, D., Gabriel, A. S., & Ellis, A. P. J. (2019). Examining the effects of menstruation on women's helping behaviour in the workplace. *Journal of Occupational and Organizational Psychology, 92*(3), 695–706.

Oster, E. (2019). *Cribsheet: A data-driven guide to better, more relaxed parenting, from birth to preschool.* New York, NY: Penguin Press.

Ruef, A. M., & Levenson, R. W. (2007). Continuous measurement of emotion: The affect rating dial. In J. A. Coan & J. J. B. Allen (Eds.), *Handbook of emotion elicitation and assessment* (pp. 286–297). New York, NY: Oxford University Press.

Volpone, S. D., Gabriel, A. S., Campbell, J. T., MacGowan, R. L., & Moran, C. M. (2019). Examining workplace support for breastfeeding women: A fuzzy set approach. In H. K. Cheung & E. B. King (Chairs), *From pregnancy to permanent motherhood: Experiences of working mothers in the field.* Symposium presented at the 32nd Annual Conference of the Society of Industrial and Organizational Psychology, Washington, DC.

Weiss, H. M., & Rupp, D. E. (2011). Experiencing work: An essay on a person-centric work psychology. *Industrial and Organizational Psychology: Perspectives on Science and Practice, 4*(1), 83–97.

Yang, L. Q., Bauer, J., Johnson, R. E., Groer, M. W., & Salomon, K. (2014). Physiological mechanisms that underlie the effects of interactional unfairness on deviant behavior: The role of cortisol activity. *Journal of Applied Psychology, 99*(2), 310–321.

CHAPTER 9

TAKE THAT DETOUR

Unexpected Influences on a Research Career

Peter Glick
Lawrence University

How do research careers take the shape they do? The answer differs for each individual researcher and, because colleagues asked me to trace the arc of my own career, this piece addresses the reasons for the paths I took, emphasizing how others influenced the choices I made about what to research. Those who are just beginning or contemplating an academic career may find it useful in some way; perhaps my 20/20 hindsight will reveal pitfalls to avoid or ways to more deliberately encourage circumstances that, for me, were sometimes simply lucky breaks. In any event, please forgive the self-indulgence talking about one's own career (even if asked by colleagues to do so) inevitably involves.

Perspectives on Gender and Work, pages 101–116

HOW MY RESEARCH INTERESTS DEVELOPED

People sometimes ask why I chose to study sexism and gender, making the (somewhat accurate) presumption that men typically show less interest in these topics. In fact, I often find myself the only man in the room or in collaborations with colleagues, who have invariably made me feel appreciated and welcomed (in contrast to research suggesting that solo women in otherwise male contexts often experience exclusion). I cannot claim any particular virtue for my choice of topics to study, other than openness to others' influence. In my case, that influence did not directly come from the usual suspects, graduate school mentors. Although they trained me well, my graduate school mentors (mainly Mark Snyder and Ellen Berscheid) at the University of Minnesota were not primarily interested in sexism or gender (although, ironically, another influential faculty member, Gene Borgida, later turned to these topics as I did). It was after graduate school that I veered toward studying sexism. The proximal influence was my students, the undergraduate psychology majors I began to teach at my first (and lasting) job as a professor at a liberal arts college with fewer than 1,500 undergraduates and no graduate programs, Lawrence University.

I had earned my undergraduate degree at Oberlin College. It was no accident that I later chose to be a small college professor. I loved the liberal arts college environment as an undergraduate and wanted to return to it. Although liberal arts colleges lack many resources large universities can provide to faculty, they possess a scale, charm, and energy I find appealing. In particular, being at a small college enabled me to treat teaching and research as complementary, rather than competing activities. This confluence occurred most directly in my research methods course, a required class for psychology majors (which my colleagues happily ceded to me). Although my approach to this course has developed over the more than 30 years I have taught it, one element has remained constant since the beginning: Students develop and test a psychologically interesting and hopefully novel hypothesis in a small experiment.

The only possible way for students to generate interesting as well as novel hypotheses is to tap their own experiences for inspiration. Life events have led to many famous social psychological hypotheses (e.g., the Kitty Genovese murder led to Latané and Darley's, 1968, bystander experiments). For students, seeking inspiration in daily life is the most viable option for generating new ideas. It's simply too difficult to become steeped in past theory and research on a topic and then immediately try to figure out what's missing or the logical next step. Indeed, a cardinal rule I developed was to forbid students from reading about past research until after they had reasoned through their own ideas. I found that reading about past theory and research before then quickly snuffed out any chance for creative, new ideas.

Exposure to the fire hose of past work leaves students overwhelmed, with the strong sense that "everything has already been done." Only after their intuitive ideas shape up do I start helping students to conceptualize and extract the relevant underlying psychological variables, figure out how their idea fits with prior theory and research, and direct them toward articles to read. Similarly, I forbid any talk about methods until after students develop an interesting concept; otherwise, they quickly jump to something "doable" without thinking about whether or why it might be worth doing.

Leaving it up to the students to find inspiration for a project is both stressful and exhilarating (at least when things come together). It forced me to be open to topics I might otherwise not have considered, shaping the direction my research took. When I started, as a very green, rookie professor in the 1980s, the vast majority of psychology majors at Lawrence were female. As a result, ideas related to sexism often emerged from their lived experiences. Thus, my students started to pull me into sexism as a research topic. When these early projects yielded interesting results, I encouraged students to continue collaborating with me, collecting additional data. Although I continued some research along lines begun in graduate school, my early publications at Lawrence evidence a shift toward understanding sex discrimination as my students and I began to find some interesting results. The first sex discrimination study my students (Cari Zion and Cynthia Nelson) and I collaborated on started as a research methods class project, but ended up in the *Journal of Personality and Social Psychology* (*JPSP*; Glick, Zion, & Nelson, 1988). Back then, a *JPSP* article didn't require seven studies involving thousands of participants, but getting into the top journal in social psychology was still quite a coup.

Cari, Cynthia, and I had found that even though stereotype-inconsistent individuating information resulted erased stereotypical trait inferences about male and female job candidates, discrimination in hiring recommendations still occurred: People still viewed a man as a better fit for a male-dominated job (sales manager) and a woman as a better fit for a female dominated job (administrative assistant). We suggested that gender categorization itself, apart from stereotyped personality trait inferences, may influence perceived fit between a candidate and a job.

I was hooked. Not only did understanding sex discrimination have important applied consequences, it proved to be a fascinating intellectual puzzle. After Cari and Cynthia graduated, I continued to follow the same line of thought. I ran two studies aimed at testing whether sex discrimination occurred due to two processes by which evaluators match candidates to jobs: stereotype-influenced trait inferences and sex categorization itself (Glick, 1991). I assessed how strongly various jobs are associated both with gender-typed personality traits (e.g., agency versus warmth) and, separately, having male versus female incumbents (i.e., perceived ratio of men to women in the job). Not surprisingly, the two are related, but not to the point that they were completely overlapping.

In Glick (1991), a first study showed that the degree to which people associated jobs with masculine personality the more prestige they assigned those jobs; these jobs also have better actual salaries. By contrast, the degree to which people associate jobs with feminine traits only weakly (though positively) correlated with perceived prestige and bore no relation to actual salaries. A second study revealed (as Cari, Cynthia, and I had argued) that business professionals matched candidates both on (a) how well candidates' perceived traits (many gender stereotypical) matched the personality traits people associate with the job, and (b) whether the candidate's sex matched the typical incumbent's sex. For example, a woman might not be hired for a "masculine" job due to stereotyped personality trait inferences (e.g., She's not tough enough) and/or simply because she's the "wrong" sex (i.e., Because incumbents are typically male). Thus, two separate discriminatory processes influence hiring recommendations.

The student collaborations also continued. Korin Wilk, Michele Perreault, and I used factor analysis to infer the underlying dimensions by which people classify occupations (Glick, Wilk, & Perreault, 1995). Two orthogonal factors emerged: prestige and gender type. The job's gender type was determined mainly by the typical incumbent's sex (i.e., Is the typical incumbent a man or woman?), confirming the role sex ratios play in job images. Although perceived occupational prestige was independent from jobs' gender type, this factor was gendered in another way: Jobs viewed as requiring stereotypically masculine personality traits (e.g., agency) were generally seen as more prestigious.

A path had been set. My students' interests had led to one study, then another, then another. Alice Eagly noticed my research and invited me to join a conference panel. Journals had started to ask me to review manuscripts related to sex discrimination, leading to my first direct contact with Susan Fiske (who later became a close collaborator on the research that elevated my career) when she was serving as a journal editor and asked me to review a paper.

By the early 1990s, I had been modestly productive and done enough to earn tenure at Lawrence. However, I had come to a crossroad in my scholarly career. I was looking to take a next step, but had little idea about what it might be. I decided to spend my post-tenure sabbatical year at a research university, attempting to forge new collaborations to revitalize and expand my research. I narrowed my choices to prominent researchers whose work I especially admired, and asked Susan Fiske whether I might spend a year collaborating with her at the University of Massachusetts (her home institution at the time). She generously agreed, which led to a career-defining collaboration and the work I am most proud to have generated.

HOW A RESEARCH CAREER TOOK OFF THROUGH COLLABORATION

My collaboration with Susan Fiske during my sabbatical exceeded any expectation I could possibly have had. Susan warmly welcomed me, arranged office space, and I settled in. Most importantly, Susan pointed me in a new direction that led to the work about which I am most proud. Because my students' influence had turned me into a sexism researcher, when Susan and I discussed what we might do together, she noted that the field needed a new sexism scale. Her suggestion was the seed that grew into ambivalent sexism theory and its associated measures, the Ambivalent Sexism Inventory (Glick & Fiske, 1996) and Ambivalence toward Men Inventory (Glick & Fiske, 1999).

I could not have turned to a better source for suggestions about possible new research directions. Susan had already shown her uncanny prescience about the directions in which social psychology should head (e.g., publishing a book that defined the then-nascent subfield of social cognition). From the 1970s to the 1990s, the Attitudes Toward Women Scale (AWS; Spence & Helmreich, 1972) had been the dominant measure of individual differences in sexist attitudes. The AWS was published in 1972, when empirical research on sexism had just begun in earnest. Before then, sexism was not even a minor topic. In his classic tome on the nature of prejudice, Allport (1954) mentioned sexism only once, in passing. Spence and Helmreich's AWS was groundbreaking and the scale had long proved its mettle (and remains a reliable and valid measure today). However, as gender roles and norms had shifted rapidly from the early 1970s to the 1990s, many items had become dated, with participants generally rejecting notions such as, "Sons in a family should be given more encouragement to go to college than daughters," leading to reduced variance in responses.

Further, newer theories about racism had created a new *zeitgeist* in prejudice research, suggesting that people hold more complex attitudes about outgroups than suggested by the definition of prejudice as an antipathy. Newer racism theories emphasized ambivalence and response polarization. Katz and colleagues (Katz, Wackenhut, & Hass, 1986) had proposed that, in addition to negative feelings stemming from racial stereotypes, Whites often sympathize with Black people as potential targets of discriminatory treatment. Gaertner and Dovidio (1986) had developed similar ideas, creating aversive racism theory. They proposed that many Whites view themselves as unprejudiced egalitarians and, as a result, bend over backwards to avoid discriminating when doing so would threaten this cherished self-image. At the same time, internalized, negative stereotypes about Black people lead Whites to engage in exclusion, avoidance, and discrimination when the situation provides a plausible nonracial excuse (thereby removing threat to their egalitarian self-image). These newer theories revealed that racism is not just the province of obviously hostile bigots, whose attitudes now became referred to as "old-fashioned racism" (McConahay, 1986), but infects liberals who view themselves as unprejudiced.

As the term "old-fashioned racism" implies, theorists viewed racial ambivalence as something new, largely a post-civil rights era phenomenon. Many White Americans' consciences were pricked when they viewed news footage of police attacking people peacefully protesting segregation laws. America's egalitarian ideals clashed with the realities of brutal racial discrimination, provoking sympathy for Blacks. Thus, in addition to ambivalence, racism theorists had focused on how racial attitudes had subsequently changed. Racism was subtle, covert, and disguised, even to the point that individuals enacting discrimination were self-deceived (i.e., viewed themselves as fair and unbiased). "Modern racism" (McConahay, 1983, 1986) and "symbolic racism" (Bobo, 1983) represented more subtle belief systems, less overt in characterizing Black people as inferior, but manifesting in opposition to policies such as affirmative action and school desegregation aimed at providing more opportunity for minorities.

Similarly, there were hints that gender attitudes might also be complex and ambivalent. Most prominently, Eagly and Mladinic (1994) had established the "women are wonderful effect." They discovered that people generally hold more positive stereotypes about women than men. Their work provided a hint that sexism might also be ambivalent.

Thus, Susan's charge to rethink how to measure sexism came at an especially fertile time, when new theories and findings had begun to transform the field's understanding of prejudice. Additionally, in retrospect, my prior training and teaching interests made me uniquely well suited to think about sexism in a different way. Although my graduate school mentors had not focused on studying sexism per se, Mark Snyder specialized in studying how people perceive each other, including the role stereotypes play in biasing person perception (and one of his classic studies on this topic involved gender stereotypes; Skrypnek & Snyder, 1982). Ellen Berscheid's early research had also focused on how stereotypes (based on physical attractiveness) bias person perception and lead to discrimination (Berscheid & Walster, 1974). Moreover, Ellen had subsequently focused on understanding heterosexual intimate relationships and, while I was in graduate school, Mark had begun collaborating with Ellen on this topic. My very first publication, coauthored with Mark and Ellen, examined individual differences in the attributes people focus on when initiating heterosexual dating relationships (Snyder, Berscheid, & Glick, 1985).

Taking classes from and collaborating with Mark and Ellen meant I was steeped in the two subfields, prejudice and close relationships, most relevant (as it turns out) to ambivalent sexism. At Lawrence, I taught seminars on each topic. In my mind, as in the field more generally, however, these topics remained in separate silos. It took a while, but as I began to pilot possible sexism items, those silos walls began to collapse and ambivalent sexism theory began to emerge.

Ambivalent sexism theory (Glick & Fiske, 1996) starts with an apparent paradox at the heart of gender relations: Men have long dominated women, while simultaneously depending on them as intimate partners. As a result, intimate heterosexual relations condition the form sexist attitudes have taken. Contemporary theories about racism and the "women are wonderful effect" had paved the way to looking for ambivalence in gender attitudes. Importantly, however, Susan and I theorized that, unlike racial ambivalence, gender ambivalence was not a recent development due to sympathy sparked by a social movement. Rather, ambivalence was baked into gender relations from the start, due to that curious combination of male dominance and heterosexual intimate interdependence. Power disparities between men and women generate hostile sexism, whereas men's interdependence on women (e.g., in heterosexual close relationships) generates benevolent sexism. Both serve as complementary ideologies, the carrot and the stick that reinforce and justify gender inequality. Benevolent sexism promises women men's provision, protection, and affection should they embrace traditional feminine roles and stay "in their place." Hostile sexism threatens punishment should women fail who instead pursue equality or powerful roles, thereby threatening men's stranglehold on status and power.

My collaboration with Susan has resulted in another highly cited theory, the stereotype content model (Fiske, Cuddy, Glick, & Xu, 1998), but ambivalent sexism theory holds a special significance for me as it marked a turning point that transformed my career. Beyond its personal impact, ambivalent sexism theory has some qualities to recommend it: An aesthetically pleasing parsimony while combined with considerable explanatory power for understanding gender relations. Specifically, the theory shows how myriad implications stem from two basic facts about gender relations (dominance and interdependence). It helps to make sense of how men can both be sexist yet genuinely love and achieve greater psychological closeness with women (typically an intimate partner) than other men.

Ambivalent sexism theory has provided a useful framework. Its associated measure, the Ambivalent Sexism Inventory (ASI), comprising separate hostile sexism and benevolent sexism scales, has shown good reliability and validity. Soon, Susan and I were collaborating with colleagues all over the world who showed interest in the theory and the measures. These collaborations showed that hostile and benevolent sexism constitute recognizable ideologies in nations around the globe (reliably measured by the ASI; Glick et al., 2000, 2004). Further, treating nation as the unit of analysis, we found that hostile and benevolent sexism go hand in hand, correlating almost .90. This finding supported the idea that benevolent and hostile sexism represent complementary tools of control: Nations in which people strongly endorsed hostile sexism invariably proved to be nations where people also strongly endorsed benevolent sexism. Most importantly, national scores on the ASI correlated with actual gender inequality as assessed by objective measures (e.g., disparities in the ratios of men and women in powerful roles in business and government).

Research spearheaded by others more fully illuminated just how insidiously effective benevolent sexism is at keeping women "in their place." Admittedly, reading others' ambivalent sexism research sparks competing emotions for me: pride (for the foundation Susan and I provided), envy (wishing I had thought of the insightful hypotheses and clever experiments others came up with), but also humility (awe at the quality of work others have produced). It has been especially gratifying to see others take up the mantle. Science is about giving things away. Researchers generate theories and methods hoping that others will gravitate toward and use them.

Here's a taste of what research spearheaded by others (with one or two collaborations snuck in) has revealed about the ways benevolently sexist attitudes and discrimination undermine women. Jost and Kay (2005) showed how benevolent sexism uniquely fosters system justification among women. Becker and Wright (2011) extended this work, revealing how merely thinking about benevolent sexism decreases women's motivation for collective action (whereas hostile sexism has the opposite effect). Consistent with system justification theory (Jost & Banaji, 1994), benevolent sexism seems to have a palliative effect on women, enhancing their perceived satisfaction with their lot despite persistent gender inequality (Connelly & Heesacker, 2012).

Hammond and Sibley (2012) found that women's expectations that men will protect and provide for them in heterosexual romantic relationships mediate benevolent sexism's palliative effects. Indeed, women who viewed their male romantic partner as engaging in benevolent behavior toward them more strongly endorsed benevolent sexism over time (Hammond, Overall, & Cross, 2016). On average, women not only find profiles of potential male partners who endorse benevolent sexism more attractive than hostile sexist men, but also more attractive than egalitarian men (Bohner, Ahlborn, & Steiner, 2010; Kilianski & Rudman, 1998). Further, when women endorse benevolent sexism, they prefer more traditional qualities in mates (e.g., the man should earn more, Travaglia, Overall, & Sibley, 2009) and more traditional gender roles within heterosexual relationships, including the idea that husbands should hold more decision-making power and that wives' careers should have less priority (Chen, Fiske, & Lee, 2009). Benevolent sexism also leads women to be more willing to accept male romantic partners' paternalistic, protective restrictions even when they negatively affect their career opportunities (Moya, Glick, Expósito, de Lemus, & Hart, 2007). All of these benevolently sexist behaviors and expectations in heterosexual romantic relationships help to cement gender inequality in place.

In the workplace, benevolent sexism similarly restricts women's opportunities. King, Botsford, Hebl, Kazama, Dawson, and Perkins (2012) showed how benevolent sexism leads to denying women critical feedback and the challenging opportunities that provide greater opportunity for promotions. Shnabel, Bar-Anan, Kende, Bareket, and Lazar (2016) demonstrated that men who endorse benevolent sexism are more likely to offer dependency-inducing (rather than autonomy-promoting) help to women (e.g., offering to do something for them rather than to provide resources to enable a woman to help herself). Further, they found that women who endorse benevolent sexism seek out dependency-oriented help from men (but not women). Dardenne and his colleagues have shown that exposure to benevolent (but not hostile) sexism in a workplace context undermines women's performance on cognitive tests (Dardenne, Dumont, & Bollier, 2007).

In sum, ambivalent sexism theory and the measures we provided proved highly generative. Others found our framework and measures useful, accelerating understanding of how benevolent and hostile sexism harm women and help to maintain gender inequality. From a personal standpoint, the opportunity to spend a year focusing solely on research in collaboration with a prominent colleague with a knack for divining productive new directions proved transformative, and suggests some possible takeaways for new researchers.

ADVICE TO SCHOLARS EMBARKING ON THEIR CAREER

Before I provide any advice, some caveats: First, researchers have to figure out what works best for them, which may not be what worked for me. Second, I have had an odd career; although I was able to produce some highly cited research, I have spent my career at a liberal arts college not a research university, making my experience a bit anomalous. That said here are some observations and suggestions.

Take a Step Back, Question Basic Assumptions, Look Beyond Psychology Journals

I remember telling one of my students, Maggie Thomas (now a tenured professor at a liberal arts college) never to lose a quality she consistently exhibited: asking questions about basic assumptions. Our training as scholars necessarily involves learning paradigms, theories, and past findings. We need that knowledge, but training and socialization into a field also create blinders (see the *Structure of Scientific Revolutions*, Kuhn, 2012). It becomes difficult to step back and question basic ideas. What we "already know" can shackle creativity and the ability to develop new perspectives. Take time to reconsider basic assumptions in the field or to read outside sources (e.g., a novel) or expose yourself to experiences that might challenge assumptions. Something that takes you outside the narrow confines of your field can shake loose new ideas.

When Susan and I began developing ambivalent sexism theory, I knew we were onto something big when our idea (sexist ambivalence) began to seem so obviously true that it boggled my mind that the field had missed it before. However, Allport (1954) had defined prejudice as an antipathy, so sexism must be hostile. Yet abundant cultural truisms pointed to benevolent sexism (e.g., "the better half") and ambivalent sexism (e.g., "can't live with them, can't live without them"). When I began compiling potential items for a new sexism scale by combing popular sources that extolled traditional gender relations, they clearly revealed subjectively benevolent attitudes that did not fit the "prejudice as antipathy" assumption. Starting anew, without strong preconceptions, generated a different view of sexism.

Another way to shake things up is by deliberately taking a contrarian perspective. As McGuire (1997) noted, the opposite of every great psychological truth is probably also true, at least some of the time and under certain conditions. Think about when and why, and you may just be on to something new. Relatedly, I make it a habit now to "assume ambivalence": People often respond in complex ways to others or to situations. Thinking about potential positive and negative responses helps me to design dependent measures that may fully capture both positive and negative reactions. I strongly recommend McGuire's article on hypothesis generation, which offers a variety of useful techniques and heuristics.

Find Your Tribe, Your Friends, and Bring Something to the Table

Research involves a very particular set of skills, figuring out new ideas, translating concepts to operations, stage-managing experiments, doing statistical analyses, writing articles, and so on. Most of us do not excel equally at all of these skills. For example, some are better theorists than methodologists and vice versa. While it's important to hone your skills and try to overcome your weaknesses, it's also fortunate that our field thrives on collaboration. Collaborators can complement strengths and help compensate for weaknesses. Further, the best ideas often emerge through brainstorming conversations with colleagues.

Finding colleagues who compensate for your weaknesses can obviously enhance the final product, but you have to provide strengths that collaborators value. For example, I'm good at synthesizing and framing theoretical ideas, writing articles, constructing measures, and interpreting patterns in data. However, I am not nearly as methodologically clever as many of my collaborators and my statistical skills have become outdated. Fortunately, I am able to work with colleagues whose strengths compensate for my weaknesses because they feel I add something to the team. Collaboration is especially important to those of us at institutions with fewer resources. Teaming with colleagues at more resource rich institutions has been critical to my successes.

Obviously, it's difficult to collaborate if you don't reach out to others. Early on in your career, you may feel inhibited about doing so. I had considerable hesitation about first contacting Susan Fiske about working with her. We had never met in person and our prior contact involved Susan asking me to review a paper for a journal. My track record at the time was modest, whereas Susan was an established star in the field. Had I not reached out to her, my research career would not have taken off as it did.

One final piece of advice about collaboration: Make it fun! People assume science is a dry, dusty, logic-fest conducted by emotionless nerds. In my experience, about half the time I spend talking with collaborators is personal rather than professional. Close collaborators inevitably become friends. The most creative and productive collaborations are usually accompanied by the most laughter. It's the personal connection as much as the scientific discovery that keeps collaborations going.

Persist

Every person with a huge h-index has experienced ample rejection. Peer review is harsh. We are all trained assassins when it comes to evaluating others' work, steeped in being critical in pursuit of academic rigor. I don't know whether this fact will make you feel better and more hopeful or worse and hopeless: The original ambivalent sexism paper (Glick & Fiske, 1996) came within a whisker of rejection after four rounds of reviews. Two reviewers were favorable, two were much less impressed, viewing it as a mere "scale development" paper undeserving of publication in *the Journal of Personality and Social Psychology*. Fortunately, John Holmes, the action editor, who cast the deciding vote, was convinced that the paper would be highly influential and generate further research.

Undoubtedly, had the paper been rejected at *JPSP*, another journal would have published it. However, publication in *JPSP* provided more immediate visibility and credibility, no doubt promoting interest in the work more quickly than would otherwise have been the case. Every time I have published in that particular journal, I have been convinced at some point that the paper was not going to make it. Persistence does not always pay off, but when it does, the victory is sweet and worth the effort.

Finally, it helps if you can shine a light on a new path that others can explore and provide tools that help others blaze new trails. Ambivalent sexism theory provided an overall framework that suggested possible new directions that others could explore. The scales Susan and I developed also provided the tools that others could easily adopt, enabling more research. Although we copyrighted the scale, by putting a © next to it and advising others to ask permission to use it (mainly so that we could keep track of the research others performed), we put the items into the public domain and always freely give permission for academic research. Give it away. Hope they will take it and cite you for it. Of course, shining that light on a promising new path requires looking ahead. However, as science fiction author William Gibson suggests, anticipating the future involves understanding the present (Rothman, 2019).

LOOKING AHEAD BY LOOKING AT THE PRESENT

When it comes to sexism, the saying "the more things change the more they stay the same" seems to apply. On one hand, the long haul has shown a steady march toward equal rights for women. Two hundred years ago, women had almost no rights in marriage. A century ago, women did not have the right to vote in the United States (though by the time this chapter gets published suffrage's 100-year anniversary will have passed). A few decades ago, it would have been unthinkable for a major political party to nominate a female candidate for president. A few years ago, a female presidential candidate won the popular vote and both the number of female CEOs and members of congress increased to the most ever.

On the other hand, the record number of female CEOs in the Fortune 500 remains under 7% (Zillman, 2019) and the record number of female members of congress or senators is still under 25% (Kurtzleben, McMinn, & Klahr, 2019). In other words, despite all the changes and hashtag challenge movements (#MeToo, #OscarsSoWhite, #TimesUp), gender inequality remains a stubborn fact. Female leaders are still cast as dislikable, penalized at work and the ballot box (Okimoto & Brescoll, 2010). Threatened by women's progress, a precarious, aggrieved masculinity has reasserted itself in politics and social life (e.g., internet trolls who harass women). Whether the arc of history will continue to bend toward gender equality, stall, or regress remains unknown.

One could argue that we have seen the future and the future is now: Progress toward gender equality will continue to contend with backlash, producing a polarized situation that provides ample research opportunities. Women will make gains, but sexist backlash will undermine those gains, with justifications for discrimination taking new forms, morphing to fit the current climate. For example, it's unlikely that Americans will go back to popularly believing that a woman's place is only in the home, not the workplace. At the same time, women will probably continue to experience workplace discrimination that targets any new development viewed as challenging men's power. For example, in reaction to the #MeToo movement, sexist men may use "fear that I'll be falsely accused of harassment" as an excuse not to mentor women at work. New whines ("men have it tough these days!") will pour from the same old sexist bottle to achieve the same old goal: limiting women's progress.

That said, I am not confident that my ability to predict the future exceeds the reliability of the Magic 8-Ball I keep in my office. An alternative view might be that as gender becomes more fluid, researchers will have to reconceptualize gender entirely. Our paradigms for studying sexist attitudes and behaviors presume a popular belief in the gender binary. Will this become hopelessly outdated as gender ceases to be an either/or category? I suspect, however, that popular belief in the gender binary will remain. Even as alternative identifications become more common, people may continue to view these as exceptions to the general rule. The gender binary has deep roots, biologically and historically, and remains a core part of individual identity for most people. Then again, rapid progress sometimes happens, such as the sea of change in attitudes about homosexual marriage, culminating in the legalization for same-sex marriage in the United States. Predicting the future is always a dicey business.

CONCLUSION

Research careers can take unanticipated turns based on unexpected influences that deflect one's path first by a little and then by a lot. In my case, being open to my students' influence turned out to be a good idea. I veered in a new direction that turned out to be fascinating. We all owe many debts to others, as I do to various mentors, colleagues, friends, and family. This chapter, however, is dedicated to the students who influenced the questions I asked and the path I took.

REFERENCES

Allport, G. W. (1954). *The nature of prejudice.* Reading, MA: Addison-Wesley.

Becker, J. C., & Wright, S. C. (2011). Yet another dark side of chivalry: Benevolent sexism undermines and hostile sexism motivates collective action for social change. *Journal of Personality and Social Psychology, 101*(1), 62–77.

Berscheid, E., & Walster, E. (1974). Physical attractiveness. In L. Berkowitz (Ed.), *Advances in experimental social psychology* (Vol. 7; pp. 157–215).Cambridge, MA: Academic Press.

Bobo, L. (1983). Whites' opposition to busing: Symbolic racism or realistic group conflict? *Journal of Personality and Social Psychology, 45*(1), 1196–1210.

Bohner, G., Ahlborn, K., & Steiner, R. (2010). How sexy are sexist men? Women's perception of male response profiles in the Ambivalent Sexism Inventory. *Sex Roles, 62*(7), 568–582.

Chen, Z., Fiske, S. T., & Lee, T. L. (2009). Ambivalent sexism and power-related gender-role ideology in marriage. *Sex Roles, 60*(11–12), 765–778.

Connelly, K., & Heesacker, M. (2012). Why is benevolent sexism appealing? Associations with system justification and life satisfaction. *Psychology of Women Quarterly, 36*(4), 432–443.

Dardenne, B., Dumont, M., & Bollier, T. (2007). Insidious dangers of benevolent sexism: consequences for women's performance. *Journal of Personality and Social Psychology, 93*(5), 764–779.

Eagly, A. H., & Mladinic, A. (1994). Are people prejudiced against women? Some answers from research on attitudes, gender stereotypes, and judgments of competence. *European Review of Social Psychology, 5*(1), 1–35.

Gaertner, S. L., & Dovidio, J. F.(1986). The aversive form of racism. In J. F. Dovidio & S. L. Gaertner (Eds), *Prejudice, discrimination, and racism.* Orlando, FL: Academic Press.

Glick, P. (1991). Trait-based and sex-based discrimination in occupational prestige, occupational salary, and hiring. *Sex Roles, 25*(5–6), 351–378.

Glick, P., & Fiske, S. T. (1996). The Ambivalent Sexism Inventory: Differentiating hostile and benevolent sexism. *Journal of Personality and Social Psychology, 70*(5/6), 491–512.

Glick, P., & Fiske, S. T. (1999). The ambivalence toward men inventory: Differentiating hostile and benevolent beliefs about men. *Psychology of Women Quarterly, 23*(3), 519–536.

Glick, P., & Fiske, S. T. (2001). Ambivalent sexism. In M. P. Zanna (Ed.), *Advances in experimental social psychology* (Vol. 33; pp. 115–188). Thousand Oaks, CA: Academic Press.

Glick, P., Fiske, S. T., Mladinic, A., Saiz, J. L., Abrams, D., Masser, B., . . . & López, W. L. (2000). Beyond prejudice as simple antipathy: hostile and benevolent sexism across cultures. *Journal of Personality and Social Psychology, 79*(5), 763–775.

Glick, P., Lameiras, M., Fiske, S. T., Eckes, T., Masser, B., Volpato, C.,& Wells, R. (2004). Bad but bold: Ambivalent attitudes toward men predict gender inequality in 16 nations. *Journal of Personality and Social Psychology, 86*(5), 713–728.

Glick, P., Wilk, K., & Perreault, M. (1995). Images of occupations: Components of gender and status in occupational stereotypes. *Sex Roles, 32*(9–10), 565–582.

Glick, P., Zion, C., & Nelson, C. (1988). What mediates sex discrimination in hiring decisions? *Journal of Personality and Social Psychology, 55*(2), 178–186.

Hammond, M. D., Overall, N. C., & Cross, E. J. (2016). Internalizing sexism within close relationships: Perception of intimate partners' benevolent sexism promote women's endorsement of benevolent sexism. *Journal of Personality and Social Psychology, 110*(2), 214–238.

Hammond, M. D., & Sibley, C. G. (2011). Why are benevolent sexists happier? *Sex Roles, 65*(5–6), 332–343.

Jost, J. T., & Banaji, M. R. (1994). The role of stereotyping in system-justification and the production of false consciousness. *British Journal of Social Psychology, 33*(1), 1–27.

Jost, J. T., & Kay, A. C. (2005). Exposure to benevolent sexism and complementary gender stereotypes: consequences for specific and diffuse forms of system justification. *Journal of personality and social psychology, 88*(3), 498–509.

Katz, I., Wackenhut, J., & Hass, R. G. (1986). Racial ambivalence, value duality, and behavior. In J. F. Dovidio & S. L. Gaertner (Eds.), *Prejudice, discrimination, and racism* (pp. 35–59). Cambridge, MA: Academic Press.

Kilianski, S. E., & Rudman, L. A. (1998). Wanting it both ways: Do women approve of benevolent sexism? *Sex Roles, 39*(5), 333–352.

King, E. B., Botsford, W., Hebl, M. R., Kazama, S., Dawson, J. F., & Perkins, A. (2012). Benevolent sexism at work gender differences in the distribution of challenging developmental experiences. *Journal of Management, 38*(6), 1835–1866.

Kuhn, T. S. (2012). *The structure of scientific revolutions.* Chicago, IL: University of Chicago Press.

Kurtzleben, D., McMinn, S., & Klahr, R. (2019, January 4). What it looks like to have a record number of women in the House of Representatives. *NPR.* Retrieved from https://www.npr.org/2019/01/04/678227272/what-it-looks-like-to-have-a-record-number-of-women-in-the-house-of-representati

Latané, B., & Darley, J. M. (1968). Group inhibition of bystander intervention in emergencies. *Journal of personality and social psychology, 10*(3), 215–221.

McConahay, J. B. (1983). Modern racism and modern discrimination: The effects of race, racial attitudes, and context on simulated hiring decisions. *Personality and Social Psychology Bulletin, 9*(4), 551–558.

McConahay, J. B. (1986). Modern racism, ambivalence, and the Modern Racism Scale. In J. F. Dovidio & S. L. Gaertner (Eds.), *Prejudice, discrimination, and racism* (pp. 91–125). Orlando, FL: Academic Press.

McGuire, W. J. (1997). Creative hypothesis generating in psychology: Some useful heuristics. *Annual Review of Psychology, 48*(1), 1–30.

Moya, M., Glick, P., Expósito, F., de Lemus, S., & Hart, J. (2007). It's for your own good: Benevolent sexism and women's reactions to protectively justified restrictions. *Personality and Social Psychology Bulletin, 33*(10), 1421–1434.

Okimoto, T. G., & Brescoll, V. L. (2010). The price of power: Power seeking and backlash against female politicians. *Personality and Social Psychology Bulletin, 36*(7), 923–936.

Rothman, J. (2019, December 9). How William Gibson keeps his science fiction real. *The New Yorker.* Retrieved from https://www.newyorker.com/magazine/2019/12/16/how-william-gibson-keeps-his-science-fiction-real

Shnabel, N., Bar-Anan, Y., Kende, A., Bareket, O., & Lazar, Y. (2016). Help to perpetuate traditional gender roles: Benevolent sexism increases engagement in dependency-oriented cross-gender helping. *Journal of Personality and Social Psychology, 110*(1), 55–75.

Skrypnek, B. J., & Snyder, M. (1982). On the self-perpetuating nature of stereotypes about women and men. *Journal of Experimental Social Psychology, 18*(3), 277–291.

Snyder, M., Berscheid, E., & Glick, P. (1985). Focusing on the exterior and the interior: Two investigations of the initiation of personal relationships. *Journal of Personality and Social Psychology, 48*(6), 1427–1435.

Spence, J., & Helmreich, R. (1972). The Attitudes toward Women Scale: An objective instrument to measure attitudes toward the rights and roles of women in contemporary society. *JSAS Catalog of Selected Documents in Psychology, 2,* 66–67.

Travaglia, L. K., Overall, N. C., & Sibley, C. G. (2009). Benevolent and hostile sexism and preferences for romantic partners. *Personality and Individual Differences, 47*(6), 599–604.

Zillman, C. (2019, May 16). The Fortune 500 has more female CEOS than ever before. *Fortune.* Retrieved from https://fortune.com/2019/05/16/fortune-500-female-ceos/

CHAPTER 10

GENDER AT THE WORK–FAMILY INTERFACE

A Collaborative Journey

Jeffrey H. Greenhaus
Drexel University

Gary N. Powell
University of Connecticut

We have been collaborating on work–family research (so far) for about two decades. Our first project was a vignette study of work–family decision-making, initially presented at the Academy of Management (AOM) Meeting (Greenhaus & Powell, 2000) and later published in *Organizational Behavior and Human Decision Processes* (Greenhaus & Powell, 2003). Our most recent project was a book that adopted a decision-making perspective to the work–family interface, *Making Work and Family Work: From Hard Choices to Smart Choices* (Greenhaus & Powell, 2017). Actually, our most recent project is this chapter, which has been a pleasure to prepare. It has provided an ideal opportunity to reflect on our long and satisfying careers (we are both emeritus professors) and our common interest in gender-related issues.

Perspectives on Gender and Work, pages 117–128

HOW DID YOU GET INTERESTED IN STUDYING GENDER AT WORK?

Although we share a commitment to understanding the role of gender in work and family life, we came at this interest through different paths.

Jeff: My PhD dissertation at New York University was a study of the role of career salience in the career choice process. I had a sense that men and women are likely to differ in the salience they attach to their career, and I diligently examined and reported sex differences in my findings. I observed that although men displayed higher career salience, women were more likely to choose a career that is ideal for them and to report greater satisfaction with their chosen career field (Greenhaus, 1971). Although my discussion offered some speculations for these findings, I now realize that I offered no theory to support my views, and the areas I suggested for future research made scant reference to men, women, or gender. In a second study based on my dissertation (Greenhaus, 1973), I found that men placed more importance on career advancement and planning, whereas women had more positive general attitudes toward work. Again, I wasted an opportunity to explain these interesting findings with sound gender-related theory.

In retrospect, I think that I had a curiosity about gender and careers but not a deep commitment to understanding what was going on. In fact, my research during the 1970s (mostly on careers and work attitudes) did not reflect an abiding interest in gender-related issues. What triggered a more serious interest on my part was an invitation by my student Nick Beutell to supervise his dissertation in the late 1970s. Nick was interested in the inter-role conflict experienced by married women juggling home and nonhome roles. I finally found an area (work–family) that was personally meaningful, and I began to believe that men and women inevitably experience the work–family interface in different ways. Remarkably, although Nick and my conceptual piece on work–family conflict in the *Academy of Management Review* (Greenhaus & Beutell, 1985) made reference to gender dynamics (for example, that the direction of role interference may differ by gender), it did not incorporate gender in our model or our propositions and was not mentioned in our concluding comments. Clearly, we realized that gender was a critical consideration in understanding work–family conflict, but we didn't advance that notion aggressively.

My focus on gender-related issues was solidified in three conceptual papers with my late colleague and friend Saroj Parasuraman: a chapter on the life-style of the woman manager (Parasuraman & Greenhaus, 1993), followed by a chapter on work, family, and gender in Gary's *Handbook of Gender and Work* (Greenhaus & Parasuraman, 1999), and an article on critical gaps in work–family research (Parasuraman & Greenhaus, 2002). Collectively, these papers made me (us) realize that one cannot understand the work–family interface without appreciating the role of gender. However, the research had to move beyond what we saw as a preoccupation with seeking main effects of employee sex on work–family outcomes such as work–family conflict, which, by the way, produced highly inconsistent findings. Instead, we believed that a more nuanced approach would acknowledge that although there are between-gender differences in work–family constructs, there are also within-gender variations that can only be understood by examining how social context interacts with gender to influence work–family experiences. We also concluded that it is at least as important—if not more important—to understand the *process* by which women and men experience the work–family interface as it is to determine whether they differ on levels of work–family conflict and work–family enrichment or enhancement.

By this time, I had begun to appreciate the complexities of gender roles as they relate to work and family, which made it a perfect time for Gary and me to establish our collaboration. More about that shortly.

Gary: I was an academic child of the 1970s women's liberation movement in the United States and elsewhere, which was in full force while I was pursuing my PhD at the University of Massachusetts (UMass). Besides being personally affected by it, I was struck by its implications for the workplace, which felt important to examine. I explored conducting research on women in management after completing my (boring) dissertation on another topic in 1976 and starting a job at the University of Connecticut (UConn) that fall. During my first week on campus, I went to the UConn library and browsed the stacks of bound journals, looking for something relevant to my interests. It didn't take too long to discover a recent article by Bem (1974), who advanced the concept of psychological androgyny as a new ideal for mental health. A light bulb went on! What if this concept was applied to the realm of management? In light of the growing proportion of women in managerial positions, would a "good manager" be seen as androgynous?

I approached my former dissertation advisor at UMass, Tony Butterfield, with the idea. We agreed to collect data to test this research question during my first semester at UConn and write a paper to submit to the 1977 AOM Meeting. The paper was accepted for presentation at AOM (Powell & Butterfield, 1977), and a later version was published in *Academy of Management Journal* (Powell & Butterfield, 1979).

However, what we found was that a good manager was overwhelmingly described as masculine (i.e., higher in masculine than feminine traits) rather than androgynous (i.e., high in both masculine and feminine traits). This finding had implications for future research on the relationship between leader and gender stereotypes in a changing societal context (the growing proportion of women in managerial positions), which Tony and I were eager to pursue.

My career as a scholar of gender issues in the workplace was off and running!

HOW DID YOU COME TO WORK TOGETHER?

The research described above was conducted independently of each other. Although we were aware of each other's work, we didn't meet until 1994 when Jeff gave a talk on social support and work–family conflict to UConn faculty and PhD students. We quickly became friends, and Jeff and Saroj invited Gary to present a paper at Drexel University's International Stein Conference on Work, Family, and the Community in the 21st Century: Issues, Challenges, and Agenda for Change, held in Philadelphia in November 1994. Gary's presentation, "The Sex Difference in Employee Inclinations Regarding Work–Family Programs: Why Does It Exist, Should We Care, and What Should be Done About It (If Anything)?" was subsequently included as a chapter in an edited book based on the conference (Powell, 1997). The chapter captured Gary's emerging interest in relating gender to work–family dynamics and decision-making, a linkage that would characterize much of our work together going forward. In the spirit of "no good deed goes unpunished," Gary invited Jeff and Saroj to prepare a chapter on work, family, and gender for his own edited book, *Handbook of Gender and Work* (Greenhaus & Parasuraman, 1999).

Even before Gary's handbook was published, Jeff and Gary sat down in 1997 at the AOM meeting in Boston to talk about actually working on some research together. We had an implicit understanding that Gary was the "gender guy" (who had become interested in work–family issues) and Jeff was the "work–family guy" (whose earlier interest in gender was re-emerging). Maybe we could come up with some creative ideas. If not, at least we would have fun. We got along very well, we shared a non-academic interest in women's college basketball (both UConn's and Drexel's teams were a treat to watch), and we had compatible writing habits and work styles (Jeff thought he was attentive to detail until he met Gary!). We figured we would give it a try, and we're still at it.

WHAT IS THE STUDY OR FINDING THAT YOU ARE MOST PROUD OF?

We are most proud of a pair of studies that were published in 2010, both of which adopted a decision-make perspective on the work–family interface. In a conceptual article published in *Journal of Management* (Powell & Greenhaus, 2010a), we reviewed the literature relating family-domain factors (e.g., family background, structure, demands and responsibilities, and supports, family-related motives and attitudes) to three types of work-domain decisions: (a) whether to start a business, a role entry decision; (b) the number of hours to devote to a job or a business, a role participation decision; and (c) whether to quit a job, a role exit decision. In our review, we found substantial evidence that family-domain factors did influence these examples of work-domain decisions, and that the impact of family-domain factors on work-domain decisions tended to be stronger for women than men.

These findings prompted us to propose a model on the effects of sex and gender on decisions at the family → work interface. Incorporating constructs from theories of the psychology of gender and identity theory, we posited that employee sex indirectly affected the impact of family-domain factors on work-domain decisions in two respects. In one path, employee sex affects the gender-related construct of femininity (women higher than men), which in turn relates positively to family role salience, which positively moderates the impact of family-domain factors on work-domain decisions. The other path links employee sex → femininity → family role salience → family-domain factors that ultimately affect work-domain decisions. We also proposed that cultural (e.g., gender egalitarianism) and population (e.g., socioeconomic status) characteristics determine the strength of the relation between employee sex and femininity.

We are particularly proud that our model provided insights into the role of sex in work–family decision-making, in particular, what we subsequently

(Greenhaus & Powell, 2012; Powell & Greenhaus, 2012) called the family-relatedness of work decisions, that is, the extent to which employees factor family considerations into work-domain decisions. We are also pleased that we identified two causal paths that distinguish employee sex from gender-related (femininity) and identity theory (family role salience) constructs. Preparing this article helped to lay the foundation for our book on work–family decision-making (Greenhaus & Powell, 2017).

The other study of which we are especially proud is an empirical study published in *Academy of Management Journal* (Powell & Greenhaus, 2010b). Again, we adopted a decision-making perspective that focused on one particular type of decision: the extent to which an employee prevents work-related matters from entering the family domain (i.e., engages in work → family segmentation) or permits work-related matters to enter the family domain (i.e., engages in work → family integration). Once again, by incorporating constructs from different theoretical perspectives, we found that employee sex → high femininity (women higher than men) → high family role salience → preferred segmentation of work from the family domain → actual segmentation of work from the family domain. Interestingly, the actual segmentation of work from family life related negatively to work-to-family conflict *and* to work-to-family positive spillover, indicating that role segmentation is a double-edge sword: It keeps out the "bad" influence of work on family (role conflict) but also keeps out the "good" influence (positive role spillover).

We are proud that these findings reinforce the importance of separating biological sex from gender and identity theory constructs, and that they provide empirical support for the indirect effect of employee sex on an important decision at the work–family interface. The findings may also help explain why some studies found that women experience less work-to-family conflict than men: high family role salience derived from women's tendency to be high on femininity triggers a segmentation of work from the family domain, which relates to lower work-to-family conflict. However, because the relation between sex and femininity, although statistically significant, was far from perfect, within-gender variations (Parasuraman & Greenhaus, 2002) in femininity might explain why some women (and men) are more likely than others to segment work from their family life.

WHAT DO YOU THINK ARE THE HOT TOPICS FOR THE FUTURE?

Most critically, we believe that gender-related similarities and differences, and gender-related issues in general, need to be re-established as central to understanding the work–family interface. It is ironic that theory and research on what used to be considered a "woman's issue" (the work–family interface) now often ignore gender issues entirely or relegate sex and gender to control variables in statistical analyses (for exceptions, see the outstanding work of Leslie, Manchester, & Kim, 2015 and Shockley, Shen, DeNunzio, Arvan, & Knudsen, 2017, who thoroughly explore gender in theoretically important ways). We believe that gender considerations should be in the foreground—not the background—of work–family research. We are not suggesting that women and men inevitably experience the work–family interface differently in every respect. Rather, because socially constructed gender continues to play a prominent role in everyday life, it is likely to influence perceptions, affect, and behavior at the work–family interface.

However, because the effects of gender may not be simple or straightforward, it is critical to determine whether gender differences are lurking beneath the surface. For example, in preparing a presentation on gender and the work–family interface at the Third Annual Invitational Journalism Work–Family Conference in Boston (Greenhaus, 2004), Jeff conducted exploratory analyses on the Families and Work Institute's 1997 National Study of the Changing Workforce (NSCW) data set that consists of more than 3,500 employees. He immediately calculated the correlation between employee sex and work–family conflict and found that there was NO relation between sex and either work-to-family conflict or family-to-work conflict. This was just what he expected (and wanted).

It didn't take much longer in statistical analyses (or testing of sophisticated theory) to discover the importance of context. Greenhaus (2004) found that when there was a very young child (less than 3 years of age) living at home, women experienced more family-to-work conflict than men. In the absence of a young child, women and men experienced the same level of family-to-work conflict. Also, when a spouse didn't spend enough time with the children (in the eyes of the other spouse), women experienced more family-to-work conflict than men. When a spouse spent sufficient time with the children, women and men experienced the same level of family-to-work conflict. Since Jeff's aim was to make a point—that gender differences in work–family conflict depend on the circumstances—and not to develop theory, he stopped there and felt that he was quitting while he was ahead.

We are not suggesting that researchers should mine data until a gender difference in a work–family variable is finally found. Rather, we encourage scholars to use (or develop) theory to determine whether there are contextual characteristics that determine whether men and women experience a particular element of the work–family interface similarly or differently. These could be personal characteristics (e.g., family identity construal; Masterson & Hoobler, 2015), relational characteristics (e.g., negotiation style; Livingston, 2014), organizational characteristics (e.g., provision of maternity and paternity, dependent care, flexibility, social, and informational supports; Greenhaus & Powell, 2017), or societal characteristics (e.g., gender egalitarianism; Emrich, Denmark, & Den Hartog, 2004).

We also urge researchers to go beyond self-reports of work–family conflict or enrichment when studying work–family dynamics and the role of gender at the work–family interface. Self-reports of work–family interdependencies require an awareness of an effect (e.g., work interfered with family) and sufficient recall of the effect to report it on a survey. Cross-domain relationships that do not rely on self-reports of work–family interdependencies can provide rich information on the work–family interface and the presence or absence of gender differences. For example, ten Brummelhuis and Greenhaus (2018) studied the impact of demands and resources in one role on the amount of social support men and women provide in another role. They collected data from both members of cohabiting heterosexual couples (Study 1) and both members of employee-coworker dyads (Study 2), and found that extensive emotional demands in one role reduced the amount of support that men (but *not* women) provided in the other role. Moreover, resources experienced in one role expanded the amount of support women (but *not* men) provided in another role. They concluded (p. 1265) that "relative to men, women prevent role demands from reducing the support they provide in another role and use role resources to enhance the support they provide in another role." One might also conclude that women experienced less inter-role interference (demands restricting support) than men and more inter-role enrichment (resources enhancing support) than men, all of this without assessing role interference or enrichment via self-reports.

In a conference presentation on designing and conducting work-life research (Greenhaus & Powell, 2019), we described this cross-domain, work–family relationship design as an *inferential* approach because work–family interdependencies (conflict and enrichment) are inferred from the presence and strength of cross-domain relationships rather than measured directly through self-reports. This approach, which is consistent with ten Brummelhuis and Bakker's (2012) Work–Home Resources Model, has provided insights into the impact of job-related tension on parenting behavior (Stewart & Barling, 1996), the impact of commute time of pregnant women on the health problems of their infants at birth (Wang & Yang, 2019), and the impact of work pressure on participation in a family activity (Greenhaus & Powell, 2003). We encourage researchers to consider using this type of design to examine work–family interdependencies more generally and gender effects in particular.

Finally, we think it is essential to incorporate the passage of time in work–family research as Allen, French, Braun, and Fletcher (2019) have persuasively advocated. Snapshots of cross-sectional relationships do not reveal the process by which men and women experience the work–family interface over time. For example, Shockley et al. (2017) found an indirect effect of gender on work-to-family conflict due to the more extensive hours worked by men compared to women. On the surface, this finding seems inconsistent with the observation that female college students expect to experience more work–family conflict when they pursue their career than do male college students (Weer, Greenhaus, Colakoglu, & Foley, 2006). What happens between college-age expectations and subsequent experiences? There is some indication that there are no sex differences in work hours until the presence of children in the family at which time mothers work fewer hours than fathers (Friedman & Greenhaus, 2000). We suggest that women are more likely to factor parental responsibilities into work-hour decisions than men (Powell & Greenhaus, 2010a) because women are more likely than men to construct their social identity around availability to their family (Greenhaus, Peng, & Allen, 2012), construing their family identity in terms of providing care and nurturance (Masterson & Hoobler, 2015). Societal norms (Powell, Francesco, & Ling, 2009) and spousal negotiation regarding the primacy of each partner's career (Livingston, 2014) undoubtedly exert influences as well. Moreover, as children grow up and leave the home, the sex difference in work–family conflict may begin to diminish or even change direction.

Our point is that what may seem like a simple bivariate relationship—between employee sex and work-to-family conflict—probably reflects a series of pressures, attitudes, and behaviors that change over time. We believe that more long-term longitudinal designs, retrospective studies, and qualitative inquiries that link gender to the evolution of careers are essential to understand what Powell and Mainiero (1992) called "cross-currents in the river of time" as people's lives unfold in their work and family domains whether segmented or integrated.

CONCLUSIONS

This chapter and book are being published at a time when some scholars have speculated that *gender fatigue* (Joshi, Neely, Emrich, Griffiths, & George, 2015, p. 1466), or weariness with researching gender issues in the workplace, has set in. Such fatigue, if it exists, may be a response to the marginalization or de-legitimation of scholarship on gender-related issues by other scholars who find them unworthy of interest (Jané, van Esch, & Bilimoria, 2018). Gender fatigue may also arise from what has been called a *postfeminist sensibility* at work (Gill, Kelan, & Scharff, 2017, p. 226). According to this sensibility, gender inequalities existed in the past (not in the present); gender inequalities occur elsewhere (not in my place of work); being a woman is an advantage (not a disadvantage); and, if any gender inequalities exist, that's just the way the world is and it needs to be accepted (Gill et al., 2017). In other words, "the problem of gender has been 'solved'" as much as it ever needed to be solved (Broadbridge & Simpson, 2011, p. 475).

In conclusion, we call for scholars of gender in the workplace in general, and of gender at the work–family interface in particular, to not let gender fatigue or other scholars who de-legitimize or marginalize your work prevail. Indeed, as scholars of these issues, we should just be getting warmed up. If our chapter encourages you to respond to this call by initially examining these issues yourself or keeping at it, we will be proud to consider your work as part of our legacy as emeritus professors.

ACKNOWLEDGMENTS

As with most of our work, we made equal contributions to the preparation of this chapter. We thank our respective spouses, Adele Greenhaus and Laura Graves, for putting up with the demands of our collaborative relationship and joining in on the rewards, which are having fun together on multiple occasions in multiple locations.

REFERENCES

Allen, T. D., French, K. A., Braun, M. T., & Fletcher, K. (2019). The passage of time in work–family research: Toward a more dynamic perspective. *Journal of Vocational Behavior, 110*(Part B), 245–257.

Bem, S. L. (1974). The measurement of psychological androgyny. *Journal of Consulting and Clinical Psychology, 42*(2), 155–162.

Broadbridge, A., & Simpson, R. (2011). 25 years on: Reflecting on the past and looking to the future in gender and management research. *British Journal of Management, 22*(3), 470–483.

Emrich, C. G., Denmark, F. L., & Den Hartog, D. N. (2004). Cross-cultural differences in gender egalitarianism: Implications for societies, organizations, and leaders. In R. J. House, P. J. Hanges, M. Javidan, P. W. Dorfman, & V. Gupta (Eds.), *Culture, leadership, and organizations: The GLOBE study of 62 societies* (pp. 343–394). Thousand Oaks, CA: SAGE.

Friedman, S. D., & Greenhaus, J. H. (2000). *Work and family—allies or enemies? What happens when business professionals confront life choices.* New York, NY: Oxford.

Gill, R., Kelan, E. K., & Scharff, C. M. (2017). A postfeminist sensibility at work. *Gender, Work and Organization, 24*(3), 226–244.

Greenhaus, J. H. (1971). An investigation of the role of career salience in vocational behavior. *Journal of Vocational Behavior, 1*(3), 209–216.

Greenhaus, J. H. (1973). A factorial investigation of career salience. *Journal of Vocational Behavior, 3*(1), 95–98.

Greenhaus, J. H. (2004, May). *Work and family as allies and enemies: Are there gender differences?* Paper presented at the Third Annual Invitational Journalism-Work/Family Conference, Boston, MA.

Greenhaus, J. H., & Beutell, N. J. (1985). Sources of conflict between work and family roles. *Academy of Management Review, 10*(1), 76–88.

Greenhaus, J. H., & Parasuraman, S. (1999). Research on work, family, and gender: Current status and future directions. In G. N. Powell (Ed.), *Handbook of gender and work* (pp. 391–412). Newbury Park, CA: SAGE.

Greenhaus, J. H., Peng, A. C., & Allen, T. D. (2012). Relations of work identity, family identity, situational demands, and sex with employee work hours. *Journal of Vocational Behavior, 80*(1), 27–37.

Greenhaus, J. H., & Powell, G. N. (2000). When work and family collide: Choices and conflict between competing role demands. *Academy of Management Proceedings, 2000*(1), B1–B6.

Greenhaus, J. H., & Powell, G. N. (2003). When work and family collide: Deciding between competing role demands. *Organizational Behavior and Human Decision Processes, 90*(2), 291–303.

Greenhaus, J. H., & Powell, G. N. (2012). The family-relatedness of work decisions: A framework and agenda for theory and research. *Journal of Vocational Behavior, 80*(2), 246–255.

Greenhaus, J. H., & Powell, G. N. (2017). *Making work and family work: From hard choices to smart choices.* New York, NY: Routledge.

Greenhaus, J. H., & Powell, G. N. (2019, May). *Examining cross-domain, work-family relationships: An inferential approach.* Contribution to the workshop Designing & Conducting Work–Life Research Event: Innovative Approaches, Challenges and Dilemmas. Liverpool, England: University of Liverpool Management School.

Jané, S., van Esch, C., & Bilimoria, D. (2018). *"Why'd you wanna study that?"* A process model of the under-legitimation of a research topic. *Academy of Management Learning and Education, 17*(4), 401–424.

Joshi, A., Neely, B., Emrich, C., Griffiths, D., & George, G. (2015). Gender research in AMJ: An overview of five decades of empirical research and calls to action. *Academy of Management Journal, 58*(5), 1459–1475.

Leslie, L., Manchester, C. F., & Kim, Y. (2015). Gender and the work–family domain: A social role-based perspective. In T. D. Allen & L. T. Eby (Eds.), *The Oxford handbook of work and family* (pp. 53–67). Oxford, England: Oxford University Press.

Livingston, B. A. (2014). Bargaining behind the scenes: Spousal negotiation, labor, and work–family burnout. *Journal of Management, 40*(4), 949–977.

Masterson, C. R., & Hoobler, J. M. (2015). Career and career: A family identity-based typology of dual-earner couples. *Journal of Organizational Behavior, 36*(1), 75–93.

Parasuraman, S., & Greenhaus, J. H. (1993). Personal portrait: The life-style of the woman manager. In E. A. Fagenson (Ed.), *Women in management: Trends, issues, and challenges in managerial diversity* (Vol. 4; pp. 186–211). Newbury Park, CA: SAGE.

Parasuraman, S., & Greenhaus, J. H. (2002). Toward reducing some critical gaps in work–family research. *Human Resource Management Review, 12*(3), 299–312.

Powell, G. N. (1997). The sex difference in employee inclinations regarding work–family programs: Why does it exist, should we care, and what should be done about it (if anything)? In S. Parasuraman & J. H. Greenhaus (Eds.), *Integrating work and family: Challenges and choices for a changing world* (pp. 167–174). Westport, CT: Quorum.

Powell, G. N., & Butterfield, D. A. (1977, August). *Sex, sex-role identification, and the good manager.* Paper presented at the annual meeting of the Academy of Management, Kissimmee, FL.

Powell, G. N., & Butterfield, D. A. (1979). The "good manager": Masculine or androgynous? *Academy of Management Journal, 22*(2), 395–403.

Powell, G. N., Francesco, A. M., & Ling, Y. (2009). Toward culture-sensitive theories of the work–family interface. *Journal of Organizational Behavior, 30*(5), 597–616.

Powell, G. N., & Greenhaus, J. H. (2010a). Sex, gender, and decisions at the family–work interface. *Journal of Management, 36*(4), 1011–1039.

Powell, G. N., & Greenhaus, J. H. (2010b). Sex, gender, and the work-to-family interface: Exploring negative and positive interdependencies. *Academy of Management Journal, 53*(3), 513–534.

Powell, G. N., & Greenhaus, J. H. (2012). When family considerations influence work decisions: Decision-making processes. *Journal of Vocational Behavior, 81*(3), 322–329.

Shockley, K. M., Shen, W., DeNunzio, M. M., Arvan, M. L., & Knudsen, E. A. (2017). Disentangling the relationship between gender and work–family conflict: An integration of theoretical perspectives using meta-analytic methods. *Journal of Applied Psychology, 102*(12), 1601–1635.

Stewart, W., & Barling, J. (1996). Fathers' work experiences effect children's behaviors via job-related affect and parenting behaviors. *Journal of Organizational Behavior, 17*(3), 221–232.

Ten Brummelhuis, L. L., & Bakker, A. B. (2012). A resource perspective on the work-home interface: The work-home resources model. *American Psychologist, 67*(7), 545–556.

Ten Brummelhuis, L. L., & Greenhaus, J. H. (2018). How role jugglers maintain relationships at home and at work: A gender comparison. *Journal of Applied Psychology, 103*(12), 1265–1282.

Wang, Y., & Yang, M. (2019). Long commutes to work during pregnancy and infant health at birth. *Economics and Human Biology, 35,* 1–17.

Weer, C. H., Greenhaus, J. H., Colakoglu, S. N., & Foley, S. (2006). The role of maternal employment, role-altering strategies, and gender in college students' expectations of work–family conflict. *Sex Roles, 55,* 535–544.

CHAPTER 11

MARCHING FORWARD

Mikki Hebl
Rice University

Quinetta, Eden, and I thought it would be a nice break (for both author and reader) to compile a series that diverged from the typical volume of research-based chapters. Instead, we wanted to create a unique compilation on gender that includes scholars' responses to four different questions: (a) "How did you get involved in conducting gender-related research?"; (b) "What gender-related research makes you most proud?"; (c) "What advice do you have for gender researchers?"; and (d) "What do you believe are 'hot topics' for future gender researchers?" I specifically chose to contribute to this volume as both an editor *and* an author because gender issues have played a prominent role in my life, both personally and professionally. So, I willingly share my journey, perspective, and advice.

MY JOURNEY INTO CONDUCTING GENDER-RELATED RESEARCH

"I think you should either go to Allegheny College and play Division III basketball or go to Smith College, an all-women's college in Massachusetts."

Perspectives on Gender and Work, pages 129–140

This was the advice that my Wayland Academy college counselor, Bruce Hunter, offered me almost 35 years ago. I remember laughing and initially thinking he was crazy. First, I had never heard of either of these two schools. Second, I certainly had no interest in playing collegiate basketball. And third, under no circumstances did I want to go to a college without men.

Of course, Bruce Hunter most assuredly was *not* crazy and, in fact, changed my life. I succeeded in talking him out of the basketball idea, but he succeeded in talking me into traveling with him one evening to attend a Smith College function held at an alumna's house. That evening, I sat surrounded by a room full of smart, strong, accomplished women who talked about how Smith had changed their lives, spurred their confidence and success, and instilled in them a profound concern for women's issues. They presented a slide show of the beautiful campus and served tea and hors d'oeuvres on white linen tablecloths, a Friday afternoon tradition at Smith College. And that evening, this girl from Pardeeville, Wisconsin—population 1,507—was sold. I applied and was accepted early decision to Smith College; 6 months later, my parents dropped me off in Northampton, Massachusetts, 17 hours (1,086 miles) away from the one town where I had spent my entire life.

When I first began meeting new classmates and housemates at Smith, I realized how sheltered I had been growing up in Pardeeville, a town where—even today—96% of people are White, 85% of people over 25 years of age (including my mother, sister, and brother) do not have a college degree, the median household income is $56,114, and 100% of the people who declare themselves to be religious are Christian. It was not surprising, then, that my first semester in college, I found these "Smithees," as a whole, to be foreign and . . . weird. Although uniformly intelligent, they were from diverse racial and ethnic backgrounds. Some ordered hamburgers from McDonalds *without the meat*; some went to synagogues, temples, and meditation centers instead of churches; some smoked pot and were "emo" before emo was cool; and many were sexually fluid. My 17-year-old self became acutely aware that a great diversity had suddenly invaded my surroundings. And with it was born the construct of feminism.

One of my earliest gender-related recollections happened within a few weeks of my first semester at Smith. I was walking down the sidewalk of Elm Street and encountered a newfound friend who was climbing onto a bus loaded full of other Smithees. She turned back to me on the sidewalk and asked "Are you coming?" She was heading to a march in Washington, and when I asked her what it was about, she matter-of-factly said, "I don't know . . . some exciting women's issue!" Would I be going to this? No, I most certainly was not going to Washington. I couldn't afford the bus ticket. My dad had given me a whole $5 dollars when he turned his car back in the direction of Wisconsin. But more importantly, I would not be getting on a bus to go to a march about which I knew nothing. And how could my friend not know exactly what she was marching for?

Flashing forward 2½ years to another gender-related experience on that same Elm Street sidewalk, I had just finished my junior year of college and summer break was about to begin. The streets were crowded with cars passing by and people packing up to go home for the summer. And standing at almost the same spot on the sidewalk, I was bidding farewell to one of my very best friends at Smith. Her name is Asma, and coincidentally, we had become like sisters, having attended both the same high school in Wisconsin and then college in Massachusetts. I would be staying on campus for the summer, and Asma was leaving to go home. As we were embracing in a hug, a carload of young men drove by shouting at us "Lesbians!"; "Dykes"; and "Get a room!" At that point, I realized I had long outgrown my freshmen fear of being viewed as a lesbian. Rather, I felt a deep connection to lesbians. So deep, in fact, that I felt umbrage, anger, and personal conviction. What should it matter if I were hugging this woman as a friend or a lover? How dare these boys insert their asinine selves uninvited into a wonderful relationship, however it was defined? I felt a palpable fury that I—and that other women and men as well—should have to endure harassment because of whom we love. I realized that day that I had evolved. I would fight for people's right to love, without sanctions or restrictions. This was something I would be getting on a proverbial bus to support for the rest of my life.

Flashing forward again, just 3 months thereafter, to another lightbulb Smith memory I have, this one shaping my career trajectory dramatically. I was sitting inside a building (John M. Greene Hall, built in 1911) along that same sidewalk on Elm Street. It was convocation—one of the first days of my senior year—and we were in this large hall, preparing to hear our college president address the class. I looked around at all the women busily catching up and chattering, yelling college cheers, and getting fired up for the new school year. I remember feeling that dreadful nervousness that sometimes accompanies my attempt to avoid just plain freaking out. I was a newfound senior and had no idea what I would be doing with myself in just 9 months. And while my classmates at Smith no longer seemed as foreign to me as they did just 3 years earlier, the majority of them (unlike me) now seemed to know exactly what they planned to do with their lives post-BA. I remember getting tunnel vision and looking around—as if in slow motion—at these smart, bright women filling the hall and thinking back to other famous Smithees who had filled these seats in this same hall years before—Sylvia Plath, Julia Child, Gloria Steinem, Mary Whiton Calkins, Betty Friedan, Margaret Mitchell, Madeleine L'Engle, and Molly Ivins. So many of these and other female predecessors dared to get on buses and head to marches with the intent of making lives better for the women who came after them. They had made something of themselves and didn't abandon their feminism along the way.

I thought back to my Smith classes where I had learned about different feminist movements. Whether for one's reproductive rights, ending violence, equal pay, educational opportunities, workplace rights, or LGBTQ rights, women had marched forward for other women. Some of these women (and allied men) marched for decades to try to gain the right to vote. Some engaged in silent protests, hunger strikes, and countless parades and protests. Some were heckled, jailed, and/or physically abused. And many of them never even got to see 19th amendment pass even though they had spent a significant portion of their lives working to make it a reality. I realized sitting there that it was my destiny—as a Smithee—to become a proverbially lifelong marcher. I would do this to pay it forward to the next generation. And whatever I would end up doing, I would also become a lifelong *ally* to women and *build* women up throughout my life.

Our Smith College President, Mary Maples Dunn, gave her convocation speech that night. This would be the single speech of hers that I ever recall with such vividness. After some perfunctory introductory remarks, she launched into asking us if there are any of us who wanted to make a difference with our lives but didn't know exactly what we wanted to do. I left the slow-motion space I had been in and shuffled back to focus on her entirely. She had a recommendation for us individuals—we should pursue academia. She told us to "consider it" as a way of doing research and teaching on a topic that we loved. She told us that given the economy, the pundits expected that there would be a boom in academic jobs (actually, there would not be), academic salaries would go way up (actually, they would not), and this would be a good occupation if we wanted to make a difference in the lives of other people (indeed, it is). I sat there thinking about what our college president was saying and felt all the possibilities—it was a way I could combine my interests in psychology, my love of advancing women's issues, and my desire to change the lives of future generations. And indeed, this is the impetus of how I began my career, interested in studying gender issues and doing applied research that would hopefully help make women's lives more equitable to those of men's. I would be willing to use a mighty pen as my sword (Wayland's motto) to help march women forward.

SOME OF MY GENDER-RELATED RESEARCH

In my 20 years in academy, I have published approximately 165 articles and chapters. I am proud of each article—because anyone who publishes knows that they are all accomplishments. And that the journals where they ultimately appear do not necessarily reflect the amount of blood, sweat, tears, and years that went into each of the projects. But in thinking about the most meaningful or special projects, I am going to briefly mention four studies, each of which makes me proud for different reasons.

The "Gay and Proud" Study (Hebl, Foster, Mannix, & Dovidio, 2002)

Two years after my arrival at Rice University (~2000), I decided to have an end-of-the-semester outdoor lab party with my graduate students and team of approximately 20 undergraduate research assistants. Our plan was to walk down to a large lawn just off campus, celebrate the semester, and reflect on what we had accomplished and learned in lab for the semester. Because our lab focused on discrimination-related issues, I thought it might be educational for the students to take part in a field study in which they possibly experienced discrimination. Then, we could discuss their firsthand experiences with discrimination at our picnic celebration. All the research assistants said they were interested in participating, so I decided I might as well get IRB approval just in case we found anything worth publishing. We called stores the week before our study to find out which ones were hiring, and then we sent each research assistant into six different stores, giving him/her a new hat to wear before each new store. This hat either had "Texan and Proud" or "Gay and Proud" printed on it, but the research assistants remained unaware of which. The research assistants always followed the same script—they asked to speak with a manager and (a) if there were jobs available, (b) if they could fill out an application, and (c) what they would be doing if they got the job. We also had them audiotape the conversations with the managers and store personnel. Upon departing the store, each research assistant completed a survey in which they indicated the amount of subtle discrimination (e.g., reduced eye contact, decreased friendliness, premature termination of the interaction, increased hostility) the manager displayed toward them. Additionally, we had independent coders later listen to and rate the audiotapes for the same sorts of subtle discrimination measures. Finally, we evaluated actual job callback rates (i.e., overt discrimination) over a 3-month period of time.

Sitting on the grass during the picnic after this study had taken place was one of the finest teaching moments I ever had and probably ever will. The research assistants uniformly loved being involved in this research. There was no other research like this going on in the Psychology Department at Rice, and they were able to step outside of a laboratory and experience bias and prejudice in the real world. Many of them spoke about being recipients of different types of discrimination. What was just as exciting was when we analyzed the data over the next few weeks, we found that, despite somewhat low levels of formal, overt types of discrimination, there were significant amounts of informal, subtle forms of discrimination to those wearing "Gay and Proud" versus "Texan and Proud" on almost every measure we assessed. The study importantly initiated what would be the start of a long research career examining the ways in which people show subtle biases and the strategies that targets and organizations might adapt to reduce these biases. Additionally, the study showed me how excited and invested students could become in the research enterprise. Some research assistants who were relatively homophobic before the start of the study became incensed when they later discovered that they were targets of bias while donning a hat identifying themselves as gay/lesbian. One of my coauthors also left an indelible mark on me—Jack Dovidio. Jack has already made history for his seminal work on intergroup relations and for being one of the most all-time prolific social psychologists. But his legacy is also being a tremendous male ally—one who helped me immensely, paved the way for our field to be more open to women, and always extends his help and support particularly to women and individuals from underrepresented groups. He was an editor on the first paper I ever got accepted at *Personality and Social Psychology Bulletin*; he graciously helped me develop our storyline for the "Gay and Proud" paper; and he has consistently provided mentorship, support, and friendship along the way. And this is what I think of when I think of the "Gay and Proud" paper—Jack's allyship.

The "Men in Speedos" Study (Hebl, King, & Lin, 2004)

A few year later, I read a study that showed different cognitive outcomes associated with men and women wearing swimsuits (Fredrickson, Robertson, Noll, Quinn, & Twenge, 1998). When women wore swimsuits, they objectified themselves, which led to worse performance (Compared to men? Compared to when women were not wearing swimsuits?) on math-related tasks. But when men wore swimsuits, no such deficits were observed. Reading the original study, I noted the incongruity in experience between a woman wearing a clingy swimsuit and a man wearing a swimsuit resembling a baggy pair of shorts. My graduate student, Jean Lin, and I decided to replicate and extend the study. In our extension, we asked men to wear Speedos, which would be a more accurate comparison condition with the typical style of women's swimsuits (at the time). Indeed, when men wore the Speedos, they too experienced deficits in their math performance and other cognitive capabilities. We published this research in *Personality and Social Psychology Bulletin* in 2004. Two things stand out about this study. One, it shows how cultural and/or societal customs (e.g., women's versus men's swimsuit norms) can produce enormous downstream gender disparities (e.g., women's deficits in cognitive performance). Surely, there must be similar downstream effects of women (but not men) wearing makeup, high-heeled shoes, and other skin-tight clothing, all of which are fairly normative for women today. Two, it was one of the first collaborations I had not only with Jean Lin, but also with this superbly talented Rice University undergraduate student named Eden King. It was not only fun to do the research and think about the implications of gendered norms, but it was also exciting to see how effective, efficient, and enjoyable it could be working together and producing. Little did I know then that some 20 years later, this undergraduate student was going to have a faculty office some 20 feet away from mine at Rice University, become a SIOP president, and continue to be one of the best people I have ever met.

The "Fatsuit" Study (King, Shapiro, Hebl, Singletary, & Turner, 2006)

The year 2018 will always be remembered as a bummer year for Eden, for me, and for the entire Rice family of industrial/organizational and social psychology scholars. The world lost Jenessa Shapiro to cancer. Jenessa was an amazingly talented scholar and one of the most upbeat personalities our field will ever see. Who else would put on a sweaty, obesity prostheses that had been worn across the years and take silly delight in the idea that she was going to get to interact with managers in stores wearing a costume that made her look eight sizes bigger than she actually was?! She would get crazy overjoyed when she met anyone in the field whose name or research she recognized. She was passionate about research, she was climbing to the top of her game, and she was so happy to empower members of underrepresented groups. She was a tenured professor at UCLA who had two research awards named after her at Rice, one before she even left campus with her undergraduate degree. She had several other awards posthumously named for her at other institutions.

And so, when I think of the "fatsuit" study, I think of Jenessa and research assistants (and Eden King, Sarah Singletary Walker, and Stacy Turner Steele). In this study, like the gay and proud study, we also entered retail stores but this time as nonobese/control or obese customers wanting help with merchandise. We examined (Study 1) the overt and subtle forms of discrimination that personnel directed toward female "shoppers" as a function of being or not being obese. Replicating the paradigm of the gay and proud study, we also examined (Study 2) whether we could reduce the bias by having obese shoppers engage in behavior that assuaged stereotypes associated with obesity. Indeed, when obese women wore a running t-shirt, carried a Diet Coke, and announced they had just completed a 5K; or when they wore nicer, upscale clothing, they experienced less subtle discrimination. We further wanted to examine (Study 3) whether there were real-world implications of this subtle discrimination, and we found that there were. Specifically, we surveyed authentically heavy women who were departing retail stores. Those who self-reported interpersonal discrimination also were less likely to recommend the store to others, spent less money at the store than they intended to spend, and were less likely to plan to return to the store. The same set of results was not found for women who were not heavy. This research is important because it shows the bottom-line consequences for organizations when members discriminate against their clientele. Our later research (Ruggs, Williams, & Hebl, 2015) showed that this effect also emerges for heavy versus non-heavy men, but the extent to which women are judged on their looks makes it more likely that women suffer additional consequences for being heavy than do men. Not only was the research itself important, but I will forever remember receiving scathing reviews (albeit along with a high-risk revise and resubmit). Eden and I were both a little daunted, but it was Jenessa who approached the reviews like a game, delighting in responses to each reviewer's comment to make the paper better. When it got accepted, it was awarded the SIOP best paper award for research led by students.

The "Gender Bias in Colloquium Speakers" Study (Nittrouer et al., 2018)

My job as a mentor to doctoral students is to try to get each one of my graduate students at least one solid "A" publication. There are many factors that go into getting that great publication, and sometimes the stars seem to align, and other times they do not. But when a student (and group of people) work so hard and long on a publication and it goes through several rounds of journal revisions, it is pure delight when it gets accepted. And so it was with Christy Nittrouer's paper that was published in the *Proceedings of the National Academy of Sciences* in 2018.

The study idea was born as I sat in the back row of a colloquium talk that was being given at Rice. The speaker was male, and I was watching him give his talk through the ponytails of many female graduate students' heads. To be sure, the speaker was good, and everyone enjoyed the talk. Six months later, I had counted four additional, similar experiences. Without realizing it, our department had chosen only men to give colloquium talks to a department comprised mostly of female graduate students. Of course, many researchers are men, and maybe this was just the way the dice rolled that year, but I wondered to myself if that were the case. Christy soon began to pursue this idea for her master's thesis. She coded more than 5,000 colloquium talks given in six different academic departments at the top 50 universities in the country within a 1-year period of time. We found that there were significantly more men who gave talks than women. But, the reviewers suggested, maybe it was because there were more men in the pool of available candidates. So, we coded all the professors in the six departments at the top 100 universities in the country (totaling something like 23,000 talks). The proportion of men giving talks remained higher than that of women. But, the reviewers suggested, maybe the gender difference was due to men inhabiting more senior and respected positions. So, we coded and accounted for professor rank. The gender difference was present within every level, from full professor down to assistant professor. But, the reviewers suggested, maybe female professors declined talks more often and/or maybe they didn't believe giving talks was as important, compared to male professors. So, we queried the women in our sample. Our results showed that women did *not* decline more talks, and they believed that giving talks was just as important as did men. The significant gender difference held—men were asked to give colloquium talks at higher rates than were women, controlling for other potential explanations. This seemingly minor difference may have major implications when one realizes that colloquium talks are often the gateways to new job offers, counteroffers, collaborations, social and professional networks, and idea and information generation and exchange. Publishing this study, which took Christy Nittrouer, Rachel Trump-Steele, Virginia Valian, Leslie Ashburn-Nardo, David Lane, and I more than four years to conduct and see to publication, made me proud that we could draw attention to an industry-wide gender discrepancy that we have the power to change.

ADVICE FOR GENDER RESEARCHERS

I presume almost every person reading this chapter has some level of interest in research on gender-related issues. To you, I say, "The water is warm"—come on in. We need you. Badly. Melinda Gates has recognized the perverse inequality that exists between men and women in our society, and she recently pledged $1 billion dollars to help level the playing field for men and women in the United States (Gates, 2019). Just as I felt toward the end of my time at Smith College, I hope you will "board the bus" with me and other researchers who are conducting gender-related research. It is critical for you to be aware of and appreciate what the female (and some male) pioneers have done in the two centuries that have preceded us. I hope you will be inspired by the number of ways you can and should pay it forward. As researchers, you can do this by getting passionate about the gender-related topic that interest you most, and then do the highest-quality research on it of which you are capable. Know that you can make a difference. Initiate research projects that identify additional barriers for and discrimination against women, however large or small they might be. Some people believe that gross gender inequities no longer exist, so it is crucial that we collect data to determine where these biases continue to exist and where they do not.

The Gender Equity Report published by the World Economic Forum (2019) recently ranked the United States an unacceptable 51st out of 179 countries on gender equity measures. Just some of the important avenues for future research can be inferred from the areas in which we are lacking worldwide. We need to better study how we can reduce biases against female politicians. We need to examine how we can reduce the maternal mortality rate within the United States. We need to investigate ways that women are able to effectively ascend to executive positions. We need to understand how we can get men to buy into the importance of paid family leave. We need to reduce toxic masculinity in the United States and reduce the violence that men show toward other men and toward women. We need to examine the intersectionality of gender and race (and other characteristics) and identify effective ways in which our destinies are not so predetermined by birth.

We simply cannot accept the present state of gender disparities. We need to learn how to best intervene to reduce inequities and identify the most effective ways to make changes. Ally research is also incredibly important. If you are male, act as allies to women. And whether you are male or female, remain discontent and active until we reach gender parity in critical life domains.

FUTURE "HOT TOPICS" IN GENDER RESEARCH

The "hottest" and most important research that should be done bridges the disparate perspectives and realities people hold within our society. We will continue to witness a breakdown in the moral fabric of our society if we do not address the current divisions between people based on politics, race, gender, and other identities. In the case of gender, equal rights should not be some preposterous, far-fetched notion. At present, women have fewer workplace opportunities, rewards, salaries, promotions, high-quality developmental experiences, endorsements, and less access to resources, social networks, and leadership positions compared to men. Women often think about and engage in teamwork, leadership, social networking, and decision-making differently than do men, likely in part due to the substantial power differences associated with their gender. Furthermore, women often vote for different candidates, place importance on different issues, and face different work/family balance realities than do their male counterparts. Research that takes the burden squarely off the shoulders of women for solving these inequities and places it more evenly on the shoulders of men, too, will pave the way for actual gender equality. Research that promotes this idea of "marching together" (i.e., allyship) is paramount to expediting gender equality.

Additionally, organizations have a role to play in realizing gender equity. Organizations must give parents paid family leave, institute affordable on-site daycare facilities, provide breastfeeding rooms, encourage employees to not only taking maternity leaves but also paternity leaves, ensure that meetings take place during the workday and not before or after school hours when the majority of childcare falls upon mothers. Organizations must self-evaluate, expose, and correct the overt and subtle gender biases that they have in place. This is not easy. Therefore, research that demonstrates how organizations can best identify and change such inequities is simply critical. Similar research is also needed in terms of revising even larger societal structures and norms. The #MeToo movement provided some insight into how ubiquitous the harassment is that women in our society, as a whole, face. But we cannot rest now that such negative, widescale behavior has been unveiled. We need to not only expose it but also correct it. And research that leads the way in showing how to effectively do this is simply critical. In short, we must continue to work together and make gender equity a reality rather than some unattainable ideal that women continue reaching toward but never realize. Join in. Let's continue marching forward.

REFERENCES

Fredrickson, B., & Roberts, T., & Noll, S., Quinn, D., & Twenge, J. (1998). That swimsuit becomes you: Sex differences in self-objectification, restrained eating, and math performance. *Journal of Personality and Social Psychology, 75*(1), 269–284.

Gates, M. (2019, October 2). Here's why I'm committing $1 billion to promote gender equality. *Time.* Retrieved from https://time.com/5690596/melinda-gates-empowering-women/

Hebl, M., King, E., & Lin, J. (2004). The swimsuit becomes us all: Ethnicity, gender, and vulnerability to self-objectification. *Personality and Social Psychology Bulletin, 30,* 1322–1331.

Hebl, M., Foster, J. B., Mannix, L. M., & Dovidio, J. F. (2002). Formal and interpersonal discrimination: A field study of bias toward homosexual applicants. *Personality and Social Psychology Bulletin, 28*(6), 815–825.

King, E., Shapiro, J. L., Hebl, M., Singletary, S., & Turner, S. (2006). The stigma of obesity in customer service: A mechanism for remediation and bottom-line consequences of interpersonal discrimination. *Journal of Applied Psychology, 91*(3), 579–593.

Nittrouer, C. L., Hebl, M. R., Trump-Steele, R., Ashburn-Nardo, L., Lane, D., & Valian, V. (2018). Gender bias in colloquium speakers. *Proceedings of the National Academy of Sciences, 115*(1), 104–108.

Ruggs, E., Williams, A., & Hebl, M. (2015). Weight isn't selling: The insidious effects of weight stigmatization in retail settings. *Journal of Applied Psychology, 100*(5), 1483–1496.

World Economic Forume (2019). *Mind the 100 year gap.* Retrieved from https://www.weforum.org/reports/gender-gap-2020-report-100-years-pay-equality

CHAPTER 12

MY GENDER RESEARCH JOURNEY

A Goodness of Fit

Madeline E. Heilman
New York University

Madeline Heilman, how did someone who looks like you wind up in a place like this!
—Senior Faculty Member

Although more than 40 years have passed, these words, phrased as a question but very much meant to be a statement, still sting. They mark the start of my gender research journey.

It was the first year after receiving my degree. I had landed a job at a revered academic institution and I was a bit starstruck with the eminence and renown of my new colleagues and uncertain about how I was going to fare among such luminaries. There I was at a get-to-know-you cocktail party, chatting with a group of doctoral students, trying my best to appear confident and relaxed, when an older gentleman whose textbook I had used as a student entered the room to join the festivities. In he strode and, looking directly at me, loudly bellowed those words questioning the appropriateness of my presence in such a rarefied setting. I wish I could report that I had a nasty comeback, a clever retort, or even a mild rebuke. But I did not.

Perspectives on Gender and Work, pages 141–154

Instead I stood mute as he sailed on by—I was humiliated and embarrassed, but silent nonetheless.

When I think back to that time, I am flooded with other gender-laced memories: the guy who called me "honey" in the first doctoral seminar I taught; the questionnaire for new faculty that asked me about activities "my wife" might be interested in joining; and the colleague who suggested that I not take my blazer off when I taught, no matter how stifling the room. It was not an easy time for women faculty, to say the least. There were very few of us, and there were constant reminders that we somehow did not belong.

This institution of higher learning had only begun allowing entry to female undergraduates a few years earlier than my arrival, so they, too, were struggling to feel a part of things. Getting wind of the fact that there was a young woman faculty member amenable to talking about "issues," many of these women made their way to my office. Often dressed in combat boots and clothing that was about as non-feminine as you can get, they came to talk about their experiences in classes, their experiences in their residences, and their concerns and fears about their post-graduation job prospects. I cannot count the number of conversations I had about how to manage one's female-ness in order to be taken seriously. These conversations involved topics as various as how to dress, how to present oneself, and how to appear smart—but not too smart. At some point, it became clear to me that we all were making assumptions about how women were going to be viewed by others in traditionally male settings. It was then that I decided to test these assumptions.

My training was as an experimental social psychologist, my doctoral mentor was Morton Deutsch, the renowned researcher on conflict and negotiation, and my research until then had followed in this path. My dissertation was about the reputational effects of threats and promises, and I had already published several papers about threats as influence attempts in top-tier social psychology journals. Embracing gender as a focus of study, and targeting work contexts in particular, was far afield of what to that point had been my scholarly pursuits and, as an untenured assistant professor, was a risky proposition. And it was not only changing scholarly focus that was risky; it was the content of that focus. In fact, after excitedly sharing my new idea with one of my favorite colleagues, he almost totally derailed me, advising that pursuing research on gender would be the "kiss of death" for a female researcher. But the pull was too great and my interest too piqued. With encouragement from my husband and my doctoral advisor, I embarked on a program of research that focused on gender bias and the obstacles women encounter when they seek to advance their careers.

That research focus has continued throughout my career; although it has pulled me in many directions, it has never ceased to sustain me intellectually. And (unfortunately) the world has never ceased to provide me with new and different issues to investigate. My initial concern was the identification of conditions that regulate when women are viewed as competent to perform roles that historically have been dominated by men—a focus that still prevails today. I later returned to my early work experiences to address the question of what happens to women when they are in fact successful in arenas that defy expectations or otherwise violate normative prescriptions and, most recently, have begun to investigate when and why women behave in ways that limit their own success. Along the way, I have spent a good deal of time considering the unintentional effects of the preferential selection of female job candidates as a remedy for bias-driven under-representation of women in leadership positions and the downside of some commonly endorsed intervention strategies designed to promote gender equality.

THE LACK OF FIT MODEL

When I began searching the literature relevant to gender bias I was very disappointed. Much of it was descriptive, reporting statistics about the dearth of women in various fields or depicting the way in which women and men were characterized by others. There was little theory devoted to this issue or research that attempted to systematically identify the processes underlying gender bias. (An exception was work by Kay Deaux [e.g., Deaux & Emswiller, 1974], in which she looked at gender effects in the context of attribution theory.) This all was a mixed blessing: I had little to go on or to build from, but I also was not constrained and could go my own way with little need to reconcile my ideas with those of others.

From my original jumble of ideas—both personal and scholarly—emerged what I consider to be the accomplishment that shaped much of what came after: my lack of fit model. I came to it early in my career, and it became the organizing principle for much of my subsequent research on gender bias. It has proved to be generative, and also amenable to revision, embellishment, and expansion in ways that furthered my research interests and provided a framework for testing my research questions.

At the core of the lack of fit model is the notion of gender stereotypes. I think of stereotypes as a structured set of beliefs about the features of a group that are associated with individuals who belong to that group. Because gender is one of the most salient human features, it often serves as a cue for these beliefs, and gender stereotypes frequently shape inferences about the characteristics of men and women as well as conceptions of how they ought to be. I have argued that gender stereotypes—both their descriptive and prescriptive aspects—form the basis of gender bias against women.

It had already been established that the characteristics of men and women are organized along two general dimensions: agency and communion (Bakan, 1966; Broverman, Vogel, Broverman, Clarkson, & Rosenkrantz, 1972). Agency comprises attributes such as achievement orientation (e.g., able, successful), assertiveness (e.g., dominant, forceful), and autonomy (e.g., independent, self-reliant); while communality denotes consideration for others (e.g., caring, helpful), sociability (e.g., friendly, likable), and emotional sensitivity (e.g., tender, sensitive). These dimensions continue to constitute the core content of gender stereotypes, which depict men as agentic and women as communal (Haines, Deaux, & Lofoao, 2016; Hentschel, Heilman, & Peus, 2019). Importantly, gender stereotypes tend to be oppositional in nature—men are seen not only as agentic, but also as lacking in communality. Conversely, women are seen not only as communal but also as lacking in agency (Diekman & Eagly, 2000).

It was clear to me that the effect of gender stereotypes on women is not simple and unequivocal. They are not always detrimental to women, and to argue otherwise is foolish. In fact, researchers have found that women are thought to be "wonderful" (Eagly, Mladinic, & Otto, 1991)—after all, what is wrong with being kind, helpful, and interpersonally sensitive? But gender stereotypes did seem to have negative outcomes for women in work contexts, contributing to the belief that women are less capable than men to perform jobs and fill roles that are historically dominated by men, and which typically are the most prestigious and high status in our culture.

As I thought about it, I realized that jobs and roles that traditionally have been occupied by men are believed to require the agentic characteristics that are associated with men. Research had corroborated this idea (Schein, 1973, 1975). If stereotypes of women diverge from these requisite attributes, it seemed reasonable to propose that they would create the perception that women are a bad fit for these positions, and that this "lack of fit" between people's conceptions of what women are like and beliefs about what is required to succeed in male-typed domains would produce expectations that women are unlikely to perform these jobs well. I posited that these negative expectations, maintained by cognitive distortion, would perpetuate the view that women are ill-equipped to handle such positions and thus promote bias against women when judgments and decisions are made. These ideas became the basis of the lack of fit model (Heilman, 1983)—a formulation that has proved to be an invaluable guide and the source of my many investigations examining the occurrence of gender bias in evaluative decision making (Heilman, 2001, 2012).

Testing the Model

The lack of fit model prompted me to embark on research identifying when perceptions of lack of fit are amplified and their effect most intense. Since both the "maleness" of a position and the degree of stereotyping affect the magnitude of the lack of fit, I and my colleagues systematically investigated each of these constructs. In these studies, gender bias was measured in various ways—by recommendations about entry decisions (selection for jobs or admission to school), position placement, or task assignments, as well as performance assessments, promotion and allocation of rewards, and suggested advancement opportunities.

Early on, I endeavored to show that bias against women was dependent on whether and to what degree a position is male in gender-type. I have looked at this in terms of occupational domain (e.g., industry vs education), specialty within an occupation (e.g., sciences vs humanities), and type of organizational position (e.g., line vs staff). In all cases, the more the position was viewed as male, the more bias was demonstrated. This is key to the lack of fit model, which specifies that stereotypes about women are not always detrimental—bias should not occur all the time; it should only occur when there is perception of a bad fit. I have repeatedly used the gender-type of the position in multiple studies over the years (e.g., Lyness & Heilman, 2006), all to show that it is perceived fit that is at the root of the bias against women I was demonstrating (see Heilman, 2012 for a review).

In addition, I have sought to demonstrate that gender bias is dependent on the salience of gender and the consequent activation of gender stereotypes. Thus, I have shown that decreasing the salience of gender by providing individuating information (Heilman, 1975, 1984; Heilman, Martell, & Simon, 1988) or stereotype-defying information about women (Heilman & Martell, 1986) can sometimes serve as an antidote to gender discrimination. I also have shown that when women are scarce in number, something that enhances the salience of gender stereotypes, the same woman is more negatively evaluated than when there are other women in her cohort (Heilman, 1980; Heilman & Blader, 2001). Moreover, I have demonstrated that being attractive, something that puts a spotlight on female-ness, can be a liability for women in male gender-typed contexts both in selection decisions and in performance evaluations (Heilman & Saruwatari, 1979; Heilman & Stopeck, 1985a, 1985b). Similar findings have been found in my studies about the effects of motherhood on evaluations—little could activate female stereotypes more powerfully than being a mother (Heilman & Okimoto, 2008; Okimoto & Heilman, 2012). I furthermore have demonstrated that a focus on diversity, which makes demographic categories salient, also negatively affects evaluations of women (Heilman & Welle, 2005).

So, in a series of studies conducted over many years, I, together with my students and colleagues, have shown that variations in either component of the lack of fit model lead to differences in the degree of bias evidenced. The worse the perceived lack of fit, the more gender bias was evident in decision making.

The Role of Expectations

I believed that the driver of these effects was the expectations that derive from lack of fit perceptions. And I also believed that these expectations, as is often the case with expectations, would persist regardless of disconfirming evidence. I thought that they would be fueled by ambiguity and maintain themselves through cognitive distortion in what people attend to, how they interpret what they see, what they remember (and forget), and how they allocate credit and blame. So, for example, I have shown that when women work in teams with men, they are given less credit for the team's success (Heilman & Haynes, 2005) and more blame for the team's failure (Caleo & Heilman, 2014) than are their male teammates—a process we have called attributional rationalization that allows people to maintain expectations of women being less competent than their male counterparts.

I also have sought to show the persistence of these expectations by demonstrating differences in the updating of evaluations of men and women (Heilman, Manzi, & Caleo, 2019). That is, even though men and women were shown to be rated equally negatively when they had clearly performed very poorly, when their performance improved, the increase in competence judgments was greater for men than for women. Similarly, even though women and men were shown to be rated equally positively when they had clearly performed excellently, when their performance declined, the decrease in competence ratings was more severe for women than for men. Evidently, people are more amenable to relinquishing perceptions of a woman's competence and more reluctant to relinquish perceptions of their incompetence. The expectations derived from lack of fit perceptions seem to stick around and have impact long after they appear to have been eliminated.

Implications for Intervention

Ambiguity provides fertile ground for the cognitive distortion that enables expectations to dominate in evaluative decision making. Thus, if negative expectations are to be overridden, a woman's competence has to be clear and undebatable, something we have demonstrated repeatedly (e.g., Heilman, Wallen, Fuchs, & Tamkins, 2004). Unfortunately, ambiguity abounds in work settings. There often is little objective performance information available, the criteria for judging performance are vague and subjective (e.g., consider the terms "cutting edge" or "charismatic"), and the structure for evaluation is often poorly defined with the result that different criteria are used for different people. Also, because of the tendency for people to work in teams, there frequently is confusion about individual contribution to a work product. These considerations provoked me to think about how the lack of fit model might be helpful in identifying interventions to alleviate bias in decision-making.

Indeed, a consideration of our work on lack of fit is suggestive of leverage points for intervention into the gender bias process. I, together with my colleague, Suzette Caleo, have sought to classify them using the model as a guide. We distinguished two sets of intervention strategies. One involved decreasing lack of fit perceptions by attenuating stereotype-based characterizations or by changing perceptions of the gender-type of the job or position, thereby short-circuiting negative performance expectations. The other involved breaking the link between the expectations of incompetence that arise from lack of fit perceptions and the gender bias it produces. This can be done by developing practices that reduce ambiguity in the information used and the processes employed to make evaluative judgments, as well as by increasing self-interested motivation to not be biased. The specifics of these suggested interventions can be found in our recent paper (Heilman & Caleo, 2018).

Focus on the Target of Bias

Currently, I have turned my focus to the target of bias instead of the perpetrator of bias. I am seeking an answer to the question of why women so often engage in self-limiting behavior—behavior that largely serves to confirm existing gender stereotypes. The blame, I believe, is not in deficiencies inherent in women, but rather in the cultural stereotypes they have internalized and the structural bias they encounter in work settings. I again believe lack of fit perceptions are central but, in this instance, in creating negative performance expectations for women themselves leading to decrements in motivation and deficits in performance and perseverance. This research follows loosely from my very early work involving women's assumptions about colleagues' views of their competence (Heilman & Kram, 1983) and women's self-derogation when working with male teammates (Heilman & Kram, 1978), which was later replicated and extended in work with Michelle Haynes (Haynes & Heilman, 2013). Again, I propose that fit perceptions, in this case about oneself, are fundamental, that they can be tempered or exacerbated, and that the resulting expectations can be quelled or fueled by ambiguity. So, here again, I find myself using the lack of fit framework to orient myself and develop my ideas.

ADVICE FOR YOUNG SCHOLARS

There are so many ways to be successful as a researcher and scholar. There are people who start with a theory and test it, and others who start with a hunch and proceed inductively—seeking a theory to shed light on what is going on. There are big picture people who see the connections between different ideas and find a way to pull them into something that is grander than its parts. There are highly focused researchers who systematically develop an idea, building outward to incorporate additional predictors, outcomes, and moderators of an effect. There are people who see contradictory findings as a starting place—trying to reconcile them and identify the key moderators that determine the conditions under which one or another effect arises. There are yet others who read about a commonly assumed main effect and, believing that there is more to the story, proceed to try to identify conditions that regulate its occurrence. And these are only some examples. All are different paths to developing a research focus, and all can lead to success. It is important to identify approaches to research that work best for you.

Although I am reluctant to give advice about the best research approach, I do think there are some general points to be made, and these are particularly relevant for those of us studying gender.

The Importance of Mediators and Moderators

Wherever you start, however you proceed, there should not only be an effort to describe and demonstrate a phenomenon; there should also be an effort to explain it. That means that there is a focus on mediating processes and the question of *why* a particular effect occurs. This type of focus is necessary to make a theoretical contribution—understanding why enables the identification of critical moderators of an effect, whether they be individual difference variables or contextual variables. In fact, there is a productive interplay between the identification of mediators and moderators—it is the interplay of *why* with *when* and *for whom.* If you have an idea about why something happens (let's say negative expectations about women's performance due to perceptions of lack of fit) then that helps you determine situations in which it would not happen (when the context is not male gender-typed or the female is not viewed through the lens of stereotypes), and people for whom it would not happen (perhaps those who do not strongly endorse gender stereotypes). Similarly, if you have an idea about when bias is likely to occur (e.g., when women are scarce in a setting or when there is little information about the woman available) or who is most likely to exhibit it (e.g., men who don't have career-oriented wives or daughters), it helps pinpoint why it is happening. The hypotheses that result from these exercises are essential to pushing an idea forward, finding the boundary conditions of observed effects, and enriching and elaborating the theory underlying the research.

This enterprise of identifying mediators and moderators is not only important theoretically; it also has important implications for practice. Long ago Kurt Lewin told us that there is nothing as practical as a good theory, and I totally subscribe to that statement. In short, understanding why something happens is essential to making it useful, because different manifestations of the same construct will have the same effect no matter how different they appear. So, if we know that lesser activation of gender stereotypes is necessary for a particular outcome, we can design a variety of interventions. Some may involve stereotype-reducing educational efforts, others may involve increasing the numbers of women in upper level positions, and yet others may focus on not isolating women structurally but rather clustering them in work units (to name a few). If I understand the mediator to be deactivating stereotypes about women, I can choose from among this array of interventions depending on the context, my resources, and the nature of the population involved. In one setting, I may intervene in a way that is seemingly unrelated to an intervention in another setting, but, in fact, the interventions *are* related because they both are embodiments of the same construct.

What Type of Research Should I Do?

There is no one type of research that is best. The research method should fit the question that is being asked. Sometimes it is appropriate to get a little information about a lot; other times it is important to get a lot of information about a little. Ideally, both experimental and correlational methods should be used in a program of research—one to nail down causal relationships between a limited set of variables, and the other to validate experimental findings or to provide a way of identifying critical variables that are out of reach in experimental work. Individual difference variables can be integrated into research as possible amplifiers or attenuators of expected effects or as predictors in their own right. Research types are not good or bad, but they can be implemented well or poorly. Fields of study are enhanced by an abundance of different types of well conducted studies.

It is important to be programmatic in your work. Simply having a great number of publications should not be your goal. What is critical is to have a line of research that follows some trajectory—where later studies build upon earlier ones, and there is a general underlying principle that guides the work. Haphazardly being opportunistic and jumping on the bandwagon to participate in disparate studies is not necessarily beneficial. This is nowhere more true than in research involving gender because gender is so fundamental a distinction between people, and is relevant to virtually every area of study. However, research about gender differences is not in the same line of research as, for example, research about gender discrimination. And research about queen bees is not in the same line of research as, for example, research about initiating negotiation. What defines the research is not just gender but the distinct ideas underlying it that often transcend gender and are relevant more broadly. So, although it is fine to have several lines of research, each focusing on gender (or other) issues, each one should be developed in a programmatic fashion. This has implications for joining in collaborative projects that stray far from your research focus. Numbers alone do not make a successful research career.

Individual Differences

Lastly, and very importantly, know yourself. Some of us can work for 16 hours in a row with no breaks, and others of us have had our fill after a few hours of work. Some of us can work in a Starbucks, and others need to work in a darkened room with minimal stimulation. Some of us can work on many different things at one time, and others simply cannot multitask when it comes to scholarship, and some of us are early morning workers and others are night owls. All of these variations are fine; it just is important to recognize your proclivities. Doing so avoids time-wasting and the frustrating feeling of getting nowhere.

Knowing yourself also means knowing your strengths and weaknesses. If you love writing introductions and hate writing discussion sections of articles (or vice versa), that is telling you something about your comfort zones as well as your way of thinking about research issues. If you are a person who cannot stand the minutia of designing a well-controlled experiment or dreads the data analysis entailed in a large correlational study, that also is something you should own. Working on what is not comfortable for you will make you a more well-rounded researcher and one who can function independently. It also will give you clues about whom you might best collaborate with on projects.

INTO THE FUTURE

I hesitate to identify topics I think are going to be the cutting edge of the next wave of gender research. I firmly believe that people should pursue questions that are of interest to them, whether popular or unpopular; after all, it is possible that your research will provide a spark for others, making an until-then ignored topic hot. But, having said this, I will try to identify a few areas that I think are ripe for exploration and should be attended to.

First, I think it is imperative that we continue to explore the subtleties of gender bias in work settings. Many studies, including some of my own, demonstrate the tenacity of gender stereotypes and the often covert way in which they exert force on decision-making. So, even when things seem okay, and gender bias is not evident and appears to be eliminated, it evidently takes very little to ignite the flames of bias once again. This suggests that we not accept superficial evidence of the demise of gender bias and the irrelevance of gender stereotypes but rather persevere in rooting out their effects whenever they occur. This is likely to entail the study of more subtle forms of workplace bias and its more downstream consequences.

It is additionally important to continue to explore the effects of intersectionality. Although work in this area has blossomed in recent years, more work is needed. It is still not clear how gender stereotypes affect women of different ages, races, ethnicities, and gender orientations. Discovering whether there are unique stereotypes for these groups that affect the expression of gender bias will expand our understanding not only of gender bias but also of bias more generally. In a workforce that is becoming increasingly diverse, and in a world in which the United States will soon be a majority minority country, I think that the urgency of this work is unquestionable.

I also think it is important to include men as the focus of our investigations. The greater job opportunities in fields that traditionally have been in the purview of women (e.g., education, health care) have resulted in some unusual unemployment patterns of late, and it is important to determine whether this is due to men turning their backs on these opportunities because they see them as a bad fit or is due to bias against them when they do pursue them. Seeing if the same principles that we know apply to women also apply to men will allow for a different type of test of our theories. Additionally, efforts should be made to understand how to engage men as allies in the fight against gender bias. This entails the study of what motivates men to support women and what obstacles they are likely to face or penalties they are likely to incur for doing so. Women need all the help they can get in the struggle for gender equality, making it all the more important to understand how to mobilize men in their favor.

Lastly, while there already has been quite a bit of work, including my own, concerning the penalties women endure when they violate stereotype-based gender norms, continuing this work is critical. As more and more women attain positions of power and prestige, there apparently are new difficulties that await them as well as old difficulties that persist, but often in a new form. What these difficulties are, when and why they come about, and what types of interventions can assuage them all are important questions for this new chapter in the history of women and work.

CONCLUDING COMMENTS

It certainly is a long way from that eminent professor's inquiry about the appropriateness of my presence in an institution of higher learning. My journey has been long, rich with discovery, and rewarding. It has been a thrill to do research that not only has theoretical importance but also is important to me personally. With the aid of students and colleagues, I have been able to systematically explore gender bias and its consequences, and to provide insights that increase our general understanding of the processes underlying bias in evaluative judgments and decisions. This research also has enabled me to contribute to thinking about how to resolve the seemingly intractable problem of women's underrepresentation in historically male work settings—a problem that morphs into new and different forms just as we believe progress is being made. But progress *has* been made and, with progress, new issues have arisen—issues that beg to be addressed. It has been an honor to be in on the early days of our exploration and exhilarating to see how our field has blossomed and continues to blossom with innovative research. I am so happy that I had the grit to shift gears so long ago and am eagerly looking forward to the next chapter of my gender research journey.

AUTHOR NOTE

Correspondence concerning this article should be addressed to Madeline E. Heilman, Department of Psychology, New York University, 6 Washington Place, New York, NY 10003. Email: madeline.heilman@nyu.edu

REFERENCES

Bakan, D. (1966). *The duality of human existence: Isolation and communion in Western man.* Boston, MA: Beacon Press.

Broverman, I. K., Vogel, S. R., Broverman, D. M., Clarkson, F. E., & Rosenkrantz, P. S. (1972). Sex-role stereotypes: A current appraisal 1. *Journal of Social issues, 28*(2), 59–78.

Caleo, S., & Heilman, M. E. (2014). Is this a man's world? Obstacles to women's success in male-typed domains. In R. J. Burke & D. A. Major (Eds.), *Gender in organizations* (pp. 217–233). Cheltenham, England: Edward Elgar.

Deaux, K., & Emswiller, T. (1974). Explanations of successful performance on sex-linked tasks: What is skill for the male is luck for the female. *Journal of Personality and Social Psychology, 29*(1), 80.

Diekman, A. B., & Eagly, A. H. (2000). Stereotypes as dynamic constructs: Women and men of the past, present, and future. *Personality and social psychology bulletin, 26*(10), 1171–1188.

Eagly, A. H., Mladinic, A., & Otto, S. (1991). Are women evaluated more favorably than men? An analysis of attitudes, beliefs, and emotions. *Psychology of Women Quarterly, 15*(2), 203–216.

Haines, E. L., Deaux, K., & Lofaro, N. (2016). The times they are a-changing... or are they not? A comparison of components of gender stereotypes, 1983 to 2014. *Sex Roles, 40*(3), 353–363.

Haynes, M. C., & Heilman, M. E. (2013). It had to be you (not me)! Women's attributional rationalization of their contribution to successful joint work outcomes. *Personality and Social Psychology Bulletin, 39*(7), 956–969.

Heilman, M. (1975). Miss, Mrs., Ms., or none of the above? Effects of instructor's title on course desirability. *American Psychologist, 10,* 310–324.

Heilman, M. E. (1980). The impact of situational factors on personnel decisions concerning women: Varying the sex composition of the applicant pool. *Organizational Behavior and Human Performance, 26*(3), 386–395.

Heilman, M. E. (1983). Sex bias in work settings: The lack of fit model. *Research in Organizational Behavior, 5,* 269–298.

Heilman, M. E. (1984). Information as a deterrent against sex discrimination: The effects of applicant sex and information type on preliminary employment decisions. *Organizational Behavior and Human Performance, 33*(2), 174–186.

Heilman, M. E. (2001). Description and prescription: How gender stereotypes prevent women's ascent up the organizational ladder. *Journal of Social Issues, 57*(4), 657–674.

Heilman, M. E. (2012). Gender stereotypes and workplace bias. *Research in Organizational Behavior, 32,* 113–135.

Heilman, M. E., & Blader, S. L. (2001). Assuming preferential selection when the admissions policy is unknown: The effects of gender rarity. *Journal of Applied Psychology, 86*(2), 188–193.

Heilman, M. E., & Caleo, S. (2018). Combatting gender discrimination: A lack of fit framework. *Group Processes and Intergroup Relations, 21*(5), 725–744.

Heilman, M. E., & Haynes, M. C. (2005). No credit where credit is due: Attributional rationalization of women's success in male-female teams. *Journal of Applied Psychology, 90*(5), 905–916.

Heilman, M. E., & Kram, K. E. (1978). Self-derogating behavior in women—fixed or flexible: The effects of co-worker's sex. *Organizational Behavior and Human Performance, 22*(3), 497–507.

Heilman, M. E., & Kram, K. E. (1983). Male and female assumptions about colleagues' views of their competence. *Psychology of Women Quarterly, 7*(4), 329–337.

Heilman, M. E., Manzi, F., & Caleo, S. (2019). Updating impressions: The differential effects of new performance information on evaluations of women and men. *Organizational Behavior and Human Decision Processes, 152,* 105–121.

Heilman, M. E., & Martell, R. F. (1986). Exposure to successful women: Antidote to sex discrimination in applicant screening decisions?. *Organizational Behavior and Human Decision Processes, 37*(3), 376–390.

Heilman, M. E., Martell, R. F., & Simon, M. C. (1988). The vagaries of sex bias: Conditions regulating the undervaluation, equivaluation, and overvaluation of female job applicants. *Organizational Behavior and Human Decision Processes, 41*(1), 98–110.

Heilman, M. E., & Okimoto, T. G. (2008). Motherhood: A potential source of bias in employment decisions. *Journal of Applied Psychology, 93*(1), 189–198.

Heilman, M. E., & Saruwatari, L. R. (1979). When beauty is beastly: The effects of appearance and sex on evaluations of job applicants for managerial and nonmanagerial jobs. *Organizational Behavior & Human Performance, 23*(3), 360–372.

Heilman, M. E., & Stopeck, M. H. (1985a). Attractiveness and corporate success: Different causal attributions for males and females. *Journal of Applied Psychology, 70*(2), 379–388.

Heilman, M. E., & Stopeck, M. H. (1985b). Being attractive, advantage or disadvantage? Performance-based evaluations and recommended personnel actions as a function of appearance, sex, and job type. *Organizational Behavior and Human Decision Processes, 35*(2), 202–215.

Heilman, M. E., Wallen, A. S., Fuchs, D., & Tamkins, M. M. (2004). Penalties for success: Reactions to women who succeed at male gender-type tasks. *Journal of Applied Psychology, 89*(3), 416–427.

Heilman, M. E., & Welle, B. (2006). Disadvantaged by diversity? The effects of diversity goals on competence perceptions. *Journal of Applied Social Psychology, 36*(5), 1291–1319.

Hentschel, T., Heilman, M. E., & Peus, C. V. (2019). The multiple dimensions of gender stereotypes: a current look at men's and women's characterizations of others and themselves. *Frontiers in psychology, 10,* Article 11.

Lyness, K. S., & Heilman, M. E. (2006). When fit is fundamental: performance evaluations and promotions of upper-level female and male managers. *Journal of Applied Psychology, 91*(4), 777.

Okimoto, T. G., & Heilman, M. E. (2012). The "bad parent" assumption: How gender stereotypes affect reactions to working mothers. *Journal of Social Issues, 68*(4), 704–724.

Schein, V. E. (1973). The relationship between sex role stereotypes and requisite management characteristics. *Journal of applied psychology, 57*(2), 95.

Schein, V. E. (1975). Relationships between sex role stereotypes and requisite management characteristics among female managers. *Journal of applied psychology, 60*(3), 340.

CHAPTER 13

IDENTITY, DIVERSITY, AND INCLUSION

My Personal and Academic Path

Sonia K. Kang
University of Toronto

LOOKING BACK: WHY I STUDY GENDER AND DIVERSITY

I am the oldest of four daughters, all born in Canada. My parents were both born in India and moved to England when they were very young (my mom at age 3 and my dad at age 13), before eventually immigrating to Canada in their 20s. I noticed early on that, within both Indian and Western cultures, having four girls was not only an anomaly, but also perceived as a very unfortunate thing. Indian people were more overtly negative and at times dramatic in their evaluation. People would openly try to console my parents for their misfortune, tsk in our general direction when we replied "no" to their question about if we had any brothers, or publicly pray at the Gurdwara (Sikh temple) that my parents might be blessed with a son, even when they were well past the thought of having more kids themselves. For my parents' part, they always shrugged off and dismissed these comments, saying that they were "silly" or "backward," and that they were happy to have four girls.

Perspectives on Gender and Work, pages 155–167

I tried to ignore these comments too, but the same kind of sentiment—that having four girls was a problem in some way—was also expressed regularly by people from outside of the Indian community. I can remember multiple times when complete strangers would see our family and make a comment like, "Four girls! Oh you poor man!" to my dad, or "Four girls! Good luck when they're teenagers!" to my mom. In addition to a multitude of other signals, these comments drove home the message that boys were better and more desirable than girls, and that we were in a particularly bad spot because there were just way too many of us.

My sisters and I also experienced the sorts of tensions that are commonly felt by second-generation immigrants and bicultural children. We grew up and went to school in predominately White communities (the city we grew up in is currently 90% White, and that number was even higher when we were young). We were constantly battling between the norms and expectations of our parents and the relatively more lax norms and expectations we perceived our White friends to be enjoying. I always felt a sense of having to hide something, either from my friends and peers at school about my Indian identity, or from my parents and family about my Canadian identity. I felt like an outsider in both settings and that feeling stuck around, even through grad school, where I felt that most people had no awareness of, or desire to understand, the massive cultural gap I was trying to bridge.

Growing up as an Indo-Canadian girl with three sisters awakened my interest in identity, inequality, and injustice. I noticed inequality everywhere and remember being interested in social justice and inclusion from a young age. I was and still am hypersensitive to seeing people be disrespected, excluded, or undermined because of their identity, whether because of their age, race, gender, social class, or anything else. My interest in many of the concepts I study are rooted in these early experiences and the desire to understand and transcend what I perceived as barriers to my own and others' self-expression and accomplishment. These interests ultimately lead me to pursue graduate studies in social psychology. I am still driven by many of the same questions that emerged in my childhood. Why do people think boys and men are better than girls and women? Why do people care so much about gender anyway? How can people from diverse backgrounds live and work together happily and productively? How can people best manage the intersections of their various social identity groups? How can environments be set up so that everyone feels valued and included?

My sisters and I are all adults now, and three of us have kids of our own. Between us, we have five boys; none of us has a daughter. The fact that we have five boys is still, in 2020, met with almost universally positive commentary, from people of all types of cultural backgrounds. When I was pregnant with my first son, Ravi, I was convinced he was going to be a girl. I *wanted* him to be a girl. Not even necessarily because I truly wanted a girl, but because I was fighting against anyone who might think that having a boy would be the preferred outcome. I could only imagine having a girl, and I was excited about the opportunity to "fix" the things that I felt were "wrong" with my upbringing. I was going to raise a strong feminist, and make sure she always felt valued and loved, and never felt like her gender meant she wasn't good enough. When I found out I was having a boy, I was terrified. I had basically no experience with boy babies; all of my sisters were girls, and most of my cousins were girls, too. I had no idea what to do with a boy! My husband was quick to remind me, "We do the exact same thing, take care of him and play with him and help him grow." I realized that despite fighting it my whole life, and despite having had similar conversations with other pregnant friends, I too had fallen victim to gender bias, assuming that only a girl could be raised to be feminist or an inequality disrupter. This completely shifted my perspective, and I realized what an amazing opportunity I had to raise a human, of whatever gender, to be comfortable and confident in his own skin and to be awake to the inequality around him. Now I have two boys, and being a mother has opened my eyes to the myriad struggles that parents face as they learn to inhabit a new identity, at home and at work. That knowledge, coupled with the desire to contribute in some small way to a society in which everyone feels valued and included, continues to invigorate my interest in gender and diversity.

A RECENT RESEARCH HIGHLIGHT: USING DEFAULTS TO ELIMINATE THE GENDER GAP IN COMPETITION

A recent study that I am particularly proud of uncovered a novel intervention for eliminating the gender gap in competition (He, Kang, & Lacetera, 2019, 2020). A robust body of research has demonstrated that, compared to men, women are less likely to participate in competition or take risks, less (over) confident, and less likely to self-promote or exaggerate accomplishments (e.g., Exley & Kessler, 2019; Flory, Leibbrandt, & List, 2015; Moss-Racusin & Rudman, 2010; Niederle & Vesterlund, 2007). However, most competitive selection processes, including those for deciding on promotions, academic admissions, and awards, require one to self-nominate and enroll in competition, which suggests that these kinds of processes could disadvantage women and create and perpetuate gender disparities in academic and professional life.

The typical organizational response to these gender disparities has fallen into two main camps. On the one hand, there have been millions of dollars spent on diversity or unconscious bias or implicit bias training (Chang et al., 2019; Leslie, 2018). These trainings are extremely widespread across the corporate world, and companies may offer them proactively or, as in the case of some high profile examples like Starbucks and Papa John's, reactively following reputation-damaging public instances of discrimination. At best, these trainings have little to no effect (Chang et al., 2019; Dobbin & Kalev, 2016; Kalev, Dobbin, & Kelly, 2006), and at worst, can be associated with a number of negative unintended consequences including reduced diversity and backlash against women and minorities (Kalev et al., 2006; Leslie, 2018). A second approach has been focused on "fixing the women," by coaching them on how to "lean in" (Sandberg, 2013), speak up, and be more assertive. Unfortunately, a classic double bind faced by professional women is that they experience discrimination for acting feminine, but also experience discrimination and backlash when they adopt the types of stereotypically masculine behaviors associated with "leaning in" (Moss-Racusin & Rudman, 2010; Phelan, Moss-Racusin, Rudman, 2008; Rudman & Glick, 1999, 2001).

The approaches mentioned above place the responsibility for both creating and solving the problem of gender discrimination onto individuals (see also Kim, Fitzsimons, & Kay, 2018). Unconscious bias training assumes that discrimination is rooted in people's minds and aims to reduce it by changing their attitudes and biases. Approaches that aim to fix the women insist that women could solve the problem of sexism themselves if they could only act more like men. Neither of these approaches works, and both completely ignore the structural and systemic biases that are built into many social systems and processes themselves.

Our work dispenses with attempts to change people's minds or fix the women and focuses instead on making structural changes to the way that the decision to compete is framed. In typical competitive processes, one must actively choose to engage, or opt-in, to compete. You have to apply for a scholarship or take some action to put yourself up for a promotion. The default response is to do nothing, specifically, to not compete. We know, however, that humans find defaults to be extremely sticky, even if they are completely arbitrary and irrelevant to the actual choice at hand (e.g., Downs, Loewenstein, & Wisdom, 2009; Johnson, Bellman, & Lohse, 2002; Thaler & Sunstein, 2009). Changing the default option can have powerful effects on behavior. For example, changing the default to one of enrollment from which people are free to opt-out has been successful in increasing rates of participation in retirement savings and organ donation programs (Carroll, Choi, Laibbson, Madrian, & Metrick, 2009; Choi, Laibbson, Madrian, & Metrick, 2002; Johnson & Goldstein, 2003; van Dalen & Henkens, 2014).

Our studies so far demonstrate that simply changing the way competition is framed—without changing anything about women themselves—can eliminate the traditionally observed gender gap. Women have been observed to compete at lower rates than men when competition is presented as an active choice with the default of not competing (e.g., Niederle & Vesterlund, 2007). We set up our experiments to compare this typical opt-in condition to an experimental condition in which the default is that all applicants are automatically enrolled in a competition but can choose to opt-out. While we observed the standard gender gap in the traditional opt-in condition, we were able to completely eliminate the gender gap in the opt-out condition: women and men stayed enrolled in competition at the same rate (He et al., 2019, 2020). Our follow-up studies show that changing the default to one of competition shifts the perception of prevailing social norms without any negative downstream consequences for performance, well-being, or the likelihood of being selected for a job. These results should be of great interest to organizations and policy-makers who are serious about structural and systemic solutions to the problem of gender disparities in participation in competition. We hope that this and similar work will convince decision-makers that we need to move beyond trying to fix the women, or any group of individuals, but instead to fix the systems that give rise to and maintain inequality (Bohnet, 2016; Fitzsimons, Kay, & Kim, 2018; Kang & Kaplan, 2019; Kim et al., 2018).

Aside from the potential these results hold for reforming the framing of competitive selection processes, I am also very proud of this work because the lead author is my PhD student, Joyce He, a brilliant researcher and fantastic collaborator. Together with our coauthor, Professor Nico Lacetera, we have been developing this work over the past few years in a truly iterative and collaborative way. We are continuing to dig deeper into our initial findings as part of Joyce's dissertation, and I am very excited about the potential these results hold for application and policy reform.

LESSONS LEARNED: ADVICE FOR JUNIOR SCHOLARS

I have three pieces of advice for junior scholars as they work to incorporate their academic identities into their already multifaceted senses of self: (a) you do you, (b) haters gonna hate, and (c) everything is temporary. I continue to work on these themes myself and have found them to be particularly relevant as a woman and person of color working in academia. I hope that they will be encouraging to students whose social identities have been traditionally under-represented in this space. As emerging scholars of diversity and inclusion, they need to know that their experiences are valid and valued and that they are not alone in their fight to understand and, ultimately, break down injustices.

First, try not to get caught up in what other people think you should do or how you should act. There are many different paths to success and there is room for many different types of people in academia. You will not last unless you carve out a path that works for you, and only you can decide what that path looks like. Despite all the terrific advice out there about how to succeed as an academic, there is no single template that works for everyone. People present advice based on what has worked *for them*, which does not mean that it will work for you. It is up to you to figure this out by experimenting and being honest about what feels right. As an example, when I first started grad school, I felt tremendous pressure to ask questions during talks. This was a completely foreign concept to me, coming from a cultural background in which power-distance is so deeply respected and from an academic background where that had not been the norm. It did not feel authentic to me and none of the constant advice I received to "just ask a question" did anything to change my mind or teach me the skill; it only made me feel bad about myself and contributed to the already strong sense I had that I did not belong. All academic skills and behaviors develop over time, and my advice is to allow yourself the space to develop these things in your own time, even if others do not. This is about meeting yourself where you are and being kind to yourself, and is probably one of the hardest things about academia. Many of us end up in academia because we are high-achievers and have very high standards for ourselves. Unfortunately, this also means that we can be particularly susceptible to guilt brought on by feeling like we are not meeting other's expectations or prescriptions. There are many different ways to get to the same place, and the way that works for you and honors your authentic self is the right way for you.

The second piece of advice basically boils down to "haters gonna hate." If people are unkind or outright mean to you, dismissive of your ideas or contributions, or undermine your sense of belonging or self-worth, please understand that that says more about them (they are an a-hole; Sutton, 2007, 2010) than it does about you. As someone who has an inherent need to feel liked, it took me years to acknowledge this as a possibility, and even though I firmly believe it now, I still sometimes find myself falling into the same trap. One particularly salient example, again from grad school, is when a senior student compared me to another student in my cohort, saying how good he thought she was but that I was not similarly cut out for the program. He told me this in a casual, off-hand way; it was nothing to him, but I obsessed over that interaction for years, trying to figure out ways to get him to take me seriously, to like me, to think I was good enough and smart enough to be in the same program. Eventually, I realized that he had absolutely no basis to make such a judgment call and that his words were meant to hurt me, or at least to undermine and shake me up a bit. It really said very little about me but spoke volumes about him. My advice here is to be open to constructive, productive, and respectful feedback—invite it, embrace it—but train yourself to dismiss immediately from your mind any personal, destructive criticisms which are meant to tear you down and make you question your worth and belonging. There are many useful books and online tools from the cognitive behavioral therapy literature to help you with quieting excessive negativity from the haters you will encounter over the course of your life.

The final piece of advice I have for young scholars is to keep in mind that everything is temporary. You might not be happy with the way things are going right now in your personal or professional life, but these things will change . . . eventually. You have a finite amount of time, energy, and motivation in any given moment, so you will inevitably find yourself working on some things and completely failing at others all the time. The hard thing is that means you feel like you are always failing because there is always something that has to fall through the cracks; no one can do everything 100% perfectly all the time. The key is understanding that the things you think you are failing at now will be the things you feel like you are excelling at in the future and vice versa. One moment you will be struck by inspiration and the next you will feel completely stuck and overwhelmed. Everything changes; nothing stays the same. Life is full of highs and lows and ebbs and flows. Sometimes you just have to ride the wave.

LOOKING FORWARD: WHERE WE NEED TO GO NEXT

Gender and diversity are fascinating research topics because they develop and evolve in a constant conversation with our broader society. As recent examples, the #MeToo movement has launched renewed activity in research on sexual harassment (e.g., Jagsi, 2018; Jagsi et al., 2016; Kensbock, Bailey, Jennings, & Patiar, 2015; McLaughlin, Uggen, & Blackstone, 2017; O'Neil, Sojo, Fileborn, Scovelle, & Milner, 2018; Ozkazanc-Pan, 2019; Rosenthalm Smidt, & Freyd, 2016; Tenbrunsel, Rees, & Diekmann, 2019; Williams, 2018; Zeigler-Hill, Besser, Morag, & Keith Campbell, 2016); social discourse around *toxic masculinity* has given rise to new work on understanding male gender and modern masculinity (e.g., Berdahl, Cooper, Glick, Livingston, & Williams, 2018; Ely & Kimmel, 2018; Jivani, 2019; Ladge, Humberd, Baskerville Warkins, & Harrington, 2015; Pascoe, 2012; Pascoe & Bridges, 2016; PettyJohn, Muzzy, Maas, & McCauley, 2019; Stiller, 2019); and the "debate" around gender pronouns has motivated examinations of transgender identity and gender fluidity, highlighting the need for future gender research to think beyond the binary to understand how traditional gender stereotypes can affect people of all genders (e.g., Airton, 2018; Beauregard, Arevshatian, Booth, & Whittle, 2018; Collins, McFadden, Rocco, & Mathis, 2015; David, 2015; Davidson, 2016; Davis, 2017; Dietert & Dentice, 2015; Elias, Johnson, Ovando, & Ramirez, 2018; Fosbrook, 2019; Fosbrook & Kaplan, 2019; Goodman & Kaplan, 2018; Martinez, Sawyer, Thoroughgood,

Ruggs, & Smith, 2017; McFadden, 2015; Mizock et al., 2018; Ozturk & Tatli, 2016; Rudin et al., 2016; Ruggs, Martinez, Hebl, & Law, 2015; Sawyer, Thoroughgood, & Webster, 2016; Winter et al., 2016; Yoder & Mattheis, 2016). While by no means an exhaustive list, I think that these three areas are ripe for continued exploration by scholars and society and that their growth and development will significantly shape the direction of research on gender and diversity in the years to come. In addition, the management of multiple identities and their intersections (Gaither, 2015; Hirsh & Kang, 2016; Kang & Bodenhausen, 2015; Ramarajan, 2014; Ramarajan & Reid, 2013) remains a critical area for future research. Future work will hopefully continue to guide us toward a richer and more meaningful understanding of intersectionality across a variety of social group identities.

Aside from these content areas, it would be fruitful for future research on gender and diversity to harness the many insights we have gained from across the behavioral sciences to design and experiment with structural interventions (Bohnet, 2016; Kang & Kaplan, 2019; Thaler & Sunstein, 2009). I think the future of our field lies in taking a solution- and intervention-based approach moving forward. Our work on gender and competition mentioned above is one example of zooming out from a particular finding—women are less likely to participate in competition—to design and test a behaviorally informed intervention that could be easily applied across a variety of contexts (He et al., 2019, 2020). Similar intervention-focused work shows that defaults can be used to eliminate the gender gap in leadership selection (Erkal, Gangadharan, Xiao, 2019); that providing precise and objective qualification criteria on a job application reduces the gender gap in willingness to apply (Coffman, Collis, & Kulkarni, 2019); that an "evaluation nudge" wherein applicants are evaluated jointly rather than separately reduces gender bias in selection (Bohnet, van Geen, & Bazerman, 2016); and, relatedly, that making hiring and selection decisions for sets of applications rather than one-by-one increases gender diversity (Chang, Kirgios, Rai, & Milkman, 2020). Each of these studies tests structural and procedural interventions, and hopefully, the field will continue this move away from attempts to fix the women or fix the minorities and focus on fixing the systems and processes that create and perpetuate biases themselves. I hope that testing new and exciting interventions with laboratory and field experiments will become the next hot topic in gender and diversity science. These types of interventions should also allow us to focus on the "I" of "D&I"—inclusion. Researchers, practitioners, and policy-makers have spent at least 30 years now focusing on increasing representation of women and minorities (diversity), with relatively little attention paid to understanding what it takes to make them feel welcome and fostering a sense of belonging (inclusion). Hopefully, a move to a more intervention-based approach will help us to make progress on the inclusion side of the story as well.

REFERENCES

Airton, L. (2018). *Gender: Your guide: a gender-friendly primer on what to know, what to say, and what to do in the new gender culture* (First Adams Media hardcover edition). Avon, MA: Adams Media.

Beauregard, T. A., Arevshatian, L., Booth, J. E., & Whittle, S. (2018). Listen carefully: Transgender voices in the workplace. *The International Journal of Human Resource Management, 29*(5), 857–884. https://doi.org/10.1080/09585192.2016.1234503

Berdahl, J. L., Cooper, M., Glick, P., Livingston, R. W., & Williams, J. C. (2018). Work as a Masculinity Contest. *Journal of Social Issues, 74*(3), 422–448. https://doi.org/10.1111/josi.12289

Bohnet, I. (2016). *What works: Gender equality by design.* Cambridge, MA: The Belknap Press of Harvard University Press.

Bohnet, I., van Geen, A., & Bazerman, M. (2016). When performance trumps gender bias: Joint vs. separate evaluation. *Management Science, 62*(5), 1225–1234. https://doi.org/10.1287/mnsc.2015.2186

Carroll, G. D., Choi, J. J., Laibson, D., Madrian, B. C., & Metrick, A. (2009). Optimal defaults and active decisions. *The Quarterly Journal of Economics, 124*(4), 1639–1674. https://doi.org/10.1162/qjec.2009.124.4.1639

Chang, E. H., Kirgios, E. L., Rai, A., & Milkman, K. L. (2020). The isolated choice effect and its implications for gender diversity in organizations. *Management Science, 66*(6), 2752–2761. https://doi.org/10.1287/mnsc.2019.3533

Chang, E. H., Milkman, K. L., Gromet, D. M., Rebele, R. W., Massey, C., Duckworth, A. L., & Grant, A. M. (2019). The mixed effects of online diversity training. *Proceedings of the National Academy of Sciences, 116*(16), 7778–7783. https://doi.org/10.1073/pnas.1816076116

Choi, J. J., Laibson, D., Madrian, B. C., & Metrick, A. (2002). Defined contribution pensions: Plan rules, participant choices, and the path of least resistance. *Tax Policy and the Economy, 16*, 67–113. https://doi.org/10.1086/654750

Coffman, K. B., Collis, M., & Kulkarni, L. (2019). *When to Apply?* [Harvard Business School Working Paper Series, Working Paper 20-2062]. https://www.hbs.edu/faculty/Publication%20Files/20-062_2d1ab2b7-432e-464a-9944-468201bcbd9f.pdf

Collins, J. C., McFadden, C., Rocco, T. S., & Mathis, M. K. (2015). The problem of transgender marginalization and exclusion: Critical actions for human resource development. *Human Resource Development Review, 14*(2), 205–226. https://doi.org/10.1177/1534484315581755

David, E. (2015). Purple-collar labor: Transgender workers and queer value at global call centers in the Philippines. *Gender & Society, 29*(2), 169–194. https://doi.org/10.1177/0891243214558868

Davidson, S. (2016). Gender inequality: Nonbinary transgender people in the workplace. *Cogent Social Sciences, 2*(1). https://doi.org/10.1080/23311886.2016.1236511

Davis, H. F. (2017). *Beyond trans: Does gender matter?* New York, NY: New York University Press.

Dietert, M., & Dentice, D. (2015). The transgender military experience: Their battle for workplace rights. *SAGE Open, 5*(2), 1–12. https://doi.org/10.1177/2158244015584231

Dobbin, F., & Kalev, A. (2016, July 1). *Why diversity programs fail.* Cambridge, MA: Harvard Business Review. https://hbr.org/2016/07/why-diversity-programs-fail

Downs, J. S., Loewenstein, G., & Wisdom, J. (2009). Strategies for promoting healthier food choices. *American Economic Review, 99*(2), 159–164. https://doi.org/10.1257/aer.99.2.159

Elias, N., Johnson, R. L., Ovando, D., & Ramirez, J. (2018). Improving transgender policy for a more equitable workplace. *Journal of Public Management & Social Policy, 24*(2), 54–81.

Ely, R. J., & Kimmel, M. (2018). Thoughts on the workplace as a masculinity contest. *Journal of Social Issues, 74*(3), 628–634. https://doi.org/10.1111/josi.12290

Erkal, N., Gangadharan, L., & Xiao, E. (2019). *Leadership selection: Can changing the default break the glass ceiling?* Retrieved from https://ssrn.com/abstract=3022386

Exley, C. L., & Kessler, J. B. (2019). *The gender gap in self-promotion* (Working Paper No. 26345). Washington, DC: National Bureau of Economic Research. https://doi.org/10.3386/w26345

Fitzsimons, G., Kay, A., & Kim, J. Y. (2018, July 30). "Lean In" messages and the illusion of control. *Harvard Business Review.* https://hbr.org/2018/07/lean-in-messages-and-the-illusion-of-control

Flory, J. A., Leibbrandt, A., & List, J. A. (2015). Do competitive workplaces deter female workers? A large-scale natural field experiment on job entry decisions. *The Review of Economic Studies, 82*(1), 122–155. https://doi.org/10.1093/restud/rdu030

Fosbrook, B. (2019, October 8). Working beyond the gender binary. *Gender and the Economy.* https://www.gendereconomy.org/working-beyond-the-gender-binary/

Fosbrook, B., & Kaplan, S. (2019). The work of trans inclusion: A case study of Amazon's Trans-Affirmative Action Program. *Rotman Institute for Gender and the Economy Research Briefs, 12.*

Gaither, S. E. (2015). "Mixed" results: Multiracial research and identity explorations. *Current Directions in Psychological Science, 24*(2), 114–119. https://doi.org/10.1177/0963721414558115

Goodman, R., & Kaplan, S. (2018). *Reconsidering gender diversity in economic development (SSIR).* Retrieved from https://ssir.org/articles/entry/reconsidering_gender_diversity_in_economic_development

He, J., Kang, S., & Lacetera, N. (2019). *Leaning in or not leaning out? Opt-out choice framing attenuates gender differences in the decision to compete* (Working Paper No. 26484). Washington, DC: National Bureau of Economic Research. https://doi.org/10.3386/w26484

He, J., Kang, S., & Lacetera, N. (2020, February 8). Addressing gender inequality via choice architecture. *VoxEU.Org.* https://voxeu.org/article/addressing-gender-inequality-choice-architecture

Hirsh, J. B., & Kang, S. K. (2016). Mechanisms of identity conflict: Uncertainty, anxiety, and the behavioral inhibition system. *Personality and Social Psychology Review, 20*(3), 223–244. https://doi.org/10.1177/1088868315589475

Jagsi, R. (2018). Sexual harassment in medicine—#MeToo. *New England Journal of Medicine, 378*(3), 209–211. https://doi.org/10.1056/NEJMp1715962

Jagsi, R., Griffith, K. A., Jones, R., Perumalswami, C. R., Ubel, P., & Stewart, A. (2016). Sexual harassment and discrimination experiences of academic medical faculty. *JAMA, 315*(19), 2120–2121. https://doi.org/10.1001/jama.2016.2188

Jivani, J. (2019). *Why young men: The dangerous allure of violent movements and what we can do about it.* New York, NY: All Points Books.

Johnson, E. J., Bellman, S., & Lohse, G. L. (2002). Defaults, framing and privacy: Why opting in-opting out. *Marketing Letters, 13*(1), 5–15. https://doi.org/10.1023/A:1015044207315

Johnson, E. J., & Goldstein, D. (2003). Do defaults save lives? *Science, 302*(5649), 1338–1339. https://doi.org/10.1126/science.1091721

Kalev, A., Dobbin, F., & Kelly, E. (2006). Best practices or best guesses? Assessing the efficacy of corporate affirmative action and diversity policies. *American Sociological Review, 71*(4), 589–617. https://doi.org/10.1177/000312240607100404

Kang, S. K., & Bodenhausen, G. V. (2015). Multiple identities in social perception and interaction: challenges and opportunities. *Annual Review of Psychology, 66*(1), 547–574. https://doi.org/10.1146/annurev-psych-010814-015025

Kang, S. K., & Kaplan, S. (2019). Working toward gender diversity and inclusion in medicine: Myths and solutions. *The Lancet, 393*(10171), 579–586. https://doi.org/10.1016/S0140-6736(18)33138-6

Kensbock, S., Bailey, J., Jennings, G., & Patiar, A. (2015). Sexual harassment of women working as room attendants within 5-star hotels. *Gender, Work, & Organization, 22*(1), 36–50. https://doi.org/10.1111/gwao.12064

Kim, J. Y., Fitzsimons, G. M., & Kay, A. C. (2018). Lean in messages increase attributions of women's responsibility for gender inequality. *Journal of Personality and Social Psychology, 115*(6), 974–1001. https://doi.org/10.1037/pspa0000129

Ladge, J. J., Humberd, B. K., Baskerville Watkins, M., & Harrington, B. (2015). Updating the organization MAN: An examination of involved fathering in the workplace. *Academy of Management Perspectives, 29*(1), 152–171. https://doi.org/10.5465/amp.2013.0078

Leslie, L. M. (2018). Diversity initiative effectiveness: A typological theory of unintended consequences. *Academy of Management Review, 44*(3), 538–563. https://doi.org/10.5465/amr.2017.0087

Martinez, L. R., Sawyer, K., Thoroughgood, C. N., Ruggs, E. N., & Smith, N. A. (2017). The importance of being "me": The relation between authentic identity expression and transgender employees' work-related attitudes and experiences. *The Journal of Applied Psychology, 102*(2), 215–226. https://doi.org/10.1037/apl0000168

McFadden, C. (2015). Lesbian, gay, bisexual, and transgender careers and human resource development: A systematic literature review. *Human Resource Development Review, 14*(2), 125–162. https://doi.org/10.1177/1534484314549456

McLaughlin, H., Uggen, C., & Blackstone, A. (2017). The economic and career effects of sexual harassment on working women. *Gender & Society, 31*(3), 333–358. https://doi.org/10.1177/0891243217704631

Mizock, L., Riley, J., Yuen, N., Woodrum, T. D., Sotilleo, E. A., & Ormerod, A. J. (2018). Transphobia in the workplace: A qualitative study of employment stigma. *Stigma and Health, 3*(3), 275–282. https://doi.org/10.1037/sah0000098

Moss-Racusin, C. A., & Rudman, L. A. (2010). Disruptions in women's self-promotion: The backlash avoidance model. *Psychology of Women Quarterly, 34*(2), 186–202. https://doi.org/10.1111/j.1471-6402.2010.01561.x

Niederle, M., & Vesterlund, L. (2007). Do women shy away from competition? Do men compete too much? *The Quarterly Journal of Economics, 122*(3), 1067–1101. https://doi.org/10.1162/qjec.122.3.1067

O'Neil, A., Sojo, V., Fileborn, B., Scovelle, A. J., & Milner, A. (2018). The #MeToo movement: An opportunity in public health? *The Lancet, 391*(10140), 2587–2589. https://doi.org/10.1016/S0140-6736(18)30991-7

Ozkazanc-Pan, B. (2019). On agency and empowerment in a #MeToo world. *Gender, Work & Organization, 26*(8), 1212–1220. https://doi.org/10.1111/gwao.12311

Ozturk, M. B., & Tatli, A. (2016). Gender identity inclusion in the workplace: Broadening diversity management research and practice through the case of transgender employees in the UK. *The International Journal of Human Resource Management, 27*(8), 781–802. https://doi.org/10.1080/09585192.2015.1042902

Pascoe, C. J. (2012). *Dude, you're a fag: Masculinity and sexuality in high school; with a new preface.* Berkeley: University of California Press.

Pascoe, C. J., & Bridges, T. (Eds.). (2016). *Exploring masculinities: Identity, inequality, continuity and change.* Oxford, England: Oxford University Press.

PettyJohn, M. E., Muzzey, F. K., Maas, M. K., & McCauley, H. L. (2019). #HowIWillChange: Engaging men and boys in the #MeToo movement. *Psychology of Men & Masculinities, 20*(4), 612–622. https://doi.org/10.1037/men0000186

Phelan, J. E., Moss-Racusin, C. A., & Rudman, L. A. (2008). Competent yet out in the cold: Shifting criteria for hiring reflect backlash toward agentic women. *Psychology of Women Quarterly, 32*(4), 406–413. https://doi.org/10.1111/j.1471-6402.2008.00454.x

Ramarajan, L. (2014). Past, present and future research on multiple identities: Toward an intrapersonal network approach. *Academy of Management Annals, 8*(1), 589–659. https://doi.org/10.5465/19416520.2014.912379

Ramarajan, L., & Reid, E. (2013). Shattering the myth of separate worlds: Negotiating nonwork identities at work. *Academy of Management Review, 38*(4), 621–644. https://doi.org/10.5465/amr.2011.0314

Rosenthal, M. N., Smidt, A. M., & Freyd, J. J. (2016). Still second class: Sexual harassment of graduate students. *Psychology of Women Quarterly, 40*(3), 364–377. https://doi.org/10.1177/0361684316644838

Rudin, J., Yang, Y., Ruane, S., Ross, L., Farro, A., & Billing, T. (2016). Transforming attitudes about transgender employee rights. *Journal of Management Education, 40*(1), 30–46. https://doi.org/10.1177/1052562915609959

Rudman, L. A., & Glick, P. (1999). Feminized management and backlash toward agentic women: The hidden costs to women of a kinder, gentler image of middle managers. *Journal of Personality and Social Psychology, 77*(5), 1004–1010.

Rudman, L. A., & Glick, P. (2001). Prescriptive gender stereotypes and backlash toward agentic women. *Journal of Social Issues, 57*(4), 743–762. https://doi.org/10.1111/0022-4537.00239

Ruggs, E. N., Martinez, L. R., Hebl, M. R., & Law, C. L. (2015). Workplace "trans"-actions: How organizations, coworkers, and individual openness influence perceived gender identity discrimination. *Psychology of Sexual Orientation and Gender Diversity, 2*(4), 404–412. https://doi.org/10.1037/sgd0000112

Sandberg, S. (2013). *Lean in: Women, work, and the will to lead* (First edition). New York, NY: Alfred A. Knopf.

Sawyer, K., Thoroughgood, C., & Webster, J. (2016). Queering the gender binary: Understanding transgender workplace experiences. In T. Köllen (Ed.), *Sexual orientation and transgender issues in organizations: Global perspectives on LGBT workforce diversity* (pp. 21–42). Cham, Switzerland: Springer International. https://doi.org/10.1007/978-3-319-29623-4_2

Stiller, C. (2019). *Modern manhood: Conversations about the complicated world of being a good man today* (First Tiller Press hardcover edition). New York, NY: Tiller Press.

Sutton, R. I. (2007, March 17). Why I wrote the no asshole rule. *Harvard Business Review.* Retrieved from https://hbr.org/2007/03/why-i-wrote-the-no-asshole-rule

Sutton, R. I. (2010). *The no asshole rule: Building a civilized workplace and surviving one that isn't* (1st trade ed.). New York, NY: Business Plus.

Tenbrunsel, A. E., Rees, M. R., & Diekmann, K. A. (2019). Sexual harassment in academia: Ethical climates and bounded ethicality. *Annual Review of Psychology, 70*(1), 245–270. https://doi.org/10.1146/annurev-psych-010418-102945

Thaler, R. H., & Sunstein, C. R. (2009). *Nudge: Improving decisions about health, wealth, and happiness* (Rev. and expanded ed). London, England: Penguin Books.

van Dalen, H. P., & Henkens, K. (2014). Comparing the effects of defaults in organ donation systems. *Social Science & Medicine (1982), 106,* 137–142. https://doi.org/10.1016/j.socscimed.2014.01.052

Williams, C. L. (2018, May 4). Sexual harassment in organizations: A critique of current research and policy. In R. Refinetti (Ed.), *Sexual harassment and sexual consent* (pp. 19–44). New York, NY: Routledge. https://doi.org/10.4324/9781315129259-3

Winter, S., Diamond, M., Green, J., Karasic, D., Reed, T., Whittle, S., & Wylie, K. (2016). Transgender people: Health at the margins of society. *The Lancet, 388*(10042), 390–400. https://doi.org/10.1016/S0140-6736(16)00683-8

Yoder, J. B., & Mattheis, A. (2016). Queer in STEM: Workplace experiences reported in a national survey of LGBTQA individuals in science, technology, engineering, and mathematics careers. *Journal of Homosexuality, 63*(1), 1–27. https://doi.org/10.1080/00918369.2015.1078632

Zeigler-Hill, V., Besser, A., Morag, J., & Keith Campbell, W. (2016). The Dark Triad and sexual harassment proclivity. *Personality and Individual Differences, 89,* 47–54. https://doi.org/10.1016/j.paid.2015.09.048

CHAPTER 14

MOTIVATING AND ENABLING GENDER BALANCE

Zoe Kinias
INSEAD, Asia

In 1993, India instituted a law that reserved leadership positions for women in randomly selected village councils. The goal of the quota was to improve gender balance, and it worked. Within the span of 8 years, the representation of women leaders in village councils increased from 5% to 40%.

And the law had another, perhaps unanticipated, impact on gender dynamics, as it shifted the career aspirations and educational ambitions of adolescent girls in India. Research later showed that, in West Bengal villages where a woman chief councilor had been appointed for two election cycles, the gender gap in career aspirations closed by 32% in adolescents and 25% in their parents (Beaman, Duflo, Pande, & Toplova, 2012). Further, the gender gap in secondary educational attainment was virtually eliminated. In just 13 years, the presence of strong female role models had changed the lives of young girls and their families.

This story demonstrates something that has always fascinated me as a person and as an academic: the degree to which psychological experiences and behavior are malleable and shaped by social, organizational, and

Perspectives on Gender and Work, pages 169–180

governmental systems. The mutual co-creation of individuals' psychological experiences and the systems and structures that surround them continually enthralls me. In particular, I am passionate about the impact that interventions—including social-psychological, organizational, and governmental—can have on gender balance in societies.

I have both systematically investigated these phenomena throughout my professional career and personally experienced them throughout my life.

COMING OF AGE IN AMERICA, EGYPT, AND GREECE

I was born and raised mostly in the United States. Early in the 1980s, when I was in primary school, my father told me that I could be president of our country one day while he could not; as I was born a U.S. citizen and he was raised in war-torn Greece in the 1940–50s and immigrated to the United States in the 1960s. I remember thinking when he spoke of me being the president that it would be my responsibility to act on behalf of our family to serve a greater good. And I remember being inspired by that idea.

However, even before I hit adolescence, I became painfully aware that presidents weren't women. I also realized that women and girls often didn't garner the same respect—or have the same rights or opportunities—as men and boys. This was true in my own home. For example, typical of many middle-class American households in the 1980s and 1990s, my brother had a computer in his bedroom, and I did not. Some scholars later attributed this social norm as a contributor to the development of gender segregation in technology and coding (Dryburgh, 2000; Fisher, Margolis, & Miller, 1997).

When I was in junior high and high school, I spent my summers in Egypt with my father, who was leading water treatment projects. There, I witnessed gender inequality that was explicit and unapologetic. Power and resources were disproportionally allocated to men. Women had limited rights and freedom, enforced both by the law and extreme social constraints. For example, grown women were expected to live with their parents, follow curfews, and regularly call home to check in on weekends—even when they were college educated and gainfully employed. Women weren't permitted to own property, aside from the (often gold) jewelry they might wear around their necks or wrists. I learned of families losing their livelihoods following the father's passing; when there were no sons, then businesses could be rightfully claimed by the father's brothers without even compensation to his wife or daughters. Women's rights had also worsened over the decades. Although state feminism of the 1960s had protected women through anti-discrimination employment laws and provision of government jobs with excellent benefits for women including childcare and maternity leave, economic and political liberalization had eroded many of women's rights and opportunities by the 1990s (Hatem, 1992). This pattern of gender imbalance troubled me. Had I known about the changes that were taking place in the village councils of West Bengal, I would have been reassured.

Witnessing the degree of inequality in Egypt heightened my sensitivity to the issues in my own country. Although I recognized that the United States was clearly more progressive than Egypt and was grateful for it, I also knew that it wasn't fully egalitarian or as meritocratic as it superficially appeared to be. Gender inequity was still present in America; it was just subtler. For example, while women were told that they could "do anything," the representation of leaders in business, government, science, and technology were disproportionately men. I do not recall exactly when it happened, but by the time I was 14 or 15, I had made a somewhat conscious decision to be more like a man—although I had a couple of beloved female friends in high school who tolerated my eccentricity, I mostly had male friends who reassured me that I was "one of the guys." Over time, this evolved so that although I remained determined to be tough like the guys, I grew to feel much more connected to and trusting of women. I explored the work of feminist writers, such as Virginia Woolf's (1929) *A Room of One's Own*, and celebrated landmark moments in gender equality, such as Ruth Bader Ginsberg's 1993 appointment as the second female U.S. Supreme Court Justice.

I came to understand that women typically had to work harder and perform better to get to the same place as men; they experience phenomena often described as "headwinds and tailwinds" (Chugh, 2018). I also came to recognize that the financial independence of women was critically intertwined with their social and personal empowerment. To have the freedom to determine their future and author their destiny, women needed to find meaningful, gainful employment outside of the home. Finally, I understood that, in order to maintain and expand our freedom, women needed to have more direct influence by leading in government and business.

I believed strongly that men and women should have the same respect, opportunities, and freedoms in life. And I wanted to contribute to that change.

MY PATH TO AND GETTING ESTABLISHED IN ACADEMIA

At university, I quickly became interested in social psychology and was mentored by two very supportive faculty members in the Honors College at Arizona State University. The first was Delia Saenz, who built her career investigating inequality through a social cognition lens (e.g., tokenism; Lord & Saenz, 1985; Saenz, 1994; Saenz & Lord, 1989) and improving the subjective experience of members of underrepresented groups. I have a vivid memory of the pivotal "ah-ha!" moment I had while sitting in her introduction to social psychology course and realizing that she was someone like me, a Latina woman—and she was a social psychology professor. Although I'm not Latina, I felt very connected to Delia's Mexican American identity, and I experienced her as a real person. This was partly because of cultural similarities between Latin and Mediterranean cultures and partly because I felt like a bit of an outsider in a White man's world. Second, Steven Neuberg was (and still is) an experimental social psychologist who utilized social cognition frameworks with an evolutionary perspective (e.g., Fiske & Neuberg, 1990; Shapiro & Neuberg, 2007) and helped set a foundation for 25 of his undergraduate students to later earn PhDs. I was one of his first undergraduates, and I learned so much from him. Delia and Steve modeled inclusion, support, and rigor for me. They substantively developed my theoretical and analytical thinking as well as my confidence as a scholar.

As an undergraduate, I began to increasingly connect with graduate students who taught me how to fund further education through teaching and research. This practical information, combined with the support I received from Steve and Delia and the identifiable role model I found in Delia, enabled me to imagine myself as a scholar. (Later, I came to deeply and academically understand the value of role models for women. See Cortland & Kinias, 2019.) As I considered PhD programs, Delia advised me to pursue a basic education in social psychology—as opposed to a more applied degree—to create more opportunities post-education. This was excellent advice. My PhD program at the University of California, Santa Barbara was very strong with respect to rigorous research methods and an emphasis on social cognition.

In graduate school, *The Nature of Prejudice* (Allport, 1954) and *Stigma: Notes on the Management of Spoiled Identity* (Goffman, 1963) as well as the then-current work on intergroup relations, especially intergroup emotion theory (Mackie, Devos, & Smith, 2000), including the target's perspective (e.g., Major & O'Brien, 2005) and culture (e.g., Kim & Markus, 1999) influenced me greatly. This inspired some of my early research projects, which focused on understandings of and emotional experiences of social groups (Seger, Smith, Kinias, & Mackie, 2009), the experience of social groups in context (O'Brien, Kinias, & Major, 2008; Simon, Kinias, O'Brien, Major, & Bivolaru, 2013), and how to facilitate resilience (Sherman, Kinias, Major, Kim, & Prenevost, 2007). Again, strong female faculty featured in my development prominently, as I worked closely with Diane Mackie, Brenda Major, Heejung Kim, and Nancy Collins, who are brilliant and provide very diverse representations of how to embody academic excellence. By the fourth year of my PhD program, I was increasingly curious about how to apply the processes that we were investigating, with thoughts such as, "What should we do as a result of what we are discovering? What can people do with this that will benefit society?"

Interested in doing more applied work in this area—including how to optimize individual and group performance—I started exploring career possibilities in business schools. This led me to a post-doctoral fellowship at the Kellogg School of Management at Northwestern University, where I had the opportunity to work with team expert Leigh Thompson (Thompson, 2008) and the esteemed diversity scholar Katherine (Kathy) Phillips (e.g., Phillips, Northcraft, & Neale, 2006; Williams & O'Reilly, 1998) who still serves as a source of inspiration for me. As I write this, I am sitting at a café in New York City where I came to see Kathy off into the next life. Our community of women and men who research and teach diversity in business schools is still reeling from the tragic loss of this positive force of nature, but I feel determined to better live by her example of strength, creative problem-solving, and embracing opportunities to educate in every way. While at Kellogg, I began translating the work of social psychologists into business skills and practices. In 2009, after two years at Kellogg, I moved to INSEAD in Singapore for a position as an assistant professor of organizational behavior.

At the time, Herminia Ibarra was the Cora Chaired Professor of Leadership and Learning in Organizational Behavior at INSEAD in Fontainebleau, having been recruited from Harvard Business School where she was already an established scholar with expertise in networks and identity (e.g., Ibarra, 1993). I did not know until many years later—while my own tenure file was under review after Herminia had moved on to London Business School—but before I joined INSEAD, Herminia had led a faculty gender diversity task force modeled after a process established to work by sociological research of organizational policies and practices (Kalev, Dobbin, & Kelly, 2006). She also represented INSEAD's organizational behavior (OB) group, both as area chair (2010–2013) and as a member of the Faculty Evaluation Committee (2010–2012). I am deeply grateful for Herminia's efforts, as they set a foundation for my current role and work at INSEAD. Today, I serve as associate professor and area chair of the Organizational Behavior Department and academic director of the INSEAD Gender Initiative (IGI). I am very proud to be the first "homegrown" woman to earn tenure within our OB department across INSEAD's Europe and Asia campuses, and also now lead our department as area chair. In my role with the IGI, which began in 2017, I have more opportunities to be of service than I ever could have imagined during my graduate school days, when I wondered how people might engender actual societal change.

They say that farming was easier for the European settlers in North America because the indigenous people had earlier established agriculture. I am keenly aware that Herminia's work, as well as that of many current colleagues and early meaningful contributors at INSEAD whom I never had the pleasure of meeting, including Edith Penrose and Erin Anderson, have made it easier for me to do what I now do for the school. I am grateful to every past, present, and future contributor to gender balance at INSEAD.

RECENT AND CURRENT RESEARCH

As a researcher, there is one project that I see as my largest contribution to gender balance theory and practice thus far. This research was motivated by a gender balance issue I observed among MBA students at a global business school. The students exhibited a gender gap in academic performance (i.e., grades), despite the fact that the men and women entering the competitive business school had the same GMAT scores. I connected this problem to one that educational psychologists had previously investigated and intervened to fix. Namely, a racial performance gap between minority and White junior high school students in America widens as minority students become aware of negative stereotypes about their groups in the context of academics, and this identity-relevant gap widening caused by stereotype threat can be eliminated by affirming children's self-systems through values reflections (Cohen, Garcia, Spfel, & Master, 2006).

I hypothesized that given the significant underrepresentation and negative stereotyping of women in global business leadership, stereotype threat (Roberson & Kulik, 2007; Spencer, Steele, & Quinn, 1997; Steele & Aronson, 1995) could explain the mysterious gender gap in performance among MBA students. To test this hypothesis and the related solution, Jessica Sim and I developed an intervention that we rigorously assessed with two cohorts of students. At the start of their MBA program, students in the self-affirmation condition completed a writing exercise in which they reflected on their own core personal values and how they manifested those values in their daily lives. The objective was for all students in this condition to be grounded with a more robust self-view. For women (but not for men), we predicted that this would translate into less self-doubt resulting from concerns about confirming negative stereotypes. Students in other experimental conditions reflected on values including those of their business school or on other people's core personal values.

Indeed, the core personal values self-affirmation intervention effectively closed the MBA performance gap through a reduction in women's self-doubt (Kinias & Sim, 2016). Because all MBAs in the intervention condition were invited to bring their affirmed selves to a new context in which women are underrepresented, the women MBAs were able to feel that their whole selves (not just the part of them that is negatively stereotyped) were part of the program and, therefore, they could perform to their ability. This research finding has also been replicated and extended at a competitive U.S. business school (Kim, Brockner, & Block, 2020), and we now provide this self-system buffering intervention to every MBA student that comes to INSEAD.

This research is meaningful for me because it developed theory in three ways: (a) it demonstrated benefits of self-affirmation to adult women with working experience who might not have been buffered because their identities are already too well established; (b) it worked for global women who could be expected to be less individualistic on average than the average American; and (b) it established an important boundary condition for values-based self-affirmation efficacy—that they must not include organizational values. This research is also meaningful to me because it adds practical value.

I am also excited about a number of other projects on which our core IGI research team is currently working. For example, in six correlational and experimental studies, Clarissa Cortland and I have found that women who recall concerns about confirming gender stereotypes are more motivated to develop gender balance within their organizations; specifically, they both state that they want more women in top leadership and take action to develop and advocate on behalf of other women (Cortland & Kinias, 2020). We, along with Chiara Trombini, are also investigating methods for engaging both men and women in efforts to develop gender balance in organizations. We continue our rigorous research on supporting the resiliency of women during identity-relevant transitions in organizational settings.

FUTURE DIRECTIONS

At INSEAD, my current role includes research, teaching, and institutional service. Because both research and impact are so close to my heart, I strive to integrate my own and others' research findings into all my teaching and institutional service work and to fold back insights from those impact conversations into my research.

Along these lines, in Spring 2019, Modupe Akinola, Michael Norton, Kathy Phillips, and I organized an intimate working conference with the goal of developing rigorous, research-based pedagogy for building diversity in business leadership through students as our touchpoints (Kinias, Akinola, Carter, Norton, & Phillips, 2019). This was a shared vision for all of us, but Kathy was the one who made it happen in many ways. Heartbreaking as it will be to continue without her, we must in her honor. The impact of effectively educating business students and executive participants on how to be inclusive—on an individual and organizational level—can be transformational, as those students and participants have a substantial immediate and long-term influence on business and society.

This speaks to a larger shift I am currently observing with respect to gender diversity, equity, and inclusion. After devoting much work to understanding and diagnosing the problem of gender imbalance, many scholars are increasingly focused on solving it.

Within the IGI, we are often approached by organizations seeking our help to address their gender balance problems. We also see growing academic interest in the systems, structures, processes, and psychological interventions that facilitate the inclusion of women. These interventions can enable organizations to increase the numeric representation of women and, in turn, the performance of organizations, teams, and boards (Joshi, Neely, Emrich, Griffiths, & George, 2015). We also see an increased focus on how gender intersects with other identities. Top diversity scholars are investigating these intersectional questions (Purdie-Vaughns & Eibach, 2008; Rosenthal, 2016) mostly in U.S. contexts, with respect to race and ethnicity (Sanchez-Hucles & Davis, 2010). There is also substantial demand from multinational organizations and business leaders for increased consideration of gender balance through a global lens.

ADVICE TO YOUNG SCHOLARS

Having been asked to advise young scholars, I say three things.

First, investigate the development of gender balance rigorously and define your research identity broadly, ensuring that your work complements mainstream topics and connects to broader audiences. For example, if your training and interests are more psychological, consider connections to fundamental frameworks such as cognition, motivation, and well-being. If your training and interests are more sociological, you might focus on gender in the context of social structures and networks. Or perhaps you are passionate about machine learning, and therefore want to focus on how to intervene on the biases inherent in and exacerbated by algorithms. Why would such an approach be useful? I suggest it because it provides essential mainstream credibility. This is because although there are noteworthy exceptions, most gender scholars must be hired into departments in which having a gender scholar is not the primary objective, and even when it is, we are hired as colleagues to others who have different interests. Therefore, we must have substantive intellectual connection with those who study other topics. Consider the model set by Mikki Hebl editing this book, whose expertise is recognized for rigorously investigating real-world discrimination and inclusion issues, including but not limited to gender. Or consider the example of Peter Glick, who complements his gender studies by investigating the social-cognitive processes of prejudice more broadly. These scholars are among the many role models featured in this volume, and I am humbled to share their company as a fellow author.

Second, if you believe it is time for change, position yourself in a place that cares about impact in addition to scholarship. That might mean, for example, working for a university that is invested in or open to pedagogic development around diversity, equity, and inclusion. If you are academically successful, that can open up opportunities to work "in the trenches" for developing gender balance within your own university. In many academic institutions our tenure is based on research productivity and impact, with some attention to effective teaching and institutional service, so we need to focus on research as a primary objective pre-tenure. And then, after achieving tenure, we can dedicate more time and energy to our impact work, such as working with colleagues and the school's leadership on inclusive practices in classes, developing courses on the content about which we feel passionate (see Harvard Business Press, 2019).

Third, identify organizational partners who want to collaborate in a way that enables the co-creation of solutions to problems. Work with those that want to develop women leaders *and create opportunities for them* to improve gender balance and better utilize talent—the organizations that really care about gender balance, rather than those who only want to "tick the box" without committing to real change. Doing this can enable knowledge-creation through evidence-based theory development and also promote knowledge-sharing in a way that benefits your career and furthers your partners' goals.

CONCLUSION

As academics, we have the privilege of opportunities to create moments—between teaching and paper revision deadlines and committee work and everything else we run around doing—to reflect on the impact we want to have through our research, teaching, professional, and personal communities. In these moments of reflection, I increasingly find myself returning to thoughts about how to create environments in which everyone, especially those who might disproportionately struggle due to gender, race, religion, nationality, and so on, can thrive. First, as role models for others, we must live and work firmly grounded in our own values and as the best versions of ourselves we can be. Beyond this, I also strive to create and embrace all opportunities to experiment with methods for motivating and creating positive change both with rigorous research methods and through observation of the dynamic systems in which I operate. May our work have impact at the scale of the Indian village councils, until such time as we are no longer needed!

REFERENCES

Allport, G. W. (1954) *The nature of prejudice.* Cambridge, MA: Perseus Books.

Beaman, L., Duflo, E., Pande, R., & Topalova, P. (2012). Female leadership raises aspirations and educational attainment for girls: A policy experiment in India. *Science, 335*(6068), 582–586.

Chugh, D. (2018). *The person you mean to be: how good people fight bias.* New York, NY: HarperBusiness.

Cohen, G. L., Garcia, J., Apfel, N., & Master, A. (2006). Reducing the racial achievement gap: A social-psychological intervention. *Science, 313*(5791),1307–1310.

Cortland, C. I., & Kinias, Z. (2019). Stereotype threat and women's work satisfaction: The importance of role models. *Archives of Scientific Psychology, 7*(1), 81–89.

Cortland, C. I., & Kinias, Z. (2020). *Stereotype threat's silver lining: Motivation for change* (Manuscript submitted for publication).

Dryburgh, H. (2000). Underrepresentation of girls and women in computer science: Classification of 1990s research. *Journal of Educational Computing Research, 23*(2), 181–202.

Fisher, A., Margolis, J., & Miller, F. (1997). Undergraduate women in computer science. *ACM SIGCSE Bulletin, 29*(1), 106–110.

Fiske, S. T., & Neuberg, S. L. (1990). A continuum of impression formation, from category-based to individuating processes: influences of information and motivation on attention and interpretation. *Advances in Experimental Social Psychology, 23*, 1–74.

Goffman, E. (1963). *Stigma: Notes on the management of spoiled identity.* New York, NY: Simon & Schuster.

Harvard Business Press. (2019). *Tackling diversity in case discussions.* Retrieved from https://hbsp.harvard.edu/inspiring-minds/tackling-diversity-in-case-discussions

Hatem, M. F. (1992). Economic and political liberation in Egypt and the demise of state feminism. *International Journal of Middle East Studies, 24*, 231–251.

Ibarra, H. (1993). Personal networks of women and minorities in management: A conceptual framework. *Academy of Management Review, 18*(1), 56–87.

Joshi, A., Neely, B., Emrich, C., Griffiths, D., & George, G. (2015). Gender research in AMJ: An overview of five decades of empirical research and calls to action. *Academy of Management Journal, 58*(5), 1459–1475.

Kalev, A., Dobbin, F., & Kelly, E. (2006). Best practices or best guesses? Assessing the efficacy of corporate affirmative action and diversity policies. *American Sociological Review, 71*(4), 589–617.

Kim, J. Y., Brockner, J., & Block, C. (2020). *Congruence between self-affirmation and self-construal eliminates the MBA gender performance gap.* (Manuscript submitted for publication).

Kim, H., & Markus, H. R. (1999). Deviance or uniqueness, harmony or conformity? A cultural analysis. *Journal of Personality and Social Psychology, 77*(4), 785–800.

Kinias, Z., Akinola, M., Carter, A., Norton, M., & Phillips, K. (2019, September 16). Integrating diversity into business education. *Knowledge.* Retrieved from https://knowledge.insead.edu/blog/insead-blog/integrating-diversity-into-business-education-12406

Kinias, Z., & Sim, J. (2016). Facilitating women's success in business: Interrupting the process of stereotype threat through affirmation of personal values. *Journal of Applied Psychology, 101*(11), 1585–1597.

Lord, C. G., & Saenz, D. S. (1985). Memory deficits and memory surfeits: Differential cognitive consequences of tokenism for tokens and observers. *Journal of Personality and Social Psychology, 49*(4), 918–926.

Mackie, D. M., Devos, T., & Smith, E. R. (2000). Intergroup emotions: Explaining offensive action tendencies in an intergroup context. *Journal of Personality and Social Psychology, 79*(4), 602–616.

Major, B., & O'Brien, L. T. (2005). The social psychology of stigma. *Annual Review of Psychology, 56*, 393–421.

O'Brien, L. T., Kinias, Z., & Major, B. (2008). How status and stereotypes impact attributions to discrimination: The stereotype-asymmetry hypothesis. *Journal of Experimental Social Psychology, 44*(2), 405–412.

Phillips, K. W., Northcraft, G. B., & Neale, M. A. (2006). Surface level diversity and decision-making in groups: When does deep level similarity help? *Group Processes & Intergroup Relations, 9*(4), 467–482.

Purdie-Vaughns, V., & Eibach, R. P. (2008). Intersectional invisibility: The distinctive advantages and disadvantages of multiple subordinate-group identities. *Sex Roles, 59*(5–6), 377–391.

Roberson, L., & Kulik, C. T. (2007). Stereotype threat at work. *The Academy of Management Perspectives, 21*(2), 24–40.

Rosenthal, L. (2016). Incorporating intersectionality into psychology: An opportunity to promote social justice and equity. *American Psychologist, 71*(6), 474–485.

Sanchez-Hucles, J. V., & Davis, D. D. (2010). Women and women of color in leadership: Complexity, identity, and intersectionality. *American Psychologist, 65*(3), 171–181.

Saenz, D. S. (1994). Token status and problem-solving deficits: Detrimental effects of distinctiveness and performance monitoring. *Social Cognition, 12*(1), 61–74.

Saenz, D. S., & Lord, C. G. (1989). Reversing roles: A cognitive strategy for undoing memory deficits associated with token status. *Journal of Personality and Social Psychology, 56*(5), 698–708.

Seger, C. R., Smith, E. R., Kinias, Z., & Mackie, D. M. (2009). Knowing how they feel: Perceiving emotions felt by outgroups. *Journal of Experimental Social Psychology, 45*, 80–89.

Shapiro, J. R., & Neuberg, S. L. (2007). From stereotype threat to stereotype threats: Implications of a multi-threat framework for causes, moderators, mediators, consequences, and interventions. *Personality and Social Psychology Review, 11*(2), 107–130.

Sherman, D. K., Kinias, Z., Major, B., Kim, H. S., & Prenovost, M. (2007). The group as a resource: Reducing biased attributions for group success and failure via group affirmation. *Personality and Social Psychology Bulletin, 33*, 1100–1112.

Simon, S., Kinias, Z., Obrien, L. T., Major, B., & Bivolaru, E. (2013). Prototypes of discrimination: How status asymmetry and stereotype asymmetry affect judgments of racial discrimination. *Basic and Applied Social Psychology, 35*, 525–533.

Spencer, S. J., Steele, C. M., & Quinn, D. M. (1999). Stereotype threat and women's math performance. *Journal of Experimental Social Psychology, 35*(1), 4–28.

Steele, C. M., & Aronson, J. (1995). Stereotype threat and the intellectual test performance of African Americans. *Journal of Personality and Social Psychology, 69*(5), 797–811.

Thompson, L. L. (2008). *Making the team.* Upper Saddle River, NJ: Prentice Hall.

Williams, K. Y., & O'Reilly, C. A. (1998). Demography and diversity in organizations: A review of 40 years of research. *Research in Organizational Behavior, 20,* 77–140.

Woolf, V. (1929). *A room of one's own.* London, England: Hogarth Press.

CHAPTER 15

REFLECTIONS ON THE STUDY OF GENDER AND DIVERSITY

An Appeal for Objectivity Over Ideology

Lisa M. Leslie
New York University

I would like to be able to say that my interest in studying gender and diversity in organizations began with a commitment to social justice. I would like to be able to say that it originated from a desire to uncover strategies for preventing bias and discrimination. I would like to be able to say that from an early age I was committed to making the world a better place for women and other disadvantaged groups. To be clear, all of these are reasons why I study gender and diversity and find meaning in doing so. But none of these are an honest characterization of the primary reason I started down this path. The reality is that I began studying gender and diversity, and continue to study it today, because I find it fascinating.

I wound up in academia in general, and studying gender and diversity in particular, due to a combination of personal interests and happenstance. I did my undergraduate work at Princeton, where students are required to write a senior thesis. At the start of my senior year, I had decided to major

Perspectives on Gender and Work, pages 181–188

in social psychology but was not otherwise drawn to any particular topic within the field. As a first step, I browsed through the list of psychology faculty with the hope of narrowing them down to a few potential advisors. I came across a faculty member who had just arrived at Princeton that fall and whose research interests included stereotyping. I remember thinking that stereotyping sounded "kind of interesting" and emailed the professor to set up a meeting. It was not until after the professor had agreed to be my advisor and we had worked together for several months that I realized I had stumbled upon arguably the world's leading expert on stereotyping—not to mention one of the brightest minds and most prolific scholars in all of social psychology—Susan Fiske.

Writing an undergraduate thesis was a transformative experience for me. I not only had a wonderful and encouraging advisor but also truly enjoyed the process. I was fascinated by the idea that people make deep-level inferences about others' traits and abilities based on surface-level information regarding the social groups they belong to and that this phenomenon could be studied scientifically. I worked harder on my thesis than I intended to, learned more from the experience than I expected to, and wrote a better paper than I needed to. I did these things not because I was committed to advancing a certain cause but because I was hooked on gender and diversity research. It was interesting and it was fun.

I enjoyed doing a thesis so much that I decided to spend the year after graduation working as a research assistant and to apply to graduate school. I ended up getting my doctoral degree in organizational psychology at the University of Maryland, where I worked with another legendary scholar—Michele Gelfand. Like Susan, Michele is not only a brilliant and accomplished scholar but also a wonderful and supportive mentor. During my first few years of graduate school I continued to explore questions related to gender and diversity but, as I approached the dissertation stage, I briefly considered moving away from this topic. I had heard that not all schools valued research on gender and diversity and that doing my dissertation on a different topic might give me more options on the job market. Yet when I started to generate different dissertation ideas, the only ideas I found interesting were related to gender and diversity. I decided that even if the topic was not widely valued—a point I return to later—I wanted gender and diversity research to be central to my scholarly identity.

I find gender and diversity research fascinating because it is complicated, nuanced, and often counterintuitive. One good example of this is a paper I published with Colleen Manchester, a colleague from when I was on the faculty at the University of Minnesota, and Patty Dahm, one of our former doctoral students (Leslie, Manchester, & Dahm, 2017). We theorized and found that, although women receive an overall pay penalty, compared to otherwise equivalent men, diversity initiatives create a pay premium for the small subset of women deemed to have the potential to reach high-level positions. Due to the prevalence of diversity initiatives, women are in high demand, but nevertheless remain severely underrepresented in the upper echelons of organizations. As a result, managers view high potential women, who have the ability to reach the upper echelons where women remain underrepresented, as more valuable for facilitating diversity goals and in turn pay them more in an effort to retain them, relative to high potential men.

This paper was interesting and fun to work on because I find the phenomenon counterintuitive. Diversity initiatives are intended to create greater equity between women and men in terms of their workplace experiences and outcomes. Thus, if working as intended, diversity initiatives should eliminate the pay gap between men and women, regardless of their potential. Instead diversity initiates create a more complicated pattern of inequity. Most women continue to receive a pay penalty, while the small subset of women deemed high potential receive a pay premium. As a result, the paper helps shed light on the complicated and nuanced nature of efforts to facilitate diversity and inclusion in organizations.

I am also particularly fond of this paper because the high potential female pay premium is one of the most robust phenomena I have ever studied and is thus practically important. The published paper includes four studies in which we find consistently supportive evidence. My collaborators and I also conducted several additional studies that did not make it into the final paper due to length considerations, but nevertheless provide convergent support. More recently, a different group of researchers, who were initially skeptical of the phenomenon, conducted a replication study (Dreher, Carter, & Dworkin, 2019). To their apparent surprise, they found evidence of a pay premium for high potential women that persisted despite the use of additional controls and different types of samples. Given the robustness of the phenomenon, it is clearly something organizational leaders should be aware of.

In all, I like this paper because I think it is interesting and important, not because I see the phenomenon as inherently "good" or "bad" for organizations. Yet when I present this paper to others, I often get one of three different evaluative reactions. Some view the high potential female premium as beneficial from the standpoint of facilitating social justice. Given that women continue to face discrimination at work, they see a pay premium for high potential women as fair and justified. They also note that compensating high potential women at a higher rate than high potential men may be instrumental for keeping them in the workforce, ensuring they ultimately reach the upper echelons, and thus helping to further shatter the glass ceiling. In direct contrast, others view the high potential female premium as detrimental from the standpoint of facilitating social justice. Women are not a protected group; rather, gender is a protected class. As a result, gender-based pay disparities constitute discrimination, even if women are advantaged by the disparity. For this reason, some view the high potential female premium as unfair and problematic. Finally, perhaps the most extreme reaction to the paper are those who find the study "troubling"—as one conference reviewer put it—on the grounds that evidence that high potential women experience advantage could be used to argue against taking action to help other women who experience disadvantage.

I, of course, have my own personal opinion regarding whether the high potential female premium does more good versus harm when it comes to facilitating social justice, but I try to avoid stating that opinion publically. As a scientist, I believe it is my responsibility to be as objective as possible when conducting research and to convey my findings in a balanced manner. Moreover, I can see how a reasonable person might have either the first or the second evaluative reaction described above. For this reason, in the paper my coauthors and I discuss reasons why the high potential female premium could be viewed as either beneficial (i.e., it may help promote and maintain gender diversity in the upper echelons) or detrimental (i.e., it can be interpreted as unfair discrimination against certain men) without coming down on one side or the other. We further note that our findings suggest leaders should be aware of the possibility that high potential women in their organization are receiving a pay premium and then decide whether it is something they want to encourage or prevent.

Although I think the two evaluative reactions we discuss in the paper are both reasonable, I find the third reaction unscientific. Given the apparent robustness of the phenomenon, it seems fair to characterize the high potential female premium as an empirical regularity; it is unlikely universal, but nevertheless seems to frequently emerge in organizations. The third evaluative viewpoint—the idea that the phenomenon is troubling because evidence of advantages for women could be used to curtail efforts to combat discrimination against women—suggests that findings that expose the realities of diversity in organizations are only worthy of study and publication if they unambiguously advance the cause of further promoting gender and diversity in organizations.

In my experience, this reaction to diversity research is not an isolated incident or specific to this one paper. I have spent much of my career studying why diversity initiatives do not always work particularly well (see Leslie, 2019 for a review). I do so because I believe that making diversity initiatives more effective requires a deep understanding of the ways in which they are both effective and ineffective, and I try to make this motivation explicit in my papers. But I have nevertheless had my work criticized—usually by anonymous reviewers—on the grounds that I am providing organizations with ammunition for cutting their diversity initiatives.

When serving as a reviewer and editor for others' papers, I have similarly witnessed negative reactions to gender and diversity research that are based on ideological objections to the research question or findings, not the quality of the research. One reviewer recommended a paper be rejected due to concerns regarding what would happen when the media got ahold of the findings. Another asked an author to explain away only the subset of findings reported in a paper that conflicted with the reviewer's own ideological beliefs as driven by statistical artifacts, rather than true effects, despite the fact that statistical artifacts were an equally likely alternative explanation for all effects in the paper. Another reviewer criticized a paper on how victims can cope with discrimination on the grounds that asking this question constitutes "victim blaming" and that the authors should instead be asking how the system can be fixed to prevent discrimination from occurring in the first place. As a final, non-exhaustive example, a reviewer objected to a paper on the effect of team diversity on performance on the grounds that organizations have a moral imperative to foster diversity. This reviewer claimed that studying the diversity-performance relationship undermines the moral case by suggesting that organizations should only focus on diversity if there is a business case for doing so.

I realize the above examples may come across as a laundry list of reviewer complaints, but I promise that is not my intent. I also want to be clear that my experience is that, although imperfect, the review process is fair, and I have never witnessed these types of ideological reactions prevent a well-executed paper from being published. At the same time, I think these examples are emblematic of a key challenge when it comes to studying gender and diversity. As I alluded to earlier, in the not-too-distant past there was a relatively common perception that less value was placed on gender and diversity research, compared to research on other mainstream topics in the field of management. Although pockets of resistance likely remain, things seem to have changed for the better and, at least in my experience, authors who focus on issues related to gender and diversity do not face additional hurdles in the publication process in terms of convincing reviewers and editors that gender and diversity is a topic worthy of study. Yet, although gender and diversity research seems to be valued in the field, the above examples suggest that scholars have deeply held ideological beliefs regarding the more specific questions and findings related to gender and diversity that have value and are worthy of study. In other words, gender and diversity scholars are relatively unlikely to be told they are studying the wrong topic, but relatively likely to be told they are asking the wrong question on that topic.

On the one hand, this is understandable. We are living in an era of increased political polarization when it comes to beliefs about not only diversity, but also any number of other social and economic issues. Ideological beliefs regarding diversity and whether and how to foster it are also often deeply personal and, at times, based on traumatic experiences. It is therefore not surprising that many management scholars have deeply held, at times, opposing beliefs regarding the most important questions and findings regarding gender and diversity. Moreover, all researchers are human and thus imperfect information processors. As a result, preventing ideological beliefs from coloring our judgments about what does and does not constitute valuable research is nearly impossible.

On the other hand, giving our ideological beliefs free rein over which questions and findings we deem valuable is bad for science. As gender and diversity scholars, our primary goal should be to gain a comprehensive scientific understanding of the nature of gender and diversity in organizations. Doing so requires we ask questions and embrace rigorous findings, regardless of whether they confirm or disconfirm our personal ideological stances. Suppressing evidence that diversity initiatives have unintended consequences is not going to help us understand why they do not always work particularly well and, in turn, how to make them more effective. Selectively explaining away findings that do not align with our ideological beliefs might make us feel better about the world, but it is not going to make those findings any less real. We should absolutely do more research on how to change the system and prevent discrimination, but changing the system is difficult (to put it mildly) and, in the meantime, there is value in understanding what victims can do to cope with the discrimination they face. The moral case for fostering diversity in organizations is valid and important, but that does not mean that understanding whether, why, and when diversity affects organizational performance is irrelevant or unimportant.

I raise all of these points because I think they help make the case for what I see as the most important advice I have for current and future generations of gender and diversity scholars. I think the secret to advancing the field lies not in researching particular gender and diversity-related questions, but in the orientation we take in determining which gender and diversity-related questions and findings have value. Producing high quality, useful science requires we all make a conscious effort to let objectivity win out over ideology when conducting our own research and evaluating the research of others. We should monitor ourselves and each other to ensure that the value of gender and diversity research is determined based on the quality of the theory and empirics, not on whether the question asked or findings align with our personal ideological stance on the world. We should be vigilant to ensure we do not suppress findings that go against our preconceived notions about how to best foster diversity or its effects, but instead embrace and try to better understand them.

Embracing objectivity over ideology is not only good for our science, it is also likely to result in more progress toward creating more diverse and inclusive organizations. I wish diversity was universally and unambiguously good and easy, but the research evidence accumulated to date does not support that is the case. Diversity can be personally enriching and enhance creativity and decision-making, but it can also be a source of interpersonal conflict and tension and exacerbate prejudice and discrimination. If it were easy, organizations would have made more progress toward diversity and inclusion by now, and there would be a lot less conflict in the world. We are likely to make more progress toward fostering diversity and inclusion if we not only highlight the upsides of diversity, but also uncover the challenges of diversity and, in turn, investigate potential solutions for overcoming them. Embracing the (at times harsh) realities of diversity is essential for understanding how to make diversity initiatives more effective.

I realize that my arguments could easily be taken out of context, so I want to emphasize a few points. I do not claim to be perfectly objective in my own research or in evaluating that of others. I am sure that my own ideological beliefs have colored my judgments as an author, reviewer, and editor. Pure objectivity is a laudable goal for science, but also one that is very difficult to achieve. In addition, I acknowledge that a plea for objectivity over ideology could be construed as hypocritical, in that this position is itself an ideological stance. Nevertheless, I do not think we are cognizant enough about the role that ideology likely plays in shaping our own scholarship and our reactions to the scholarship of others, and I think we should all be more vigilant in trying to minimize it.

I also want to acknowledge and respect that others may (perhaps vehemently) disagree with me. I began studying gender and diversity because I found the topic fascinating, not because I had a particular agenda in mind. After becoming immersed in gender and diversity research, and particularly abundant evidence of persistent prejudice and discrimination, I now study gender and diversity both because I continue to find it fascinating, and because I believe it is imperative that we make organizations fairer and more just. At the same time, my initial motivation for studying gender and diversity likely contributes to my belief that ideology should be minimized. I realize that scholars with different origin stories, who perhaps began studying gender and diversity with the goal of solving a particular problem or advancing particular agenda, might see things differently, and I respect their opinions.

I nevertheless stand by the position that embracing objectivity over ideology is not only good for science, but also likely to do the most good in terms of facilitating diversity and inclusion. Although prejudice and discrimination persist, it is an exciting time to be a gender and diversity scholar. In just the last few decades the legitimacy and popularity of the topic has grown immensely, likely due at least in part to the increased prevalence of gender and diversity-related social movements in society and diversity initiatives in organizations. But there is still much to be done and so we, as gender and diversity scholars, are likely to be in business for a long time to come. Let's not be afraid to embrace the complexity and nuance that comes along with studying gender and diversity at work. Let's be open to and accepting of the full range of questions to be asked regarding the nature of gender and diversity at work, as well as its antecedents, consequences, mechanisms, and boundary conditions. As gender and diversity scholars, let's be open to findings that support diverse ideological stances. Let's be vigilant in not letting ideology get in the way of good science. Doing so is key to understanding how to facilitate a more diverse and inclusive world.

AUTHOR NOTE

Correspondence regarding this chapter should be directed to Lisa M. Leslie, New York University, Stern School of Business, Tisch Hall, Suite 717, 40 W 4th Street, New York, NY 10012. Phone: 212-998-0455; Email: lleslie@stern.nyu.edu

REFERENCES

Dreher, G. F., Carter, N. M., & Dworkin, T. (2019). The pay premium for high-potential women: A constructive replication and refinement. *Personnel Psychology, 72*(4), 495–511.

Leslie, L. M. (2019). Diversity initiative effectiveness: A typological theory of unintended consequences. *Academy of Management Review, 44*(3), 538–563.

Leslie, L. M., Manchester, C. F., & Dahm, P. C. (2017). Why and when does the gender gap reverse? Diversity goals and the pay premium for high potential women. *Academy of Management Journal, 60*(2), 402–422.

CHAPTER 16

HOW DO YOU SOLVE A PROBLEM LIKE MARIA?

My Journey as a "Pracademic"

Isabel Metz
University of Melbourne

The question posed in the 1965 film, *The Sound of Music*, befits me; from the compliant girl to the troublesome woman. I gradually became a square peg in a round hole on my way to adulthood. I aspired to career success and financial independence; lofty heights for a woman living in a traditional, Latin macho culture. In an environment where families are more likely to live in the same suburb than in different countries, I left the family home (in Europe) young, worked my way through university (assisted by a scholarship) in a far-away continent (Africa), graduated as a computer scientist, and started to build a career in a large bank in yet another continent (Australia). In the bank, I followed a winding but upward path from IT analyst to marketing manager and to operations senior manager. While on this path, I also completed a company-sponsored Master of Business Administration degree. And then my career path became windier, and I found myself starting the career climb all over again.

Perspectives on Gender and Work, pages 189–207

Late in the 1990s, I decided to exit that corporate career in banking to commence a PhD in gender and careers. I thus became, what I herein call, a *pracademic*. Pracademics commence their academic career after a stretch in business, government, or not-for-profit organizations; they enter the world of academia later in the life-cycle. Unbeknownst to me, however, my timing was off. At the turn of the 21st century, neither organizations nor top-tier academic journals were particularly attentive to an organizational conundrum: women's persistent scarcity in management despite their educational attainment and increased workforce participation. Most men, and many women, felt the "women issue" had been addressed in most developed Western countries. We had anti-discrimination and affirmative action legislation, and there was an increasing proportion of women at low and middle management levels (Mor Barak, 2017). Therefore, the consensus was that gender equality would follow in senior management and executive positions in due time. Yet, two decades later, this prediction is mostly unfulfilled worldwide (World Economic Forum, 2020).

Herein, I provide a glimpse of how my lived experience as a "corporate woman" at the turn of the century triggered a pracademic career with a key research interest in gender diversity in organizations. But what happens inside organizations parallels what happens outside them. Therefore, in deciding to exit a corporate career to investigate women's barriers and facilitators to advancement in banking in the late 1990s, I fortuitously benefitted from a slow, but increasing, social awareness of women's abysmally slow progress in management. I explain this serendipity in four sections, starting with how I became interested in gender and careers research and ending with possible future hot topics in this area.

THE MAKING OF A PRACADEMIC: THE CURIOUS INCIDENT OF WOMEN'S SCARCITY IN LEADERSHIP

Banking at the end of the 20th century was a bleak work environment for professional women. We traversed normalized macho behavior daily, overt sexism, scarcity of role models in leadership, and a systemic blindness to gender biases and discrimination. For instance, as an IT professional early in my work life, I regularly encountered skepticism about my competence. As a result, I have numerous personal stories supporting Ridgeway's (2001) expectations states theory. For illustrative purposes, I recount three. One day I was charged with installing an additional piece of hardware (a circuit board) in a senior manager's personal computer. To do so, I had to open his computer. Despite not having met or provided IT assistance to this person before, I immediately encountered fierce verbal and physical opposition to do so. He declared that I was not sufficiently experienced, qualified, or capable to undertake the task. The encounter culminated in the senior manager posing as a human barrier between me and his computer. After much persuasion (which included offering to pay for computer damages, should they eventuate), I performed my job under his unabashed vigil. On another occasion, my manager received a letter from a peer praising my work performance; he laughed and dismissed the commendation as a sign of his peer's clear infatuation with me.

Towards the end of my stint in banking, I was placed in a front-line, lending role as part of the prerequisite training and development to assume top leadership positions in the organization. It was during this stage that my presence in a male-dominated environment (and a lending "rookie" at that) seemed to generate the most overt hostility and resentment. My assigned "mentor" was not only at a more junior level than I but had also been recently knocked back for promotion. Further, his team was understaffed. Not surprisingly, he was not inclined to spare resources to enable my training and development and, ultimately, advancement. He instructed his team not to spend time showing me the "ropes" in lending. As quaint as these stories may now seem, the experiences were often disconcerting at the time. This type of work environment was not unique to banking, which provided credence to estimates published in 1996 that it would take women 177 years to be equally represented in management in Australia (Hede & O'Brien, 1996).

Although some sections of banking continue to be unwelcoming to women (Metz, 2011), there is greater awareness and lower tolerance for incidences of inappropriate behavior towards women in banking than during the pre-social media period of the 1990s (e.g., Christodoulou, 2019). I, like many of my contemporaries, was only semi-aware of the pervasiveness of the challenges women faced and of any concomitant redress mechanisms. Faced with incomplete information, self-doubt crept-in and career aspirations ebbed away. I increasingly attributed my negative work experiences and setbacks to personal shortcomings.

However, not all work experiences and interactions were challenging or disheartening. I advanced from information systems analyst to manager, and then rotated to management and senior management positions in retail and corporate banking. I had been identified as a *high potential officer* and was being groomed for top leadership positions in the bank. Nevertheless, a feeling of discomfort developed; some things just did not add up. For example, the high potential officer group comprised 50 employees but only two were women; that's a mere 4% female representation in the most coveted group in the organization. This men-to-women ratio was unsettling partly because over 60% of the banking workforce was female (Metz & Tharenou, 1999). How then was it possible that only two female employees were "worthy" of being in the high potential officer group? I also puzzled over the scarcity of women in leadership, their demeanor, and high visibility. Not only were female leaders rare, but they seemed far from being the positive female role models that women at lower levels expected them to be. The few women in managerial positions were highly visible and scrutinized by both men and women at all organization levels. Men were likely to see female managers as representatives of all women, and aspiring career women were likely to look up to them as epitomes of career advancement possibilities. Generally, neither group's perceptions of their female leaders were flattering. The term *queen bee* had successfully crossed over from the academic to the practitioner lexicon. The term problematizes the relationships of women at work, with particular focus on senior women's lack of support for peers and junior colleagues. Yet, no equivalent term exists for senior men nor are male relationships at work similarly subject to scrutiny and negative generalizations.

Eventually, I had more questions than answers. Had I been set up to fail? Were my work experiences unique or were they commonplace among women in banking? Why was I often the only female senior manager in the room? Why were there few women in management in banking? Why were senior women's work and personal reputations so public? Were some of these women really "queen bees," and how did successful men escape equivalent notoriety?

To answer these and other questions about the barriers and facilitators of women's career advancement in Australian banking, I decided to do a PhD. The confluence of the most recent poor implementation of my career plan and the ever-present unwelcoming work environment for women prompted that decision. Despite pre- and post-exit interviews with human resources, where I made my recent disappointments and future professional plans clear, the official company announcement attributed my resignation to family responsibilities. I was both surprised and frustrated with this corporate spin, which perpetuates perceptions that women are more committed to family than to work and "opt-out" of promising careers. These perceptions can be detrimental to women's careers because they negatively influence people management decisions, such as selection and promotion, about female employees. Thus, I added to my basket of questions: "Is the widely held belief that women leave work for family responsibilities myth or reality?"

I did not set out to do a doctorate to become an academic or for lofty aims. I merely intended to examine a puzzling organizational phenomenon: women's underrepresentation in leadership positions. The chief motivation was to make sense of my corporate career experiences. I naively believed there was a rational and elegant explanation for women's scarcity in leadership and, consequently, a fail-proof solution. I was going to find that solution. Almost two decades on and with the benefit of hindsight, I'm aware this is a life-long endeavor. I also now realize how being passionate about a topic, and topic complexity and metamorphosis, can lead to a life in academia.

HALF A LIFE IN ACADEMIA STUDYING GENDER AND CAREERS: HOW FAR HAVE I COME?

The decision to examine a puzzling organizational phenomenon somewhere in the middle of one's adult working life can be exciting and challenging. We take time off whatever we are doing to examine a phenomenon that interests and mystifies us. However, doing a PhD full time can also be a lonely, slow, and all-consuming endeavor, often described as rowing a boat alone in the middle of the ocean. True to this description, there were times during my exciting PhD adventure when I wondered why on earth I swapped the known for the unknown. In particular, I questioned the soundness of my judgment to exchange financial security and a promising (albeit challenging) career for a frugal and uncertain life as a doctoral student. In addition, I underwent a steep adaptation curve as academic environments are, in a myriad of ways, very different from corporate ones. Yet, I found that those lengthy and lonely periods during which not much seemed to happen were punctuated by progressive goals and small achievements, such as passing confirmation, getting one's first conference (and then journal) paper accepted, obtaining a satisfying survey response rate, or realizing that one's survey measures demonstrated sound reliability and validity.

Further, the decision to do a PhD at the cusp of the 21st century on the barriers and facilitators of women's advancement was somewhat problematic. Unbeknown to practitioners like me, an extensive body of knowledge in this area already existed. Years later, I and Savita Kumra summarized and sorted this body of knowledge into three distinct time periods while trying to make sense of the popularity of books with career advice for women such as Sheryl Sandberg's (2013) "Lean In." The article was published in the *Academy of Management Perspectives* in the hope that it would "ultimately be useful to women's career advancement via the research that it will instigate, the detailed practical implications that it will encourage, and the student audiences that it will inform" (Metz & Kumra, 2019, p. 90).

Possibly and partly due to this vast literature, the topic of women's career advancement was perceived by both practitioners and many academics to be done and dusted. As a result, there was a drought of women in management studies being published in some of our most coveted academic management journals at the beginning of the 21st century, such as in the *Academy of Management Journal* (Joshi, Neely, Emrich, Griffiths, & George, 2015). There was also little interest among Australian corporations in participating in women in management research. Neither of these conditions augured well for a doctoral student's dreams of producing a ground-breaking PhD that would solve the "women's scarcity in leadership" puzzle. Luckily, I was oblivious to both of these unfavorable academic research conditions. I also had a PhD supervisor whose appreciation for the topic matched my inquisitiveness. I'm grateful that my supervisor, Professor Phyllis Tharenou, fully accepted and encouraged my desire to investigate the barriers and facilitators to women's advancement in Australian banking. This was the title of my doctoral thesis. The fact that this title remained exactly as proposed in my initial correspondence to her is a testament to her complete support.

My intent to return to banking after completing my doctoral studies never eventuated. Phyllis remarked at our first meeting that I would never find a job in banking after doing a PhD on women's advancement in the sector. Whether this premonition was correct or not is irrelevant for she planted the seed of doubt. Doubt in a future corporate career revival, combined with a growing appreciation for research, led me to a serendipitous academic career.

As a result of the peaks and valleys of the gender and careers topic since the turn of the 21st century, my research program resembles a human system in that its parts are distinct but interlinked. At its center is my doctoral dissertation, like a heart at the center of the human body nourishing all its parts. From this center, overlapping interests emerged and will likely continue to emerge over time (see Figure 16.1). For example, one research

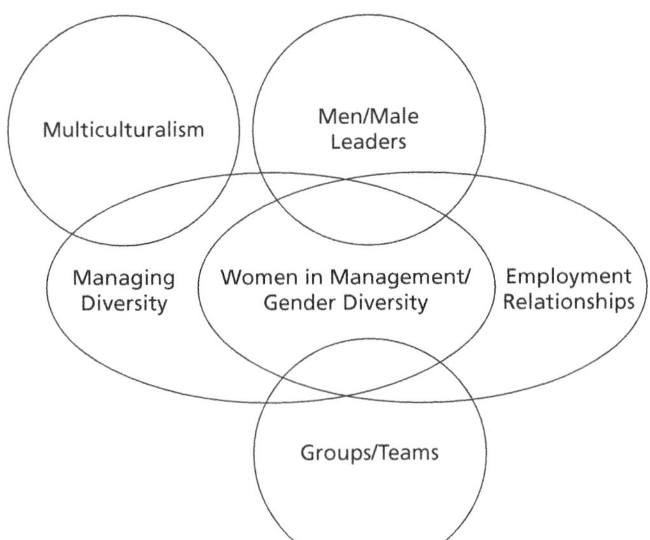

Figure 16.1 Overlapping research interests.

stream is diversity and inclusion in organizations; another is organizational change; and yet another is human resource management. Just as with the human body, these "parts" (or research streams) are intertwined and each part makes only a small contribution to solving the puzzle of women's scarcity in leadership.

Women's scarcity in management is a complex issue; the more we know, the more we realize there are unexamined aspects to it. Scholarly giants in this field have fittingly compared women's nonlinear paths to "cross-currents in a river" (Powell & Mainiero, 1992), "kaleidoscopes" (Mainiero & Sullivan, 2005), "labyrinths" (Eagly & Carli, 2007), and "off-ramps and on-ramps" (Hewlett, 2007). While I consider individual-centered explanations in my work, as a past practitioner, I have always been particularly interested in the role that nonindividual factors such as peers and bosses, organizational structures, and cultures play in women's nonlinear paths. As a result, I started by investigating the relative contribution of individual (e.g., length or type of work experience), interpersonal (e.g., mentors and social networks), and organizational factors (e.g., career development opportunities) to women's career advancement. In one of my early publications, I found (with Phyllis Tharenou) that human capital most explained women's advancement in banking (Metz & Tharenou, 2001). Human capital represents the knowledge and skills that people accumulate over time such as education, company tenure, training, and work experience (Becker, 1993). However, when women were asked (using two open-ended questions) what were the five or fewer major events that helped and the five or fewer major events that hindered their career advancement most, Phyllis and I found that social capital seemed to matter more to women's advancement at high than at low levels. Social capital is "the ability of actors to secure benefits by virtue of membership in social networks or other social structures" (Portes, 1998, p. 6). Thus, this finding led us to conclude that "women's advancement to high levels is partly beyond their control because it can depend on decisions made by men, who may be influenced by nonwork factors such as stereotypes" (Metz & Tharenou, 2001, p. 334).

In fact, male resistance to gender initiatives and men's feelings of threat when faced with pro-diversity organizational messages were subsequently identified as forces that hinder gender equity change. Common explanations for male resistance are self-interest in preserving the status quo and feeling that their talent and effort are being attacked (Frank, 2016). A rationale for feeling threatened is the perception that pro-diversity organization philosophies and initiatives diminish men's work status and opportunities; that is, some males believe that in a pro-gender diversity organization, they would be treated unfairly because anti-male discrimination would prevail (Dover, Major, & Kaiser, 2016).

However, evidence of anti-male discrimination is hard to find. Based on analyses of gender gaps over time, the World Economic Forum (WEF) estimates that it will take almost 99.5 years for the overall global gender gap to close (WEF, 2020). Male resistance to gender equality in the workplace is a considerable contributor to the slow progress women have made in leadership positions in Western societies, particularly at senior management and at executive and board level, despite decades of research and workplace interventions. Male peers and superiors can undermine, undervalue, and upset women's work efforts and contributions. The collective and cumulative effect of such workplace behavior can be devastating for women. A female banking executive recently described this effect to me as "the death by a thousand cuts."

Thus, while people broadly agree that gender inequality exists, many men still believe in traditional gender roles. In the 2018 survey snapshot of 2,122 Australians mentioned above, 88% of the participants agreed that gender equality is a problem and 65% believed men have more opportunity than women to earn the main household income. Despite this widespread awareness of gender inequality, more than one-third of the male respondents believed in traditional gender roles and that the government was already doing enough to promote gender equality. Furthermore, younger generations are not immune to persistent biases and stereotypes; 30% to 35% of millennials and Gen Z males believe that men are more ambitious and more suited for leadership than women, and childcare is best done by women (Evans, Haussegger, Halupka, & Rowe, 2018). These findings are concerning, for two reasons. First, they are likely to underreport the prevalence of traditional gender roles and negative stereotypes of working women in the population. Increased social awareness and attention on gender inequality in leadership might enhance social desirability in individual responses. Second, the survey's findings are concerning because men's gender roles beliefs can hinder women's work opportunities (Hoobler, Wayne, & Lemmon, 2009). After all, men are still likely to be the decision-makers in recruitment, selection, and allocation of work opportunities.

Female resistance to gender diversity initiatives can also contribute to women's slow progress. Some of this resistance may come from women who believe in traditional gender roles, such as that women should be the primary caregivers and men the primary breadwinners. For them, the status quo is as it should be. However, the resistance more often referred to is from seemingly unsupportive senior women and female peers. Yet, the prevalence and reach of this form of resistance is equivocal. While the media spotlights such resistance as evidence of the Queen Bee Syndrome, much of the academic literature offers alternative explanations for this apparent conflict between women at work (e.g., Bickel, 2014; Kulik, Metz, & Gould, 2016). For example, my colleagues and I decided to explore how women's well-being in organizational contexts is enhanced or diminished by other women. We uncovered a complex picture. On one hand, based on a review of the social categorization and social identity literatures, women should indeed benefit from working for and with other women. On the other hand, a review of the status characteristics and relational demography literatures revealed economic and personal costs of doing so. We concluded, "Female supervisors in male-dominated work environments experience identity tensions that motivate them to disengage from their gender group—with negative consequences for female subordinates' well-being," and surmised that "women will experience the greatest well-being benefits from working with, and for, other women only when organizations experience gender balance across all levels of the hierarchy (but especially at the top)" (Kulik et al., 2016, p. 201).

As social awareness of gender inequality, legislation, and work conditions have evolved, so too have some of the barriers and facilitators to women's career advancement. For example, Carol Kulik and I explained how overt forms of discrimination have been replaced by more subtle ones due to anti-discrimination legislation (Metz & Kulik, 2014). Later, Savita Kumra and I sketched a picture of facilitators of positive social change, such as gender equity advocacy by prominent men and regular media issue spotlighting (Metz & Kumra, 2019). So, given persistent old barriers (e.g., negative gender biases), emerging new ones (e.g., perceptions of anti-male discrimination), and changing environments (e.g., technology and new forms of work), we are likely to still be a long way to solving the amorphous enigma of women's "rocky climb" up the career ladder (Metz & Kulik, 2014). Not surprisingly, therefore, while personal pride in a study or finding has been fleeting, my motivation to search for answers has endured.

NAVIGATING LIFE AS A PRACADEMIC

As pracademics enter the world of academia later in the life-cycle, they tend to be older and more distant from contemporary academic teachings than their younger counterparts. These deficits are materially and personally challenging. For instance, materially, a pracademic's academic profile (e.g., list of publications, academic honors, and awards) might never be comparable to the academic profiles of their chronological peers whom they admire and aspire to emulate, and it may even fall behind those of their (chronologically) younger doctoral cohort peers. Consequently, a pracademic's self-esteem is regularly under siege because of the real difficulties with starting afresh in a new profession.

Therefore, I caution pracademics of the potential downside of peer comparison. I suggest assuming a rational perspective when pracademics compare their academic profile with the profiles of colleagues. Remember that time in the business world is time forever lost to building one's academic resume. Further, as second careerists, pracademics are likely to be part of the "sandwich generation" unlike their younger doctoral cohort peers. This is a stage of life when individuals (often women) juggle both children's and ageing parents' demands for time and care (Cravey & Mitra, 2011). But there are downsides of carrying out multiple roles with scarce resources, such as low or deteriorating performance (Kahn, Wolfe, Quinn, & Snoek, 1964). Time is often a scarce resource and the time demands placed on the "sandwich generation" are rarely deferrable. As a result, more time spent attending to heightened family demands is less time spent on deferrable responsibilities such as research.

Another challenge might be the gap between pracademics and chronologically younger cohorts in the start and progression of their academic career. As older doctoral graduates, pracademics might encounter ageism at the recruitment and selection stage. Ageism is discrimination based on age, and it is prevalent in many professions and across countries (Ayalon & Tesch-Römer, 2018). Once employed, time-poor pracademics might also experience delayed tenure and promotion relative to their more time-rich colleagues. Unsuccessful tournaments in job search, tenure, and promotion are likely to foster, at least some of the time, self-doubt, despondency, and low self-esteem. So, how can pracademics counteract unfavourable circumstances to attain personal and professional fulfillment in academia? With the benefit of hindsight, I illustrate three things that helped me navigate pracademia and enjoy some serendipitous outcomes.

First, wishing aloud for a mentor can be beneficial. At the beginning of my academic career, I mused to my first head of cluster, Professor Carol Kulik, that I felt I would gain from having a senior faculty mentor to work with and learn from, "Just as do men and women in corporate," I said. I was not even clear as I spoke what that mentoring would look like. She inquired: "Are you asking me to be your mentor?" I thus found myself in a bind. If I said no, I would be truthful but potentially rude. If I said yes, I would be untruthful, possibly flattering, and potentially obnoxious. I went for truth and said that she would make a great mentor, but I was not thinking of anyone in particular at the time. As it turned out, Carol became a wonderful mentor to me, providing me with instrumental and socio-emotional advice and practical support, for which I'm forever grateful. She asked me to join her, Christina Cregan, and Michelle Brown on an Australian Research Council (ARC) grant to investigate how psychological contracts might link HRM practices and organizational effectiveness. This collaboration was "a first" for me in several ways: my first ARC grant, my first real foray into human research management, and my first team collaboration as an academic.

Second, finding the sweet spot between one's instrumental goals and research passions (particularly ones with bleak prospects of publication) can facilitate tenure and advancement in academia. As passionate as I was about gender and careers, this research area was somewhat marginalized at the turn of the century. As an early career researcher, it was necessary to diversify around my core area of interest to survive as an academic. Despite my hesitant foray into other research areas, there were upsides of doing so. For instance, I was able to take advantage of unexpected collaborative opportunities and to immerse myself in new literatures. Both outcomes were exciting as they gave me the variety I craved: working with esteemed colleagues in an array of interesting topics. In hindsight, I can see the common thread in the various research streams, although I was not conscious then of a particular overarching research strategy. I suspect, however, that changing research streams in the sole pursuit of instrumental outcomes (such as tenure) might be motivationally unsustainable or intrinsically dissatisfying. Thus, I suggest welcoming opportunities for collaborative research that might broaden and support an early pracademic's core interests. This approach allows immersion in potentially exciting and enduring new research topics, while riding the waxing and waning of a focal one.

Third, switching off once a week can be a life saver. Academics are often under relentless pressure to publish, obtain research grants, engage with industry, deliver in teaching, and demonstrate service to one's institution and to the academic profession. These professional demands apply regardless of each individual's personal circumstances. Early career pracademics, however, likely juggle multiple roles. As they try to perform at an acceptable standard in multiple areas of responsibility, pracademics are particularly at risk of work overload. Work overload can lead to stress-related health outcomes, such as burnout and low performance. Thus, switching off once a week is not only necessary to maintain productivity, it may be a life-saving strategy. My "life-saver" has been making every Saturday an electronics-free day. This practice was difficult to implement, however, as it required a lot of self-discipline to not check emails, mobile, or use any type of electronics. Despite the challenges of fully "disconnecting" one day a week, I believe that doing so is as important to one's academic longevity and success as are, for example, uninterrupted blocks of manuscript writing time.

SO, WHAT MAKES ME STILL GET OUT OF BED EACH DAY? POSSIBLE FUTURE HOT TOPICS

My hope as the 20th century set and the 21st began was that gender inequality in the workplace would not be a topic worth talking about by the time my children entered adulthood. Disappointingly, that hope has not been realized as of 2020, although after years of dinner discussions, I'm sure my children would say it is not a topic worth talking about. Further, gender and careers is more salient as a topic in the public discourse than before, partly due to social media. However, this increased prominence albeit necessary is insufficient for positive change to occur. Prejudices and gender stereotypes persist about career women amongst older and younger generations alike. For example, a 2018 survey snapshot of the Australian population (Evans et al., 2018) revealed that, in general, more than 1 in 3 men believe in traditional gender roles. This statistic is fairly stable across generations: 35% of Gen Z males (who are aged between 18 and 23) believe childcare is best done by women, and 25% of female and 29% of male millennials (who are between 24 and 38 years old) believe women become less likeable when they take on leadership roles. In addition, for over a decade, I have been hearing the same objections to gender diversity and gender diversity initiatives from some of my students in every cohort; in fact, few students are vocal advocates of gender equality in leadership. These objections range from the undermining of meritocracy to the negative impact of gender diversity initiatives on "deserving" women (e.g., "'But then people are not selected on merit"). Thus, although there has been some positive change in the last two decades, that change has been disappointingly small. Nevertheless, inroads made so far sustain my hope that gender inequality in the workplace will eventually be a non-topic. Simultaneously, current progress makes me get out of bed every morning, because there is much still to be done before positive change is satisfactory and difficult to reverse.

My colleagues and I have made various recommendations for future research on gender diversity in the workplace since the year 2000. To avoid repetition, Table 16.1 includes a sample of these research suggestions. As can be seen from Table 16.1, some of our proposals encourage researchers to cross organization levels and national boundaries.

To this list, I add a couple of potentially fruitful research streams in the area of gender and careers. In doing so, I leverage Riger and Galligan's (1980) call for scholars to examine the "interaction of both person- and situation-centred variables" (p. 908), because their call is as relevant today as it was 4 decades ago. Specifically, I recommend we spotlight more assiduously than before what happens at the interpersonal level in every examination, recommendation, and intervention evaluation. Making work environments more inclusive and welcoming of women, and changing the gender composition at all organization levels and spheres of the economy, requires *everyone*'s commitment. This is a conspicuous assertion that often overlooks inconspicuous obstacles; from the benevolent sexist to the oblivious bystander. Moreover, such inconspicuous impediments are not the sole dominion of the traditionally privileged or of the older generation, because they often reflect lack of awareness and habitual behavior. I illustrate these

TABLE 16.1 Examples of Previous Recommendations for Gender Research

Recommendation(s)	Reference(s)
Large, longitudinal research into the relative importance of personal, interpersonal, and organizational level factors.	Metz (2003); Metz & Kumra (2019)
Shift to a focus on gender similarities (FGS) in research to broaden the appeal and applicability of recommendations, and thus, stimulate organizational change.	Metz & Simon (2008)
Investigate the influence of social environment (e.g., networks and mentor support) and male hierarchies on women's career advancement across organizations of different sizes and in different industries.	Metz (2009)
Obtain a more nuanced understanding of negotiations between dual-earner couples, and between individuals and their supervisors, to reduce or cope with work family conflict in non-Western countries.	Kailasapathy & Metz (2012)
Extend the examination of the interactive effects of gender diversity and work family (WF) programs on organizational performance to various management levels and across different national cultures; also broaden the focus from WF to work–life programs and to work–life climate.	Ali, Metz & Kulik (2015)
Use theoretical perspectives to predict the direction of male/female differences in leadership outcomes. Further, devote more consideration to the mediating variables between gender in leadership and outcome variables; study non-financial outcomes (e.g., internal group processes) and small-medium size organizations.	Kulik & Metz (2017)

blind spots with an incident from one of the diversity and inclusion classes I recently taught at postgraduate level. I explained how microaggressions, such as subtle insults and slights often disguised as jokes, can have a detrimental impact on the targets. Immediately after, a 30-something minority MBA student (he represented 3% of the class based on country of origin) shared his consternation at realizing that he had unintentionally been an accomplice to this form of workplace behavior. He recounted experiencing racist micro- and macro-aggression himself. As a result of his experiences, he had volunteered to lead the gender diversity initiative in his organization. Yet, he had been unaware of, and an unwitting contributor to, some forms of microaggressions directed at his female colleagues. This student's experience exemplifies some of the complexity and difficulty in organizational gender diversity change because it requires heightened personal awareness and constant vigilance.

The organizational change literature explains that change is often difficult because there are forces that drive change and forces that hinder it. Furthermore, we know from this literature that transformational change is usually top–down, and difficult to introduce and "bed down." *Bedding down* involves institutionalizing the new way of doing things so it becomes part of the culture or "DNA" of the organization. Making an organization more gender diverse and inclusive is a form of transformational change. It needs to be initiated by a highly placed champion (e.g., the CEO) and supported by the genuine commitment of successive CEOs and their top leadership team if it is to become part of the DNA of the organization. Based on cases of gender diversity in leadership initiatives, such as at Deloitte (Pellegrino, D'Amato, & Weisberg, 2011) and at IBM (Childs, 2005), we expect this premise to apply to gender diversity change in organizations. After all, highly placed individuals such as CEOs have the decision-making power to introduce change. But not all CEOs are genuine advocates of gender diversity nor are their efforts sustainable. Thus, empirical studies are needed to ascertain the importance and form of CEO advocacy to gender diversity in organizations relative to other factors (e.g., HR policies and practices). The possibilities in this "CEO research stream" are vast and include empirical examination of antecedents of CEO's advocacy (e.g., personal factors), explanatory intervening mechanism (e.g., legacy motivators), contextual factors (e.g., succession and promotion procedures, such as KPIs on evidence of commitment to gender diversity), and the presence of supporters and enablers (e.g., a committed top management team and board of directors).

Further, CEOs need not act alone. Although in some command and control organization cultures, such as those found in the military, a leader's mandate might be blindly followed, most leaders do not affect sustainable change on their own. The organizational change literature predicts that a necessary factor for successful change is the formation of coalitions. An emerging phenomenon are the male-only and gender mixed groups advocating for gender equality in leadership (e.g., Metz & Kulik, 2015). It is unknown, however, if this recent development is ephemeral or enduring, effective or not. Thus, this area of collective, high-profile gender equality advocacy is a budding avenue of research in the situation-centered sphere.

Moreover, for sustainable change to occur in organizations, it is necessary, but insufficient, that the drivers of change surpass the resisters; resisters need to be reduced or eliminated altogether. Gender in management research started by focusing on increasing the drivers of gender diversity change in leadership. For example, women were advised to get more, different, or broader education and work experience; organizations were advised to implement interventions targeted at women. This is known as the "fix the woman" period (Metz & Kumra, 2019) and continues to be an integral part of contemporary research and recommendations to practice. However, we now need to focus our efforts on fixing others; the many men and some women who actively or passively resist gender equity in organizations.

Therefore, research is needed to gain a comprehensive understanding of how we can reduce resistance to gender equity change. This understanding is key to progress and to ultimate gender equality in leadership. Efforts to date to reduce resistance, such as showing empirical evidence supporting the business case for gender diversity and unconscious bias training, have clearly not been completely successful. After more than five decades of women in management and gender diversity studies and recommendations, women continue to be underrepresented in leadership almost everywhere. For instance, women still comprise only 40.7%, 37.8%, 36.3%, 16.8%, and 14.8% of legislators, senior officials, and managers in the United States, Australia, the United Kingdom, China and Japan, respectively (WEF, 2020). Unconscious bias training might not reduce biases and might even enhance them (Noon, 2018; Williamson & Foley, 2018). Organizations' diversity efforts, such as gender diverse panels in hiring and promotion processes, can also lull decision-makers (who are still mostly men) into complacency, thus allowing those biases to reign (Castilla & Benard, 2010). And providing compelling evidence for the business case for gender diversity might win the head but not the heart of detractors. Therefore, another line of inquiry is to empirically examine what are the bundle of practices that will win the hearts of the dominant, "in-group" members who are usually men—worldwide. Is it communication of the "why" and buy-in (Kotter's 4th step for successful change; Kotter [2012])? If so, what combinations of delivery channels and communication content are most effective? Or is it including men in the organizational gender equity initiatives (Kotter's 5th step)? If it is, what inclusion efforts are most effective, and do they vary across contexts and cultures? Is it providing carefully facilitated forums for in-group and out-group members to debate the pros and cons of change? Is it providing opportunities for resisters to voice their objections, fears, and beliefs in psychologically safe one-on-one or group settings? Or is it all or a combination of these and other practices? Having this information will likely help organizations reduce male, and some female, resistance to change and increase returns on their gender diversity and inclusion efforts.

The current level of social awareness of gender inequality combined with women's inroads in education attainment and work participation (Metz & Kumra, 2019; WEF, 2020) suggests a gap in our understanding of the reasons for women's persistent scarcity in leadership positions. A good place to start investigating this gap is by focusing on men. Most men *state* that they endorse gender equality (Diversity Council Australia, 2017; Metz & Kulik, 2015), although it is unclear how or under what circumstances they act on that belief. Further, the Australian Gender Equality Attitudes 2018 survey snapshot (Evans et al., 2018) reported that 42% of men believed that men and boys are increasingly excluded from measures to improve gender equality. It is unclear, however, what the participants exactly meant; for example, were they excluded from the consultation on, or from availing of, those measures?

It is possible that men are in some way being discouraged from participating in work gender equality efforts. The family studies and work-life literatures suggest that, for example, there are social taboos around men taking parental leave and requesting to work flexibly. It seems that men who would like to work flexibly are twice as likely as women to have their requests turned down (Sanders, Zeng, Hellicar, & Fagg, 2016). Further, government legislation has the potential to be a driver or a barrier to gender equity change through the legislation that it enacts or fails to enact (Metz & Kulik, 2014).

In conclusion, my perspective of the scarcity of women in leadership has always been informed by my own experiences as a corporate woman. These experiences led to a focus on structures (e.g., HR practices) and context (e.g., interpersonal factors and culture). Also as a pracademic, I have been and continue to be interested in questions of practical importance that lead to increased industry engagement and to narrowing the research-practice gap. Thus, what still gets me out of bed every day is the realization that solving the conundrum of women's scarcity in leadership is unfinished business.

The literature on gender and careers is vast, yet gender differences at work prevail in many areas (e.g., leadership, pay, and power) and across countries (WEF, 2020). The focus on the men and women who are passive about or resist gender diversity change is only one possible future area of research that might increase industry engagement by addressing an important ingredient of sustainable competitive advantage: the attraction and retention of the best people from the *full* talent pool. Therefore, issues such as men's feelings of being excluded from measures to improve gender equality need to be investigated and addressed. If not, gender stereotypes will likely persist and continue to contribute to the slow change in gender equality at work. Another potential stream of research is investigating how government legislation and initiatives influence (a) households' "choices" in the allocation of their combined resources and (b) decision-makers' perceptions and stereotypes of women's commitment to work. Again, this is an important line of enquiry because we know that gender social roles and stereotypes are difficult to change and detrimental to women's careers (Gloor, Li, Lim, & Feierabend, 2018; Hoobler et al., 2009; Metz & Tharenou, 2001). We also know that successful transformational change, such as gender equity in leadership change, requires overcoming the biggest obstacle of all: Most men's, and some women's, recalcitrant open or subtle resistance to gender diversity efforts in the workplace. Why? Because, as previously mentioned, making work environments more inclusive and welcoming of women, and changing the gender composition at all organization levels and spheres of the economy, requires *everyone*'s commitment. Thus, we need to be less concerned about solving "a problem like Maria" and more with solving "a problem like Manuel."

REFERENCES

Ali, M., Metz, I., & Kulik, C. T. (2015). The impact of work–family programs on the relationship between gender diversity and performance. *Human Resource Management, 54*(4), 553–576.

Ayalon, L., & Tesch-Römer, C. (Eds.). (2018). *Contemporary perspectives on ageism.* Cham, Switzerland: Springer International.

Becker, G. (1993). *Human capital: A theoretical and empirical analysis with special reference to education* (3rd ed.). Chicago, IL: The University of Chicago Press.

Bickel, J. (2014). Why do women hamper other women? *Journal of Women's Health, 23*(5), 365–367.

Castilla, E. J., & Benard, S. (2010). The paradox of meritocracy in organizations. *Administrative Science Quarterly, 55*(4), 543–676.

Childs, J. T., Jr. (2005). Managing workforce diversity at IBM: A global HR topic that has arrived. *Human Resource Management, 44*(1), 73–77.

Christodoulou, M. (2019, August 30). ANZ executives accused of "manhandling" female analyst at boozy golf course party. *ABC News.* Retrieved from https://www.abc.net.au/news/2019-08-30/anz-executives-manhandled-a-female-analyst/11460102

Cravey, T., & Mitra, A. (2011). Demographics of the sandwich generation by race and ethnicity in the United States. *The Journal of Socio-Economics, 40*(3), 306–311.

Diversity Council Australia (M. Flood & G. Russell). (2017). *Men make a difference: How to engage men on gender equality.* Sydney: Diversity Council Australia.

Dover, T. L., Major, B., & Kaiser, C. R. (2016). Members of high-status groups are threatened by pro-diversity organizational messages. *Journal of Experimental Social Psychology, 62,* 58–67.

Eagly, A. H., & Carli, L.L. (2007). Women and the labyrinth of leadership. *Harvard Business Review, 85*(9), 63–71.

Evans, M., Haussegger, V., Halupka, M., & Rowe, P. (2018). *From girls to men: Gender equality attitudes 2018 Survey snapshot.* 50/50 by 2030 Foundation. Canberra, Australia: University of Canberra. Accessed from https://www.5050foundation.edu.au/gender-equality-attitudes/

Frank, R. H. (2016). *Success and luck: Good fortune and the myth of meritocracy.* Princeton, NJ: Princeton University Press.

Gloor, J. L., Li, X., Lim, S., & Feierabend, A. (2018). An inconvenient truth? Interpersonal and career consequences of "maybe baby" expectations. *Journal of Vocational Behavior, 104,* 44–58.

Hede, A., & O'Brien, E. (1996). Affirmative action in the Australian private sector: A longitudinal analysis. *International Review of Women and Leadership, 2*(2), 15–29.

Hewlett, S. A. (2007). *Off-ramps and on-ramps.* Boston, MA: Harvard Business School Press.

Hoobler, J. M., Wayne, S. J., & Lemmon, G. (2009). Bosses' perceptions of family-work conflict and women's promotability: Glass ceiling effects. *Academy of Management Journal, 52*(5), 939–957.

Joshi, A., Neely, B., Emrich, C., Griffiths, D., & George, G. (2015). Gender research in AMJ. *Academy of Management Journal, 58*(5), 1459–1475.

Kahn, R. L., Wolfe, D. M., Quinn, R. P., & Snoek, J. D. (1964). *Organizational stress: Studies in role conflict and ambiguity.* New York, NY: Wiley.

Kailasapathy, P., & Metz, I. (2012). A study of negotiations of exchange relationships in family and at work in Sri Lanka. *Journal of Social Issues, 68*(4), 790–813.

Kotter, J. P. (2012). *Leading change.* Boston, MA: Harvard Businsess Press.

Kulik, C. T., & Metz, I. (2017). Women at the top. In M. A. Hitt, S. E. Jackson, S. Carmona, L. Bierman, C. E. Shalley, & M. Wright (Eds.), *The Oxford handbook of strategy implementation* (pp. 239–281). Oxford, England: Oxford University Press.

Kulik, C. T., Metz, I., & Gould, J. A. (2016). In the company of women: The well-being consequences of working with (and for) other women. In M. Connerley, & J. Wu (Eds), *The handbook on well-being of working women* (pp. 189–207). Dordrecht, Netherlands: Springer.

Mainiero, L.A., & Sullivan, S.E. (2005). Kaleidoscope careers. *The Academy of Management Executive, 19*(1), 106–123.

Metz, I. (2003). Individual, interpersonal, and organisational links to women's advancement in management in banks. *Women in Management Review, 18*(5), 236–251.

Metz, I. (2011). Women leave because of family responsibilities: Fact or fiction? *Asia Pacific Journal of Human Resources, 49*(3), 285–307.

Metz, I., & Kulik, C.T. (2014). The rocky climb: Women's advancement in management. In S. Kumra, R. Simpson & R. Burke (Eds.), *The oxford handbook of gender in organizations* (pp. 175–199). Oxford, England: Oxford University Press.

Metz, I., & Kulik, C.T. (2015, December). *Champions of change: Why some CEOs champion gender diversity.* Paper presentation at the 29th ANZAM Conference, Queenstown, New Zealand. https://www.anzam.org/wp-content/uploads/2018/03/2597_110.pdf

Metz, I., & Kumra, S., (2019). Why are self-help books with career advice for women popular? *The Academy of Management Perspectives, 33*(1), 82–93. https://doi.org/10.5465/amp.2016.0152

Metz, I., & Simon, A. (2008). A focus on gender similarities in work experiences in senior management. *Equal opportunities international, 27*(5), 433–454.

Metz, I., & Tharenou, P. (1999). A retrospective analysis of Australian women's representation in management in large and small banks. *International Journal of Human Resource Management, 10*(2), 201–222.

Metz, I., & Tharenou, P. (2001). Women's career advancement. *Gender & Organisation Management, 26*(3), 312–342.

Mor Barak, M.E. (2017). *Managing diversity.* Thousand Oaks, CA: SAGE.

Noon, M. (2018). Pointless diversity training: Unconscious bias, new racism and agency. *Work, Employment and Society, 32*(1), 198–209.

Pellegrino, G., D'Amato, S., & Weisberg, A. (2011). *The gender dividend: Making the business case for investing in women.* Retrieved from http://sites.asiasociety.org/womenleaders/wp-content/uploads/2012/01/The-Gender-Dividend.pdf

Portes, A. (1998). Social capital. *Annual Review of Sociology, 24,* 1–24.

Powell, G. N., & Mainiero, L. A. (1992). Cross-currents in the river of time: Conceptualizing the complexities of women's careers. *Journal of Management, 18*(2), 215–237.

Ridgeway, C. L. (2001). Gender, status, and leadership. *Journal of Social issues, 57*(4), 637–655.

Riger, S., & Galligan, P. (1980). Women in management. *American Psychologist, 35*(10), 902–910.

Sandberg, S. (2013). *Lean in: Women, work and the will to lead.* New York, NY: Knopf.

Sanders, M., Zeng, J., Hellicar, M., & Fagg, K. (2016). *The power of flexibility.* Boston, MA: Bain & Company. Retrieved from https://cew.org.au/wp-content/uploads/2016/07/BAIN_CEW_REPORT_The_power_of_flexibility_Boosting_gender_parity-vF.pdf

Williamson, S., & Foley, M. (2018). Unconscious bias training: The 'Silver Bullet' for gender equity? *Australian Journal of Public Administration, 77*(3), 355–359.

World Economic Forum. (2020). *Global gender gap report 2020.* Retrieved from http://www3.weforum.org/docs/WEF_GGGR_2020.pdf

CHAPTER 17

RESEARCHING AND WRITING WHAT MATTERS MOST

Stella M. Nkomo
University of Pretoria, South Africa

Getting to research and write about what matters most is often difficult because we are too often pushed or feel pressured to take the instrumental path to becoming a scholar (Adler & Harzing, 2009; Alvesson & Gabriel, 2013; Tourish, 2019). It is not easy to get off that path, but early in my career, I was fortunate to study what mattered most to me. The work I am most proud of is my coauthored book with Ella L. J. Edmondson Bell, *Our Separate Ways: Black and White Women and the Struggle for Professional Identity* (Bell & Nkomo, 2001). Researching and writing the book unfolded over an 8-year period. But getting to this project came from my life journey. My initial inclination towards writing this chapter was to write from a distance. However, it was impossible to answer the prompting question, "How did you get interested in studying gender at work?" without sharing parts of my life story. My impetus for studying gender is probably not unique. It is no coincidence that most research on gender is done by women and that on women of color by women of color. What may be unique, though, is the particular paths we have taken to becoming a gender researcher and the

Perspectives on Gender and Work, pages 209–220

factors that have influenced the formation of our research identities (Bell & Nkomo, 1999; Cunliffe & Karunanayake, 2013).

MY STORY

I grew up in New York City at a time when busing was used to achieve racial integration. Although I lived in a poor Black and Hispanic neighborhood in the Bronx, we were bused to a White middle-class school. It was the beginning of my experiences of being a solo. At the time, high schools had different paths for the college bound versus those of us who had to get a job. For boys, it was the vocational track. For girls, it was the commercial track, which meant becoming proficient in typing and shorthand. I was one of the fastest typists and best stenographers in my graduating class but the job interviews were not forthcoming. I desperately needed a job to help my father who was trying to support a family of 10 children from a minimum wage salary. So I boldly tagged along with one of my White classmates to her interview at a large commercial bank. I was reluctantly allowed to take the job tests and could see the human resources person was doubtful I possessed the skills declared. After performing very well, I was hired to work at one of their branches in downtown Manhattan. I was the first Black secretary to be hired by the branch and was a curiosity not only to my boss but also to the mainly White customers.

This began what would be continuing experiences of being a solo Black woman in organizations and institutions dominated by White men. As young White male interns regularly came to the bank to learn about branch operations, I became keenly aware of not just the gender but also the racial disparity in who could be a manager. In the 5 years I worked in the branch, there was not a single White woman or Black woman among the interns. It was a time when an 1965 article published in the *Harvard Business Review* reported on a survey of 2,000 male and female executives that found 41 % of respondents “seemed to believe women are not only a special kind of people . . . but also that they have a special place which is not in the ranks of management” (Bowman, Worthy, & Geyser, 1965, p. 15).

I decided then to pursue further education. After completing my undergraduate degree at night, I had initially thought I would teach high school but then decided to pursue an MBA. Becoming a corporate executive seemed to be a way to break the race and gender barriers I had observed in the bank. My solo experiences continued throughout my quest for higher education. I was the only Black woman in my MBA class. My path had another turn, though. A chance conversation with one of the lecturers led me to naively believe that pursuing a doctorate would provide a greater means to making social change, through the opportunity to educate others and create knowledge.

Further education changed my life, and I believed it would do the same for others. I was the first Black woman admitted to the doctoral program at the School of Management, University of Massachusetts. There were 14 doctoral candidates in my class, nine men and five women.

I entered my doctoral studies with the goal of conducting research on the experiences of Black managers in corporate America. However, I was advised not to pursue this topic for my dissertation. Instead, I was told to produce a study on an *important* topic if I wanted to earn a doctorate. It was not a significant topic for the majority but for me and others like me, it was part of being in the world. I abandoned my topic and took the instrumental, survivalist path and produced a mainstream dissertation of formulaic research that I can barely relate to today. According to the Digest of Educational Statistics, the number of Black women earning doctorates in the field of business and management in the early 1980s in the United States was in the single digits (Snyder, 1987). After completing my doctorate and landing a position as the first Black woman tenure-track assistant professor in the business college, I produced the three perfunctory publications expected from a dissertation.

THE EPIPHANY

Breaking from my dissertation research, I embarked on what I had really wanted to study—the career experiences of Black managers. Armed with the positivist, quantitative skills acquired during my doctorate studies, I conducted survey research with Taylor Cox Jr., a pioneer in the field of race and diversity in organizations on the status of Black managers in corporate America (Blake-Beard, Finley-Hervey, & Harquail, 2008). Along with one of the completed surveys was a letter from a Black woman manager who shared her pain of being a solo in a Fortune 100 corporation. Clearly, the survey could not capture all of what she was experiencing in her organization. Her letter ended with "I'm trying to be in control of my situation and hang in there until things improve. Right now, I must say mentally it is very difficult" (Nkomo, 1988). To this day, I still wonder if she was able to survive the hostile, organizational climate in which she was employed.

I realized two things that day. First, the contents of the handwritten letter affirmed what I was coming to understand. The story of Black women in management had to be told. It was about much more than my personal experiences. It was an exclusion with consequences for so many Black women, like the author of the letter. Second, I found my scholarly voice, my preferred epistemology for creating knowledge (Nkomo, 2016). Quantitative methods alone were going to be inadequate for understanding the meaning and experience of being a Black woman manager in organizational spaces steeped in racism and patriarchy. I decided then to focus on the experiences of Black women from an intersectional lens and to employ qualitative methods that would reveal the embodied, subjective, and intersubjective realities of race and gender in the workplace (Tomkins & Eatough, 2013).

At the time, research on women in management was at a nascent stage. The gender and diversity in organizations division did not exist and women in management was an interest group struggling for legitimacy (Nkomo, Bell, Roberts, Joshi, & Thatcher, 2019). Women in management research was about White women, although the adjective White was never explicitly used in the scholarship (Nkomo, 1988). Gender essentialism dominated women in management theory and practice—an assumption that the experience of gender could be studied independent of other categories of difference like race. It was also a time when the preferred language was sex not gender (Ely & Padavic, 2007).

I then teamed up with Ella L. J. Edmondson Bell who had completed her dissertation on the bicultural life structures and stress among Black women (Bell, 1986) and Toni C. Denton[1] whose doctorate focused on supportive relationships among Black women as a coping mechanism for career stress (Denton, 1987). We embarked on an ambitious research project to tell the life stories of Black professional women in corporate America that had been largely invisible in a way that all who read them would understand the complex layers of what it meant to be marginalized, always the first, smart, strong but assumed to be just the opposite. From the outset, our primary focus was not on journal articles but on writing a book that would be read by the very women we were studying and the leaders of America's corporations. We wanted to contribute to changing the situation of Black women professionals.

THE LIFE JOURNEYS OF WOMEN IN CORPORATIONS PROJECT

At about the time we conceptualized the project, the Rockefeller Foundation announced a grant competition for research on changing gender roles in post-industrial societies. To our delight, we received a grant to conduct research (referred to as "ground breaking" by the reviewers of our application) on the effects of race and gender identity on the life course and career experiences of Black and White women managers in the United States corporate sector. We were humbled by the award as only 15 out of 600 submissions were funded. Subsequently, we also received additional funding from the Ford Foundation. This second funding affirmed the importance of the research and came at a time when we had been discouraged by some academic colleagues when presenting our work at management conferences where work on gender was scarce and that on race virtually invisible. At one Academy of Management annual meeting, the validity of the project was challenged (i.e., the research was too "subjective"), and one very senior White male professor cautioned us that we were placing ourselves into a research ghetto and would probably never get tenure.

The research design for the project was a mixed methods approach of life history interviews and survey data. We chose life history interviews because we believed it was important to embed the women's life stories within the social and historical contexts in which they unfolded. Departing from what we referred to as the parachute approach—only focusing on women's career experiences—that dominated research on professional and managerial women, we posed six questions in the study (Bell & Nkomo, 2001, p. 19):

1. What are the women's early life stories?
2. How did race, gender, and social class affect key developmental aspects of their lives?
3. What are the effects of gender, race, and social class over the course of their lives?
4. What role conflicts do the African-American women experience as a result of their bicultural life structures?
5. How do gender, race, and social class affect the women's work experiences, upward mobility, and career satisfaction?
6. How do women managers negotiate their work, family, and community roles and their interrelationships among them?

Initial efforts to gain access to the women managers and professionals were met with caution from corporations. So we turned to women's networks and professional associations who proved eager to assist. In the end, snowball sampling gave us access to 120 women for the interview phase of the project. Surveys were completed by 825 women. The research design was so different from what I had been trained to produce as a doctoral student. The life history interviews, which led the methodology, represented a departure from the positivist, quantitative sterile methods that had been forced upon me during my doctoral studies. We spent about eight hours with each woman as she shared her early life story to her current career.

Working on the project was emancipatory and challenging at the same time. I was finally enmeshed in what I had always wanted to study and write about. It was not easy though. I was comfortable with the survey, but interviewing the women evoked anxiety. As a quantitatively trained researcher, I had fears about my ability to do the research and how I would make sense of it. I struggled with the intimacy of being in the women's personal spaces and listening to their life stories shared so openly. I had to abandon the idea of scientific neutrality. Collecting and analyzing the data not only meant reliving and reflecting about my own life but angst about my authority to speak for other women. I came to understand the meaning of co-inquiry and reflexivity in qualitative research. I felt (as did most of the team) an enormous responsibility of trying to speak for others and honoring the authenticity of their lives and voices. Ella, however, was a clinically and qualitatively trained researcher who felt differently. She had the foresight to assign readings for the team. I read them with earnest. Yet it was only when I began the interviews that I fully realized what Michelle Fine (1994) meant when she reminds qualitative researchers that

> we are in relations with the contexts we study and with our informants, understanding that we are all multiple in those relations and to never forget the importance of being reflexive about whose story is being told, why, to whom, and with what interpretations and consequences. (p. 72)

Interviews with the women were intense and literally meant we had 120 individual biographies. It took some time, as is common with qualitative work, to figure out how to tell their stories without losing the complexity of their lives. Birthing the book, as Ella and I often said, was painfully difficult at times but, ultimately, the most fulfilling research project of my career (Bell & Nkomo, 1999). The greatest joy comes from the feedback we continue to receive from women of all backgrounds about how their own lives and careers resonate with the stories of the women in the research. Although the print version is no longer available, Harvard Business School Press recently released a digital version of the book.

KEY FINDINGS

Our Separate Ways in the title of the book captures the theme of the main finding of the research. The women came to the corporate workplace not just from separate paths but from what Kate Rushin (2000) calls *separate definitions* formed out of the juncture of race, gender, family background, geographical location, social class, culture, and the sociohistorical context in which they grew up (Bell & Nkomo, 2001). Social class and geographical spaces featured more strongly in their early lives. Overall, though, the study confirmed that the intersection of race and gender was important to understanding the experiences of women in management—from career entry, advancement, work, and family to how they negotiated their careers and the obstacles encountered. The general invisibility of race in research on women in management at the time was reflected in what we heard from the White women we interviewed. While gender featured in their stories, race was silent. The words of one interview summed up what we learned, "Race just wasn't on my radar screen" (Bell & Nkomo, 2001, p. 84).

The career experiences of Black and White women were inextricably intertwined because of their different social locations relative to the White men who dominated the organizations in which they worked. Consequently, there were significant qualitative differences in access to the power and privileges of being a manager. Gender discrimination was a barrier to advancement for all the women in our study. However, Black women encountered the additional barrier of racism, facing a concrete wall rather than a glass ceiling (Bell & Nkomo, 2001, p. 139). In short, the experience of gender discrimination depends on a woman's race. Black women experienced what we called *racialized sexism*—daily doses of it that had both material and psychological costs (Bell & Nkomo, 2001, p. 137). Although both groups of women had similar educational backgrounds and experience, the Black women experienced a slower rate of promotion. White women had advanced further up the corporate hierarchy compared to Black women.

Not only did the women travel separate paths, they also made different choices about how to navigate their careers and to change the workplace. The two groups of women responded differently to the organizational cultures they encountered. It was a source of tension in how they related to one another in the workplace. We found one of the widest gulfs between them resulted from their disparate experiences and understandings of race. For the Black women, racial identity was a source of strength; while White women were generally unaware of the significance of race in their own lives and careers. Black women also expressed much more awareness of racism and sexism in their companies and were much more willing to speak out against injustices. The White women were less vocal and believed they could fit in by doing the right things and performing well. We attributed these findings to the difference in the women's social location to White men, who were dominant holders of corporate power. To the extent White women share membership in the same racial category, they believed access to the organization power system was possible and that conforming was better than challenging the status quo. On the other hand Black women understood their outsider status and had no delusions about their hard work and good behavior easily yielding advancement into the power system (Bell, Meyerson, Nkomo, & Scully, 2003).

Lessons Learned

I hope sharing my journey to doing the kind of research that matters will be helpful to young scholars embarking upon an academic career. I have learned a few things along my journey. First, it is important to find one's scholarly voice—not the voice taught in doctoral education or the one that will guarantee tenure and promotion but the one that comes from one's beliefs about what is important. Finding one's scholarly voice means claiming an area of curiosity and embracing a definition of truth that is right for you (i.e., developing an epistemological stance). This does not mean a researcher should be stagnant in the methodologies of scholarship but research philosophy, research identity, and the desired impact of one's scholarship is a choice. I produced my best research when I embraced what I believed mattered most for changing the status of Black women in the workplace. I found my research identity doing the project and thereafter committed my scholarship to giving visibility to marginal voices in management and organization studies. This path is not easy for gender and diversity scholars because even though there is more research on gender (and race to a lesser degree) in organizations, it is still not yet considered mainstream (Jané, van Esch, & Bilimoria, 2018). I continue to hear from young scholars who feel pressure to abandon their interests in gender or to cloak them within more digestible packages.

Second, get close to the phenomenon you are studying. I could not have gained the rich insights to the intersection of race and gender without having had the opportunity to listen to the women's stories. Deep understanding of the phenomenon you are studying enables you to think more clearly about how to answer, "Why is this important and for whom?" Finally, I would underscore the importance of finding one's scholarly community. Research can be a lonely endeavor without the opportunity to collaborate with others with similar interests. As my journey demonstrates, teaming with Ella and Toni not only brought intellectual enrichment but emotional and motivational support at a critical time in the early years of my career. Working together also buffered us from the hostile reception our work sometimes received in the academy.

FUTURE GENDER RESEARCH

In writing this chapter, we were asked to offer ideas about "hot" gender topics. I offer two that I believe need more attention. The first one emanates from one of the major findings reported in *Our Separate Ways*. The relationship gulf between women of color and White women that impedes solidarity for achieving gender equality. At the time, we were quite distressed about what we had learned from the interviews and surveys in the study. More recently Ella and I did a podcast for Harvard Business School on the theme of sisterhood in the workplace. More research is needed about how women can forge meaningful relationships in society and the workplace across the many divides that separate us from race and class, sexual identity, ideological differences to our locations within the coloniality of power that positions the global North above the global South (Connell, 2007; Mignolo, 2007; Mohanty, 2003; Westwood, Jack, Khan, & Frenkel, 2014).

Although women, especially in "developed" countries, are present in high numbers in the workforce, we have not been able to translate our numbers into a source of power. These gulfs have also played out in broader society. The unity displayed by women across the world during the 2017 historic women's march after the inauguration of President Donald Trump was remarkable and estimates placed the number of marchers at between 3 to 4 million (Waddell, 2017). Marshalling the twin themes of intersectionality and inclusion, the organizers attempted "to bring the reality of living in bodies marked by social difference into a common voice of dissent" (Moss & Maddrell, 2017, p. 614). But the unity of the day could not overcome the divisive fault lines that prevent women from acting relationally to achieve gender equality. Of course, there are complex reasons why the show of solidarity could not be sustained. However, in respect to the workplace context, it raises a neglected question in our research on gender in organizations: "How can women build coalitions and sisterhood in the workplace as a means to gender equality?"; "Why is it difficult for women to see the interconnections among the different forms of marginalization that separate them?"; and "How can we foster understanding among women of the possibilities of collective action for engendering workplace equality for all women?"

Second, much more research is needed on *undoing gender inequality*. The research of the past several decades has done an excellent job of theorizing the problems of patriarchy and gender inequality in the workplace. What we know less about is how to disrupt them. I believe thinking (theorizing) and doing should be inseparable in our scholarship. Too often we give lip service to practice but much more research is needed on how to achieve gender equality in the workplace. I would urge scholars to take up the ethnographic work done by Ely & Meyerson (2010) and others on undoing gender in organizations. Pursuing this topic would also provide opportunities to employ underutilized methods like action research, ethnography, and case studies.

Finally, we need to revitalize research on sexual harassment in the workplace. The #MeToo movement made it clear that sexual harassment is not a thing of the past, and its current manifestations provide opportunities to explore new questions about what constitutes sexual harassment (and whose harassment counts) in the context of gender, race, class, and power dynamics in organizations.

CONCLUSION

We do not always get an opportunity to share the experience of doing research or the personal reasons for choosing the topics we study. Although this is the case, it does not mean that scholars don't engage in some form of identity work in constructing, negotiating, and maintaining a research identity. I believe it is important to reflect upon why one has chosen a particular approach and epistemology for the research undertaken. But answering the question, "Who am I as a researcher, and what do I want to study?" requires more than simply choosing an ontological and epistemological approach that ensures publications. I did my best work when I found my scholarly voice, pursuing research questions that mattered most to changing the status of women in organizations. Gender (along with other axes of social difference) remains a major source of inequality in society and in the workplace. Ultimately, the research we do has to matter and be more than armchair theorizing if the knowledge we generate will make a difference.

NOTE

1. Toni left the project early for personal reasons.

REFERENCES

Adler, N. J., & Harzing, A. W. (2009). When knowledge wins: transcending the sense and nonsense of academic rankings. *Academy of Management Learning & Education, 8*(1), 72–95.

Alvesson, M., & Gabriel, Y. (2013). Beyond formulaic research: In praise of greater diversity in organizational research and publications, *Academy of Management learning & Education, 12*(2), 245–263.

Bell, E. (1986). *The power within: Bicultural life structures and stress among Black women* (Unpublished doctoral dissertation). Case Western Reserve University, Cleveland, Ohio.

Bell, E. E., & Nkomo, S. M. (1999). Postcards from the borderlands: building a career from the outside/within. *Journal of Career Development, 26*(1), 69–84.

Bell, E. L., & Nkomo, S. M. (2001). *Our separate ways: Black and White women and the struggle for professional identity in corporate America.* Cambridge, MA: Harvard Business School Press.

Bell, E. L. E., Meyerson, D., Nkomo, S., & Scully, M. (2003). Interpreting silence and voice in the workplace: A conversation about tempered radicalism among black and white women researchers. *The Journal of Applied Behavioral Science, 39*(4), 381–414.

Blake-Beard, S. D., Finley-Hervey, J. A., & Harquail, C. V. (2008). Journey to a different place: Reflections on Taylor Cox, Jr.'s career and research as a catalyst for diversity education and training. *Academy of Management Learning & Education, 7*(3), 394–405.

Bowman, G. W., Worthy, N. B., & Greyser, S. A. (1965). Are women executives people? *Harvard Business Review, 43*(4), 14–28, 164–178.

Connell, R (2007) *Southern theory: The global dynamics of knowledge in social sciences.* Cambridge, MA: Polity.

Cunliffe, A. L., & Karunanayake, G. (2013). Working within hyphen-spaces in ethnographic research: Implications for research identities and practice. *Organizational Research Methods, 16*(3), 364–392.

Denton, T. C. (1988). *Social support among black professional women: Rituals of restoration* (Unpublished doctoral dissertation). Case Western Reserve University, Cleveland, OH.

Ely, R. J., & Meyerson, D. E. (2010). An organizational approach to undoing gender: The unlikely case of offshore oil platforms. *Research in organizational behavior, 30,* 3–34.

Ely, R., & Padavic, I. 2007. A feminist analysis of organizational research on sex differences. *Academy of Management Review, 32*(4), 1121–1143.

Fine, M. (1994). Working the hyphens: Reinventing self and other in qualitative research. In N. K. Denzin & Y. S. Lincoln (Eds.), *Handbook of qualitative research* (pp. 72–82). Thousand Oaks, CA: SAGE.

Jané, S., Van Esch, C., & Bilimoria, D. (2018). "Why'd you wanna study that?" A process model of the under-legitimation of a research topic. *Academy of Management Learning & Education, 17*(4), 401–424.

Mignolo, W. D. (2007). Coloniality of power and de-colonial thinking. *Cultural Studies, 21*(2/3), 155–167.

Mohanty, C. T. (2003). *Feminism without borders: Decolonizing theory, practicing solidarity.* Durham, NC: Duke University Press.

Moss, P., & Maddrell, A. (2017). Emergent and divergent spaces in the Women's March: The challenges of intersectionality and inclusion. *Gender, Place & Culture: A Journal of Feminist Geography, 24*(5), 613–620.

Nkomo, S. M. (1988). Race and sex: The forgotten case of black female managers. In S. Rose & L. Larwood (Eds.), *Women's careers: Pathways and pitfalls* (pp. 133–150). Westport, CT: Praeger.

Nkomo, S. M. (2016). Finding my scholarly voice: Making the invisible, visible. *Journal of Corporate Citizenship, 62,* 11–13.

Nkomo, S. M., Bell, M. P., Roberts, L. M., Joshi, A., & Thatcher, S. M. (2019). Diversity at a critical juncture: New theories for a complex phenomenon. *Academy of Management Review, 44*(3), 498–517.

Rushin, K. (2000). Word problems. *Callaloo, 23*(1), 190–191.

Snyder, T. D. (1987). *Digest of education statistics.* Washington, DC: Center for Education Statistics (OERI/ED).

Tomkins, L., & Eatough, V. (2013). The feel of experience: Phenomenological ideas for organizational research. *Qualitative Research in Organizations and Management: An International Journal, 8*(3), 258–275.

Tourish, D. (2020). The triumph of nonsense in management studies. *Academy of Management Learning and Education Journal, 19*(1). https://doi.org/10.5465/amle.2019.0255

Waddell, K. (2017, January 23). The exhausting work of tallying American's largest protest. *The Atlantic*. Retrieved from https://www.theatlantic.com/technology/archive/2017/01/womens-march-protest-count/514166/

Westwood, R., Jack, G., Khan, F., & Frenkel, M. (Eds.). (2014). *Core-periphery relations and organization studies*. Basingstoke, England: Palgrave Macmillan.

CHAPTER 18

GENDER DEMOGRAPHICS AND ORGANIZATIONS

An Ongoing (and Possibly Unending) Research Agenda

Pamela S. Tolbert
Cornell University

STUDYING GENDER AND WORK: ORIGINS OF MY INTERESTS

A sequence of influences led me to study gender relations in the workplace. The first, and broadest, was the general *zeitgeist* when I started college in the early 1970s, one that was strongly influenced by the preceding decade. In 1963, Betty Freidan published her treatise, *The Feminine Mystique*, famously discussing "the problem that has no name." As it turned out, the problem did in fact have a name, sex discrimination, one called out later that year in the Congressional enactment of the Equal Pay Act. A flood of subsequent literary analyses (e.g., Bird, 1968; Greer, 1970; *Ms. Magazine*, first issued in 1972; Steinem, 1963) and legislative actions (e.g., the Civil Rights Act of 1964, including Title VII prohibiting sex discrimination in employment,

Perspectives on Gender and Work, pages 221–231

and the founding in 1972 of the ACLU's Women's Rights Project, led by Ruth Bader Ginsberg) soon followed. Thus, during my precollege years, both legal and literary forces were vigorously fanning the flames of what has been labeled the second wave of feminism, and I was not insulated from this. It's hard to say exactly how I became aware of the problems of unequal pay, limited promotion opportunities, and frequently dismissive treatment of women at work, though I assume these issues were covered in various news media. Symptomatically, within a year of beginning my undergraduate studied, I had roped my boyfriend (a graphic designer and illustrator) into designing the logo for the Tulsa Area Coalition for Equal Rights, a group that I joined trying to help pass the sadly ill-fated Equal Rights Act in Oklahoma.

My duly raised consciousness undoubtedly contributed to my attraction to studying sociology as an undergraduate (reinforced by the fact that it was the only class in which I received an "A" my first semester). Understanding the bases and consequences of social inequality was a well-established quest in sociology. Unfortunately, up through the 1970s and even beyond, many sociologists conceptualized social inequality as a problem that affected only (or at least primarily) men, as evinced by the surprisingly large number of analyses aimed at explaining earnings inequality that were based on men-only samples, without even the slightest nod to the obvious limits of such sampling procedures. But economic and social inequalities tied to gender slowly began to be addressed in the discipline, often in classes bearing some version of the title, Marriage and the Family. One of the faculty teaching such a class served as a supervisor of my senior honors thesis which, as I recall, was aimed at explaining why sex discrimination occurred. (I offer a belated tip of the hat to her for her tolerance of such an overbroad and under-comprehending question—this is not so very uncommon among undergraduates, I have come to understand.)

My decision to pursue a PhD in sociology was driven, at least in part, by knowledge of gender inequities that I had picked up in my undergraduate studies. Nearing graduation and finally facing up to the question of how I would make my living as the daughter of a woman who had struggled to support her family post-divorce, *not* earning my own living was not on the options table), I remember seriously considering only a handful of female-dominated occupations: being a public school teacher, a social worker, or a librarian. I did not explicitly reflect on the processes that led me to focus on these choices (nor why I had picked sociology rather than engineering as a major), but I did recognize that they were female-dominated occupations and had learned—probably in a class on marriage and the family—that such occupations were inevitably and significantly underpaid compared to similarly skilled male-dominated occupations. I had turned into a good student in college and acquired some interest in doing research; hence,

I decided that becoming a professor would allow me to use my academic abilities and help dodge what I now think of as the XX economic discount (chromosomally speaking).

The awareness of the links between gender and economic outcomes that I gained in my undergraduate years also affected other career choices. I had proposed focusing on two fields, marriage and the family and urban sociology, in my applications to graduate schools. But once I began graduate work, I came to realize that the former, in particular, was a female-dominated specialty within the discipline, and that the same gender effects operating *across* occupations could be found *within* occupations. Thus, I decided instead to adopt organizations as an area of concentration since, based on a seminar I took early in my graduate studies, the research in this area seemed fairly interesting, and most of my fellow students in the class were male (which I took to indicate that this area had legitimacy within the discipline). That was a lucky choice for several reasons. One is, as I came to realize and now try to impress upon my students, organizations are both the main sources of problems and solutions in the world, so understanding the forces that drive organizations is a critical quest for social sciences. In addition, it gave me a range of academic job options, and it was a poor job market in sociology when I completed my PhD. However, the choice also reflected an irony that I only later recognized: My interests in research on gender inequality, and information I gleaned from this research, led me to avoid focusing my research on gender.

Two circumstances helped me untangle this conundrum. One was a sociology seminar on data analysis that I took with Professor Don Treiman, who did research on social stratification, including gender-based stratification (see, e.g., Treiman & Roos, 1983). Many of the examples and assignments in this class required empirically addressing questions related to this topic. This experience both reinvigorated my interests in studying gendered social problems, and assuaged what can only be called my status anxieties about pursuing these interests. In the discipline, *stratification* had, and continues to have high prestige as a field of study. This may be partly because it suggests concerns with social inequality writ large (versus small, partisan concerns with one's personal disadvantages as a woman or a minority). There are other, multicollinear aspects of the field that may also affect its status: It is dominated by cutting-edge, quantitative analytic approaches, has many male scholars, and substantively overlaps with research done by economists. In any case, positioning research on gender under this broader rubric provided me with psychological license to pursue it.

A second influence on my decision to follow my interests in studying gendered problems was a lunch meeting I attended with other women graduate students in the department, one organized to introduce us to Professor Jessie Bernard, a famous feminist sociologist, who was visiting UCLA. (See, among other examples, Bernard, 1968, 1972). By way of introduction, we went around the table identifying ourselves and the topics we were studying. At the end of the round, Jessie looked at us in perplexity and asked why none of us were studying anything to do with gender (which had become strikingly clear in our self-descriptions). Our explanations ultimately boiled down to one common theme: Studying anything to do with gender was fatal to gaining recognition as a "real" scholar. In response, she noted that if everyone was afraid to study the topic, it would never *become* legitimate. That struck me as a good point, and ultimately, this very brief encounter was important in encouraging me not to sublimate genuine intellectual interests to careerist concerns.

Finally, as a just-beginning junior faculty, I encountered two publications that allowed me to recognize the logical links between my interests in studying organizations and in studying gender inequality. One was the now-iconic book by Professor Rosabeth Kanter, *Men and Women of the Corporation* (1977), an ethnographic study of the relationships, social perceptions and processes in a firm that led to truncated opportunities for women's mobility within the firm. A second, which is equally iconic in my view, was an article published in the *American Sociological Review* by Baron and Bielby (1980), making the case that, if one wanted to understand enduring social inequality, it is necessary to study organizations, since organizational decisions—hiring, pay-setting, promoting—are the central mechanisms through which broad patterns of inequality are produced and reproduced (see also Hacker, 1979). That this observation could possibly qualify as an epiphany may seem surprising, but in the 1980s, the overlap between organization scholars and gender scholars was razor thin. This overlap has widened over time, though I admit to being surprised that it is not wider by now. Especially for those interested in understanding forces that affect organizations, gender seems an obvious focus—how it affects the founders and top management, the workforce, and constituents are oddly under-explored.

STUDYING GENDER AND WORK: MY RESEARCH ON THE EFFECTS OF CHANGING GROUP PROPORTIONS

In any case, intrigued by Kanter's arguments about the effects of variations in group gender composition, and inspired by Bielby and Baron's call for more attention to organizations' role in social stratification, I began to explore the relations between various features of organizations and outcomes linked to gender inequality, most often focusing on the effects and determinants of gender composition in organizations.

With few exceptions, my empirical work on gender has been located in the context of higher education organizations. I used data from colleges and universities for my dissertation, which drew upon institutional theory (see Meyer & Rowan, 1977; Zucker, 1977) to explain the presence and absence of certain administrative offices in higher education organizations. One non-substantive finding I gleaned from this research is that these organizations have a massive footprint in terms of longitudinal, publicly available data, collected by both government agencies (e.g., the Department of Education's annual survey, known as the Integrated Postsecondary Education Data System) and nongovernmental ones (e.g., the Chronicle of Higher Education's annual faculty salary survey). And, importantly, data relevant to gender inequality—earnings, distribution of faculty at different organizational ranks, and so on—are often broken down by male and female (although individual level data are not always available). Still, if one is interested in studying variables above the individual level, higher education organizations can be a data goldmine.

Thus, in my first publication on gender differences in organizations (Tolbert, 1986), I examined the effects of various characteristics (size, prestige, revenues, etc.) of colleges and universities as potential determinants of the gap in the salaries of male and female faculty. In this study, average faculty compensation, as well as the magnitude of the differences in average compensation for men and women (within ranks), were treated as properties of an organization. The economists to whom I presented the paper reacted very negatively (which is, I would say, a wildly understated description) because this approach ran counter to their disciplinary assumption that individual wages are largely, if not entirely, a function of individual productivity. From this perspective, treating compensation as an organizational characteristic is nonsensical. Nonetheless, not being an economist nor constrained by such assumptions, I persevered in publishing it and was gratified to discover later, in the compensation literature on "pay leaders" and "pay laggards," that others also saw merit in examining compensation as an organizational-level property (see Rynes & Milkvich, 1986; Gerhart & Rynes, 2003). As far as I can tell, however, few if any studies on pay strategy have focused on the problem that gender differences in compensation may pose to measurement of the central concept (e.g., Brown, Sturman, & Simmering, 2003).

In my initial study, an important predictor of the size of gender-based pay gaps within colleges and universities turned out to be the representation of women among the faculty: The greater the proportion of women, the smaller the gap. Examining influences on the average salary of male and female faculty separately suggested that this was because the average salary of women was not strongly affected by their being in larger, more prestigious, research institutions—that is, those likely to be pay leaders—but the average salary of men was. (Thus, akin to findings from studies on the effects of education on earnings, men received higher returns to being located in "better" organizations). This was not what I expected, given Kanter's arguments about the consequences of increasing the representation of women in groups (which were, admittedly, at a different level of analysis and did not address compensation, per se). At the least, the results suggested that variations in gender composition were associated with more than the normalization of women's presence in a given setting, or increases in opportunities for intergroup interaction that might lessen biases. Puzzling over other ways in which gender composition could affect organizational outcomes led me to carry out a number of subsequent empirical and theoretical studies, working with various students and colleagues (e.g., Duguid, Loyd, & Tolbert, 2012; Lawrence & Tolbert, 2007; Tolbert, Graham, & Andrews, 1999; Tolbert & Oberfield, 1991).

Among these is one that used longitudinal data collected from the American Sociological Association's annually published *Guide to Graduate Departments* to examine whether and how variations in the representation of women in a department affected the likelihood that faculty members would stay or leave (Tolbert, Simons, Andrews, & Rhee, 1995). In retrospect, I like this study for several reasons. One is that it made a good use of existing archival data, compiled for non-research purposes, but with great demographic data on a national set of comparable organizational work groups over time. The ASA guide, which was created to provide information to aspiring sociology graduate students, provides a list of current faculty members, their rank, and areas of interest, along with other information of interest to applicants—tuition costs, financial aid, recent PhD recipients, and so on. Almost all departments with a PhD program submit this information to the ASA annually. We drew a sample of 50 departments, and by comparing the year-to-year list of faculty members for a 12-year period (1977–1988) for each, we were able to construct a dataset with measures of the number, rank, and gender of faculty member who left and those who were hired into the department each year, as well as the total number of faculty and proportion of women in the department at assistant, associate, and full professor ranks.

Another reason I like the study is because, in line with Davis's (1971) classic prescriptions for making research interesting, it set up a comparison between two competing hypotheses, each focused on group proportions and intergroup relations. Both were long-standing and both had garnered a body of empirical support, but to my knowledge, they had not been examined cheek to jowl. The first hypothesis (contact hypothesis), was premised on a classic argument (Allport, 1954) about the role of individuals' interactions with members of other social groups (defined by race, gender, or other common in-group/out-group characteristics) in reducing prejudices and discrimination. It posited that in departments with relatively larger proportions of women, women would face a more favorable social climate and the likelihood of turnover by women faculty would be lower. The second hypothesis, which had been examined mostly in work on race discrimination (e.g., Blalock, 1957), was premised on two key assumptions. The first was that competition for social resources typically entailed intergroup conflict (similar to social identity theory; see Tajfel, 1970). The second was that relative group sizes importantly affected such conflict. Specifically, it suggested that intergroup conflict increased as the size of competing groups approached parity, because the growth of a socially subordinate group entailed a progressively greater threat to a dominant group's control of resources. Hence, the derived hypothesis (competition hypothesis) was that women in departments with relatively larger proportions of women would face a more hostile environment; thus, these departments would have *more* turnover among women faculty.

The results of our analyses provided support for the competition hypothesis, and specifically, indicated a curvilinear relation between the proportion of women faculty and the likelihood that women would leave the department. That is, the rate of turnover among women, particularly women at the assistant level, increased as the proportion of women in a department increased until, by our calculations, that proportion reached about 40–50%.[1] The curvilinear relationship is in line with arguments made earlier by proponents of a competition perspective (e.g., Blalock, 1957). Presumably, once the proportion of social minorities in a group crosses a threshold, allowing them to combat discrimination by the dominant group effectively, intergroup conflict will decline. Interestingly, increases in the proportion of women in departments had little effect on the rates of turnover among male faculty—if anything, this appeared to *reduce* tenured men's likelihood of turnover.

I found—and still find—these results to be provocative, which is another reason that I like the study. The notion that increases in the representation of a social minority[2] can create a sense of threat among the members of a socially dominant group, a threat that is not necessarily reduced by social contact, fits with some of my own observations. But both the findings and the theoretical framework that they provide support for are far from unambiguous.

STUDYING GENDER AND WORK: FUTURE WORK ON STILL-PUZZLING EFFECTS OF GROUP PROPORTIONS

There are many questions about how group proportions, and especially *changes* in proportions, affect group relations that remain unanswered. These questions have practical importance, because many of our social policies aimed at addressing stubbornly persistent social inequalities are predicated on increasing pressure on organizations to desegregate (or become more diverse, in current terminology). Recognition that increasing diversity will not necessarily lead to decreasing intergroup biases and conflict, as implied by simpler versions of social contact theory, has led to a small cottage industry on increasing inclusiveness, typically aimed at surfacing implicit biases and stereotypes held by individuals, and making them consciousness of the pernicious consequences of these. But we have comparatively little empirical knowledge of the long-term effectiveness of efforts to increase organizational inclusiveness, especially in terms of behavioral changes or material indicators (e.g., reduced turnover or demographically linked differences in compensation). And relatedly, the theoretical and research foundations of such efforts need to be better-developed, including enhancing our knowledge of the contextual conditions that are apt to affect the outcomes of such efforts (see Cheng et al., 2019; Roberson, Ryan, & Ragins, 2017). Revisiting and expanding search on group proportions can contribute to this.

For example, our discussion in the 1995 paper followed the usual logic of a competition perspective in at least implicitly assuming that it was the male faculty in a department who felt threatened by the increasing representation of female faculty and created an environment leading to women's departures, but it is possible that this change may have had symbolic or status implication for the department as a whole that affected reactions of women, as well as men. Some work has acknowledged that the proportion of social minorities in a group can be related to competition *among* the minority members (see Kanter, 1977). Generally, this is presumed to occur when there is a sole social minority in a group, a token, who has become invested in the uniqueness of that status (see Duguid, Loyd, & Tolbert [2012] for a review). But this phenomenon has been addressed by relatively little research (perhaps because it is a discomfiting possibility for many of us), and how it might be affected by varying group proportions, or other group and contextual characteristics deserve more study. To my knowledge, the question of whether such reactions are typically obviated or reduced by greater numerical representation has not been adequately answered (if it has been answered at all).

In this context, a related, more complex problem for research involves untangling more materialist from more psychological explanations of the effects of variations in group proportions on intergroup relations. As suggested by social contact theory, social stereotypes and biases may be easier to reduce when the representation of different subgroups is relatively balanced, because opportunities for cross-group interaction may provide disconfirming evidence for these (particularly in the context of consciously made efforts to raise people's awareness of such stereotypes and biases). However, insofar as the stereotypes and biases reflect or are tied to underlying concerns about group social status, which may be increased when the representation of subgroups becomes more balanced, they may be much harder to reduce through contact and increased psychological awareness. Thus, understanding the relation of group demography to the interactive effects of competition and cross-group interaction merits attention by scholars.

Finally, a much, much more complex problem for research involves both theoretically and empirically specifying the links between group proportions, attitudes, and perceptions of both social minorities and social dominants and behavioral outcomes. Most research on group composition to date has focused on *either* attitudinal outcomes, suggesting implications for behavior, *or* behavioral outcomes, drawing inferences about attitudes. Saying that it is difficult to get data to examine these links ridiculously understates the case, but there are some possibilities for undertaking this challenge. Many organizations regularly conduct personnel surveys assessing climate or related attitudinal conditions, and one can imagine finding an obliging organization with such data over time that would also allow access to data on work group composition and work group and individual outcomes (like turnover, or change in leadership, etc.).

CONCLUSIONS

As noted by Baron and Bielby (1980), understanding social inequality requires identifying and studying organizational conditions that are systematically linked to group-based differences in individual achievements—getting hired, getting promoted, getting higher or lower levels of compensation. Variations in group proportions may affect all of these, and hence, it is one key aspect of understanding the forces that affect gendered outcomes and relations at work. And as pointed out to me long ago by Jessie Bernard, we need people to delve into these forces. My aims here thus are to encourage more work on the specific, unanswered questions about the impact of gender demography in organizations, and more generally, to encourage more research on all sorts of issues involving gendered aspects of organizations.

NOTES

1. Note that in our data, less than a handful of departments had that level of female representation so that estimate should be treated with a reasonable amount of skepticism.
2. I use *social minority* to refer to members of groups that are assigned low status within the larger society, that is, are seen as less competent or lacking desirable qualities, based on particular characteristics (see Ridgeway, 2019). *Numerical minorities* refers to members of groups that constitute a smaller pro-

portion of an encompassing, larger group. Most research, including mine, has focused on cases where social minorities are also numerical minorities.

REFERENCES

Allport, G. W. (1954). *The nature of prejudice.* New York, NY: Addison-Wesley.

Baron, J. N., & Bielby, W. T. (1980). Bringing the firms back in: Stratification, segmentation and the organization of work. *American Sociological Review, 45*(5), 737–765.

Bernard, J. (1968). *The sex game.* Englewood Cliffs, NJ: Prentice Hall.

Bernard, J. (1972). *The future of marriage.* New York, NY: Bantam Books.

Bird, C. (1968). *Born female: The high cost of keeping women down.* New York, NY: McKay.

Blalock, H. (1957). Percent non-white and discrimination in the South. *American Sociological Review, 22*(6), 677–682.

Brown, M. P., Sturnman, M. C., & Simmering, M. J. (2017). Compensation policy and organizational performance: The efficiency, operational and financial implication of pay levels and pay structure. *Academy of Management Journal, 46*(6), 752–762.

Cheng, S., Corrington, A., Dinh, J., Hebl, M., King, E., Ng, L., . . . Traylor, A. (2019). Challenging diversity training myths: Changing the conversation about diversity training to shape science and practice. *Organizational Dynamics, 48*(4), 1–11.

Davis, M. (1971). That's interesting: Towards a phenomenology of sociology and a sociology of phenomenology. *Philosophy of the Social Sciences, 1*(4), 309–344.

Duguid, M., Loyd, D. L., & Tolbert, P. S. (2012). The impact of categorical status, numeric representation and work group prestige on preference for demographically similar others: A value threat approach. *Organization Science, 23*(2), 386–401.

Gerhart, B., & Rynes, S. L. (2003). *Compensation: Theory, evidence and strategic implications.* Thousand Oaks, CA: SAGE.

Greer, G. (1971). *The female eunuch.* New York, NY: Bantam Books.

Hacker, S. L. (1979). Sex stratification, technology and organizational change: A longitudinal case study of AT&T. *Social Problems, 26*, 539–557.

Kanter, R. M. (1977). *Men and women of the corporation.* New York, NY: Basic Books.

Lawrence, B., & Tolbert P. S. (2007). Structure, norms and outcomes: Organizational demography and individual careers. In H. Gunz and M. Peiperl (Eds.), *Handbook of career studies* (pp. 399–421). New York, NY: SAGE.

Meyer, J. W., & Rowan, B. (1977). Institutionalized organizations: Formal organizations as myth and ceremony. *American Journal of Sociology, 83*(2), 340–363.

Ridgeway, C. (2019). *Status: Why is it everywhere? Why does it matter?* New York, NY: Russell Sage Foundation.

Roberson, Q., Ryan, A. M., & Ragins, B. R. (2017). The evolution and future of diversity at work. *Journal of Applied Psychology, 102*(3), 483–499.

Rynes, S. L., & Milkovich, G. T. (1986). Wage surveys: Dispelling some myths about the "market wage. *Personnel Psychology, 39*(1), 71–90.

Steinem, G. (1963, May). A bunny's tale. *Show Magazine,* 99–114.

Tajfel, J. C. (1970). Experiments in intergroup discrimination. *Scientific American, 22,* 96–102.

Tolbert, P. S. (1986). Organizations and inequality: Sources of earnings differences between male and female faculty. *Sociology of Education, 59*(2), 227–245.

Tolbert, P. S., Graham, M., & Andrews, A. (1999). Causes and consequences of variations in groups' gender composition. In G. Powell (Ed.), *Handbook of gender studies* (pp. 179–202). Thousand Oaks, CA: SAGE.

Tolbert, P. S., & Oberfield, A. A. (1991). Sources of organizational demography: Faculty sex ratios in colleges and universities. *Sociology of Education, 64*(4), 305–317.

Tolbert, P. S., Simons, T., Andrews, A., & Rhee, J. 1995. Effects of gender composition on faculty turnover. *Industrial & Labor Relations Review 48,* 562–579.

Treiman, D. J., & Roos, P. A. (1983). Sex and earnings in industrial society: A nine nation comparison. *American Journal of Sociology, 89*(3), 612–650.

Zucker, L. G. (1977). The role of institutionalization in cultural persistence. *American Sociological Review, 42*(5), 726–772.

ABOUT THE EDITORS

Eden King is the Lynette S. Autrey Professor of Industrial-Organizational Psychology at Rice University. She is pursuing a program of research that aims to make work better for everyone. This research—which has yielded over 100 scholarly products and has been featured in outlets such as the *New York Times, Good Morning America,* and *Harvard Business Review*—addresses three primary themes: (a) current manifestations of discrimination and barriers to work-life balance in organizations, (b) consequences of such challenges for its targets and their workplaces, and (c) individual and organizational strategies for reducing discrimination and increasing support for families. In addition to her scholarship, Dr. King has partnered with organizations to improve diversity climate, increase fairness in selection systems, and to design and implement diversity training programs. She is currently serving as co-editor of the *Journal of Business and Psychology.*

Quinetta Roberson is the John A. Hannah Distinguished Professor in Management and Psychology. Prior to her current position she was an endowed chair at Villanova University and tenured professor at Cornell University. She has been a visiting scholar at universities on six continents, and served an appointment as director of the science of organizations program at the National Science Foundation (NSF). Dr. Roberson has published over 40 scholarly journal articles and book chapters, edited a *Handbook of Diversity in the Workplace,* and served as an associate editor at the *Journal of Applied Psychology.* She also has over 20 years of global experience in teaching courses, facilitating workshops, and advising organizations on how to drive performance through diversity, inclusive cultures, and leadership. Her work is

Perspectives on Gender and Work, pages 233–234

informed by her experiences as a financial analyst and small business consultant prior to obtaining her doctorate. She earned her PhD in organizational behavior from the University of Maryland, and holds undergraduate and graduate degrees in finance.

Mikki Hebl is the Martha and Henry Malcolm Lovett Professor of Psychology and Professor of Management at Rice University, where she has been for the last 19 years. She graduated with her BA from Smith College and her PhD at Dartmouth College. She is an applied psychologist whose research focuses on workplace discrimination and remediation. Her particular area of expertise is in the area of gender discrimination. She has published over 125 articles, received 20 teaching awards, been awarded major NIH and NSF funded grants, and recently received both the lifetime award for Gender and Diversity in Organizations at the Academy of Management (2014) and the national Cherry Professor of the Year Award (2016).